Inner Messiah, Divine Character

Inner Messiah, Divine Character

NARRATIVE APPROACHES
TO BE BEYOND BEST

BENJAMIN YOSEF

RESOURCE *Publications* · Eugene, Oregon

INNER MESSIAH, DIVINE CHARACTER
Narrative Approaches to Be Beyond Best

Resource Publications
An Imprint of Wipf and Stock Publishers
199 W. 8th Ave., Suite 3
Eugene, OR 97401

www.wipfandstock.com

ISBN 13: 978-1-62564-888-4

Manufactured in the U.S.A.   07/09/2014

In Memoriam

Art Campbell
&
La Forza del Destino

Contents

Acknowledgements

As with all creative processes that seek to populate this world with positive ideas and empowering messages, this book represents the cumulative impact of many great teachers and scholars on my thought processes. First and foremost, I must acknowledge the extraordinary support, guidance, and intellectual prowess of Professor Donald Capps at Princeton Theological Seminary. In addition to his unbound knowledge on this subject matter and nurturing teaching style, Professor Capps provided mission critical encouragement and direction throughout this endeavor.

Along with Professor Capps, I must mention those Princeton professors with the most profound influence on my knowledge about ancient esoteric subjects, such as Professor Peter Schäfer at Princeton University and Professor James Charlesworth at Princeton Theological Seminary. Their dedication to and achievement in their respective fields, supplemented by their engaging and inspiring teaching styles, truly facilitated my acquisition of knowledge and my ability to distill important practical lessons from ancient scriptural and mystical texts.

Of course, friends and family played instrumental roles in this book's completion. From my parents' obligatory patience and encouragement to my friends' willingness to discuss ideas, this book did take a community to complete. In particular, I must thank a few key players who helped bring scholars and books to my attention, such as Professor Alex Kaye, David Newton and Marcelo Meir Schor (who shared some late-night discussions about some "things" and pointed me to some rabbinic sources that supported my notion about the *Inner Messiah*'s theological significance).

Finally, a major factor on the quality and diversity of my scholarship throughout my entire time in Princeton warrants a special note of gratitude. One of the secret, hidden treasures of Princeton Theological Seminary, our reference librarian, Kate Skrebutenas, was instrumental in the initial phases of this book's research, along with its forthcoming sequel, *Inner Messiah, Divine Leader.*

Regardless of those names enumerated or left silent, my gratitude for this book's creation can only be surpassed by my appreciation for its readers who dedicate the time and effort to extract from its pages some wisdom to help bring about positive changes in their lives, both individually and collectively.

Benjamin Yosef

Princeton, NJ
April 7, 2014

Introduction

SOMEHOW THIS BOOK HAS come within our physical embrace and its allusion to a novel character with the promise to transform our ordinary life story into an extraordinary existence has attracted our attention. Whether through some cosmic occurrence, intellectual curiosity, or other catalyst, we have all arrived at this time upon the same page—this page. This particular tangible page and its expressive language are the masters of our attention and our imaginations at the moment, as well as the ultimate arbiter to determine how many subsequent pages will enter our consciousness, both individually and collectively.

Stop! Look up, look down, look left, and look right. Really, stop and breathe right now! Now, wait, how can we be looking right if you are reading this sentence? If we observe this interrogative punctuation and thought without proper pause, we are already ignoring this book's advice and instruction! How could this book and its insights ever help to reorient our thinking process and to discover our superlative *Self*? Do we really want to acquaint, or better phrased reacquaint, ourselves with our *Divine Character* that can potentially transform all aspects of our lives? Or, do we choose to persist in the comforts of mediocrity and self-delusion that permanently disenfranchise our dreams and hopes from loftier pursuits? Well, our ability to attain some aspect of the superlative within our life story will be based upon our willingness to submit our selves and thinking processes to the thoughts and reflections highlighted by this book. As presented within these pages, the convoluted thoughts and ideas of all *levels* of intellectuals, sages, psychologists, and celebrated thinkers have been distilled to their bare essence to help us to attain our goals in their fullest sense and to facilitate their pursuit and attainment.

Our narrative character is a rather elastic construct that uses various modes of communications to transcend the boundaries of conventional communications, academic disciplines, or other demarcations. To identify that aspect of our narrative character that can be universally applied and accepted, this book attempts to revisit our identity and self-awareness as a narrative phenomenon that requires us to embrace a narrative perspective that will help us to differentiate between the personalized self (uppercase *Self*) and the generic self (lowercase *self*) within our creative expressions, especially our storytelling. These pages have been carefully filled with scholarly observations and innovative insights to help us, both reader and author, understand why we have allocated the time and energy to read these pages and to distill their wisdom to improve our lives—especially our sense of *self* and its ability to experience personal, professional, and spiritual satisfaction in all aspects of our lives. The identity that can transcend these barriers requires three distinct analyses of the *Self* and its current status so as to reformulate a new, improved self-awareness to overcome crippling negativity. In particular, the ability of an individual to embrace the potential of its *Divine Character* and to concretize ambitions associated with that potential becomes an important goal and outcome of this three-part *Be Beyond Best* process set forth below.

PROCESS PART I—DISCOVERING THE "BE" WITHIN OUR BEING

"In the beginning," the opening of the *first* verse of the *first* chapter of the *first* book in the Bible provides the commencement for this exercise. Consider that before we understand what truly needs to change in our lives, we need to understand a few firsts in our own personal narratives. This book will help us become intimately acquainted with the term *narrative* and its character formation as the ultimate transformative phenomenon within our self-awareness. Through recollection and reflection, our narratives will help us to revisit those moments and memories in our lives upon which subsequent events, dreams, and ambitions are built. In those early, nascent moments, we have touched the building blocks of our own personal, unique creation stories that have allowed us to create the lives we are currently living. Unfortunately, the ravages of every day living, the distractions of earthly pursuits, the competition for success, and the maintenance of status quo have taken their toll. Hence, we may have acquired this book to help bring us to the next phase of our own life stories. To achieve this, we must think about how to "BE" in the fullest, purest sense without life's follies depreciating our spirits, our hopes, and, most importantly, our perspectives!

To *Be Beyond Best*, the first part of our identity analysis is learning how to "Be" in an optimal state of existence. Clearly, this process will have a miraculous component attached to its attainment in light of the feelings that have brought us to the confines of this book's pages. Though, as both a reader and a believer in our own survival skills, the transformative term *miraculous* does not necessarily equate with impossible. To that end, we are to embrace the possibilities of the infinite states of being, some of which we experienced, some of which we dreamt, and some of which we are still gestating.

Each mode of being is inexorably linked to each other through our own knowledge of what's it like to *Be* within each of those states. As a result, we are strongly encouraged to remove our selves from any thought, idea, or other limiting intention that impairs our abilities to *Be* at complete rest with our inner most thoughts, ideas, and creations that are not tainted by any external experiences. There exists an aspect of our selves that is void of any worry, self-doubt, or fear that existed before anything else existed within our selves. It is that *Self*, which we shall refer to as the "innocent self," that must be retrieved prior to exploring other possible self-expressions of our identity that will create a shift in our life at this time. The "innocent self" represents the initial *Self* in its purest form and expression without the hurts and disappointments of every day existence and other weightier filters.

While the art of being cannot be considered a permanent goal to replicate in future identity expressions, the innocent self provides an important canvass to compare personality changes and their impact that we have acquired since the inception of our identities and their current modes of expressions. The *difference* between who we were and what we have become will help us have great insight into the factors that help us *Be* and the intended and unintended consequences of those factors on our own identity expressions. In turn, we will have a chance to evaluate the contours and patterns of our decision-making processes and revisit those decisions that have diverted us away from an optimal existence. Hopefully, the whole experience will teach us how to *Be* in a particular moment in time, place, and thought so as to understand how the gradual evolution from the first decision/action in helping us arrive at that moment can help us extract its full possibilities to achieve an optimal outcome.

PROCESS PART II—REFORMULATING OUR POTENTIAL TO SEE BEYOND ORDINARY EXPECTATIONS

The next part of this self-analysis requires an intensive evaluation of our goals and ambitions and the benchmarks we employ to determine our own successes at goal achievement. The measurement of our life's achievements, especially the goals and dreams we have attained, requires careful consideration and differentiation between objective and subjective measurements. Regardless of our own objectivity, the role of personal prejudice and perspective on such matters presents a challenge for goal formation and achievement. For example, we all wish to earn a certain amount of success during our lifetime, whether monetary, celebratory, or other laudatory demarcation. The actual realization of such goals all comes down to one major factor—how realistic our relationship is between reality and the possibilities contained with that reality for our own lifetime.

Only a chosen few have *never* heard the words "Are you out of your mind?" when opining about some of our more deluded ambitions. Yet, we are all able to pursue the most outlandish things even against the most sage advice. The infinite frontier between possible and impossible inspires our thoughts and pursuits in the most cunning way because that frontier's location is neither known nor discernable in our consciousness. It represents a very important factor in our decision making process because the role of chance in the achievement of our goals cannot be underestimated. We are always wandering within that infinite frontier between the possible and impossible in the formation and achievement of our goals and ambitions and what truly determines what can be considered possible and impossible is mostly the convergence of a chance coincidence—the application of conditioned survival skills to a foreseen scenario with unforeseen circumstances. To circumvent that role of chance, we must think about achieving a sense of *Self* that is *Beyond* anything ordinary and provides an additional boundary in the ambition formation and achievement process.

Creating a space for the *Self* that is *Beyond* anything that was initially conceived for a particular purpose is a most creative exercise in deciphering among multiple scenarios for happiness, contentment, and resilience. We can conceptualize this particular space as the merger between the possible and impossible, i.e., the impossible possible or the possible impossible. Regardless of the juxtaposition of those two words, the intended meaning is the same. While all things can be possible with God or some notion of the Divine, all things can also be possible with an idea or ambition that is *Beyond* the ordinary. Because we are striving for something *Beyond* the usual and known, we will experience an outcome without a binary success or failure method of analysis. Rather, we can transform the outcome and learn from its consequence on our own identity and projection of *Self* throughout the entire exercise.

In essence, we are exercising our strength, no matter our weaknesses or our perceived weaknesses, to achieve something that exceeds established boundaries, whether real or imaginary. As a result, the barriers to change and to grow should no longer become a limiting obstacle. Instead, those barriers should become motivational fodder for our dreams and ambitions as we undertake ways to analyze our identities in relation to the current boundaries and to the possibilities of our imaginations. Each condition achieved *Beyond* a limitation represents a manifestation of the potential within our selves to live *Beyond* states of perceived optimality and to celebrate our personal victories over mediocrity.

PROCESS PART III—BUILDING EXERCISES TO UNDERSTAND AND TO ACHIEVE OUR "BEST"

Implicit within the statements above, we must recognize the causal connection between our current surroundings and our current perspective on our future possibilities. Unfortunately, the pace of life has not only taken its toll on the hopes and dreams of all of us, but has left a big hole in the most precious gift of our lives—a true, unique sense of the *Self*. While many commentators, authors, and scholars have identified the adverse effects of consumer culture, conspicuous consumption, and exploitative media, the "individual" and its contribution to the social, political, economic, and social historical continuity of humanity have been relegated to the importance of the "now" and the anticipation of "the next big thing." All corners of our culture, both domestic and international, have been infiltrated with ephemeral "tissue" interests—grabbing our attention for a moment without any particular long-term benefit or consequence.

The power of 140 characters from a basic Twitter account can ignite a viral frenzy over the most inane celebrity topic and saccharine theme. With the explosion of social media's popularity, individuals are compelled to project an image of the *Self* in words and images through a plethora of social media outlets to garner attention for all sorts of superficial personality endeavors. The pressure to present a *Self* and to connect with a larger community has created an intense, unnecessary competitive mentality that has ultimately shifted our focus away from our individual importance in the historical narrative to our quest for individual attention (most likely, personal and professional validation) in the "now." As we glance over these words, we all are encouraged to reflect upon our life decisions that have been made with this type of myopia. For example, have we ever entered a relationship because our friends and family encouraged us to suppress our reservations and to focus on the obvious benefits to our long-term happiness and security? Or, have we ever accepted and stayed at a job or profession for immediate financial gain and sacrificed our long-term personal and professional satisfaction? Even more distressing, have we compromised our personal faiths and belief systems to pursue commercially generated needs and desires at the detriment of our spiritual well being and peace? If we answered in any degree of the affirmative to the foregoing, we should pay particularly close attention to the scenarios set forth in this book to avoid relapsing into undesirable, sub-optimal decision-making practices.

Though we may never meet in person or have cause to socialize in the future, this book represents a collective exercise for our combined interests in improving our selves and our roles for the overall societal "good." Any message or thought that empowers the individual at the expense of another person, institution, or idea does not help propel our overall perspective into a positive zone of existence. Rather, the message that gains strength or encouragement through degrading its predecessor creates more problems than it solves since those predecessors will become our enemies and divert precious intellectual resources from attaining a superior outcome that can have far-reaching consequences beyond our individual selves, prejudices, fears, and egos. In other words, we need to refocus our focus on creating a superlative sense of *Self*, the optimal, superlative *Self*, that recognizes and embraces the power of diversity as we *all* search for a superior collective existence. This perspective will start to help us reconceptualize our personalized identity, i.e., *Self*, as a unique, dynamic character that interacts with and is influenced by various narratives throughout our individual and collective existences.

THE NARRATIVE APPROACHES AND THEIR CLASSIFICATIONS

Throughout this book, we will become well acquainted with three narrative classifications that have the most influence on the development and execution of our character as embodied by our *Self*. As a threshold matter, we must reorient our thinking to conceive of our lives as an amalgam of personalized "story-acquiring" and storytelling phenomena. The *acquisitive* phenomenon represents the penultimate life activity and transforms all our life experiences, interactions, circumstances and dreams into some form of imaginative content and creative expression. The *telling* phenomenon allows us to share this content and expression with others and to define a place within a greater collective storyline.

To understand these phenomena and their power to transform our lives, we will work with three narrative classifications. First, we must think about how we describe our own character to others and ourselves. We shall call this narrative approach, our *personal narrative*. As we can appreciate, our *personal narrative* will undergo tremendous transformation from this approach as we analyze our *Self* within this narrative construct and distill new insights about our current life situations. Second, we will think about what stories inspire us to dream beyond the ordinary and to escape the rational burdens of our everyday existence. For that purpose, we shall revisit our personal faith systems, or lack thereof, and classify those stories and their inspirational powers as the *Sacred Textual Narrative*. The *Sacred Textual Narrative* will help us to search for new inspirations from old texts as we seek to understand the origins of our divine character and its quest for connection to the original act of creation.

Finally, we shall call how our *personal narrative* interacts with our generic *self* and our individual *Self* through the much larger, more important overarching historical narrative of all civilization, the *Grand Historical Narrative*. Through reimagining and repositioning our attention on the elongated timeline of the *Grand Historical Narrative*, we may come to understand *why* the "me-against-the-world" mentality has not really placed our society in a position to appreciate our collective roles in helping all peoples understand the magic and mystery of the *Grand Historical Narrative* and its origins in the Divine or the "absolute beginning," at *time minus one*, that can be found in our *Sacred Textual Narrative*.

The thought of our lifetime, or any particular moment in our life, having such power and consequence to evoke fear, anxiety, dread or pain becomes somewhat inconsequential when we compare the actual time-quantity of our lifetime and its moments to the *Grand Historical Narrative*. For example, if we were fretting about our boss or spouse for some significant moment of time, then we were squandering significant moments in our own lifetime that only add to our insignificance on the timeline of the *Grand Historical Narrative*. The additional insignificance does not come from the negative feelings and emotions about a particular situation and their dilatory impact on our ability to find happiness. Rather, the disconnectedness originates with our separation from the power of creation and our lack of appreciation of that power to create our superlative existence, i.e., *Sacred Textual Narrative*. It is that very disconnectedness that separates us from enjoying our lives and moments in the time allotted within our own personal timelines to formulate an optimal *Self* through merging our narrative approaches into a singular, unified story about our superlative *Self* and its control over all these narrative constructs.

Regardless of our personal convictions and faith preferences about our application of the *Sacred Textual Narrative*, we are all invited to unlock the power of the term *creation* and its creative capacities within our imaginations and our possibilities. Of course, religious-oriented scholars and practitioners have usurped these terms for theological exposition and exploitation to validate their religious agendas. Despite that unfortunate misappropriation, these terms encapsulate powerful language that must be reclaimed by all individuals, regardless of their religious views and personal prejudices, to reorient the debate toward a "collective" understanding of the Divine and the Divine's presence in the world today.

Many self-help and New Age authors, not all, are determined to resurrect the past and to revisit faith practices that challenge modern faith belief systems. Yet, such authors rarely evaluate the inter-relationships between modern faith practices and their predecessors and continue to promulgate an unnecessary contempt that preempts meaningful, contemplative or mutually beneficial exploration. Scholarship appears to be changing this thinking and, hopefully, will eventually redefine the parameters of the debate.[1] More importantly, the ancillary benefits of this scholarship include among other things, our thirst for certainty to life's voluminous unknown.

Our Elusive Quest for Certainty

History may teach us many things about our origins, especially our consistent and persistent quest to embrace and to control the uncertainties in every day existence and beyond. Looking back at the power of religions to mobilize civilizations and to create great artistry as far back as the Ancient Egyptians to modern-day theological thinking, a strong pattern emerges—the quest to attain certainty over life's inevitable sufferings. Major religions have always dealt with that inevitable, inescapable part of life known as mortality. Whether pyramids, reincarnation beliefs, or other religious victories over death, most religions and their *Sacred Textual Narratives* are crafted around that singular life event to give both purpose and certainty to every aspect of our existence and its eventual demise.

Today, the quest for certainty appears to have become dislodged from the larger collective exploration for a universal understanding about all *creation* as the dominance of the individual emerged. Hence, human life itself has become a puzzle that requires all of us to search for the ultimate "thing" to shift our discomfort to comfort as we search for the ways to attain, maintain and project our well-being to ours selves and the world around us.[2] Through the confluence of social media, consumer spending and other cultural norms, we have become acculturated to accept certainty in new ways to avoid dealing with unmarketable inevitabilities that could disrupt our consumer culture. For example, if we were more mindful about our eventual passing before a life threatening diagnosis or incident, we might reorient our spending habits, work ethics, and leisure activities to reflect their "true opportunity cost" on our overall existence. To put this into perspective with the benefit of hindsight, how many people would have rushed to work early on 9/11 and continue to commute into NYC had the true terror of that day would have been revealed on 9/10? If we all had full, complete information about unforeseen accidents, how would that information impact our behavior? Would we have done something or everything differently?

1. See, generally, Bellah, *Religion in Human Evolution.*
2. Critchley and Webster, "Gospel according to 'Me,'" 8.

While we are not necessarily attuned to the gifts of prophecy, we are seeking ways to minimize the uncertainties associated within our lives, whether working to amass savings, acquiring appropriate insurance policies or undertaking other intellectual and practical ventures. In our thinking process, we are acting according to our primal instinct to survive that has now been supplemented by our capitalist culture to achieve beyond the comparative and to attain the superlative. Through this process of acquisition, even academic knowledge, we have conditioned ourselves to understand our inevitabilities and to weigh opportunity cost within the broader social confines, rather than according to our own individual decision-making processes. Thus, uncertainty and its pejorative connotations have become akin to a treatable diagnosis. This diagnosis appears to require us to undertake an active search for a marketable panacea, to accept our control over the search as certainty and to distract us from recognizing our lack of control over the inevitable outcome as uncertainty. We will reevaluate this relationship between certainty and uncertainty through our ability to create within and beyond our lifetime with our *personal narrative* and its relationship to both the *Sacred Textual Narrative* and the *Grand Historical Narrative*.

RECOMMENDED READER PREPARATION

So, let us begin, not so much in the beginning, but where our thoughts and quests have taken us—to this page and its print. Not so much a singular moment in time—a continued exercise for understanding and desire for individual betterment. Regardless of our current relationship with the Divine, institutional affiliations, ritual practices and, most importantly, the *Sacred Textual Narrative*, we are strongly encouraged to read the first chapter of the first book of the Bible, Genesis 1:1—2:3, to become acquainted with, at least, the literary construct of the term *creation*. Whether or not our personal views of the Genesis narrative impinge the literary majesty of its structure and depth to conceptualize the "beginning," we must recognize the *Sacred Textual Narrative's* attempt to provide a definitive and superlative account of this historical moment. In doing so, we can craft our own narratives with the same expansive literary structure and intention as we recall our own sacredness (regardless of its origins), its relationship to creation and the power of creation to help us embrace and deploy that sacredness to reclaim our *Divine Character*.

Attitude Check-Up

To prepare for the lessons set forth in this book, we will need to lay out its premise with particular attention to our current attitude and mood about two basic things. The first attitude check-up is to evaluate our attitude toward the "Divine," "Karma," "Mystery," "Magic," "Synchronicity," "Déjà vu," "God," or any other similar construct. Perhaps, we will have a very visceral reaction to a particular term or we will become inundated with a flood of complex emotions. Whatever our reaction, all reactions are valid and require contemplation for our personal growth and consequential change. Hopefully, we will apply our emotional reactions and understand how we can improve our lives, our knowledge about *Sacred Textual Narratives*, our *personal narratives*, and their input into the *Grand Historical Narrative*.

While we are gifted with the power of free will, we must never surrender the *power* of our decision-making process, not the decision-making process itself, to comport with a particular groupthink mentality. Suffice it to say, the power of *creation* rests within our power to make decisions that somehow reflect our role in the power of *creation* since every decision we make and undertake causes us to create *something*, whether new, old or recycled. Yet, most of us do not always approach the decision-making process with any sort of awe or appreciate how the sacredness of our decision-making helps us renew our relationship with both the Divine *and* the power of *creation*. Thus, our second attitude check-up requires us to identify and to conceptualize how we make decisions, from life-altering career and romantic decisions to mundane food choices in our supermarkets. All that decision-making capacity, even the simple act of uttering a single word or sigh, must be evaluated from this paradigm.

So, do we all make decisions all the time? Most likely, yes! So now, the decision that is most relevant and pressing for our undertaking is why are we reading this book? That's right, why are we reading this and what motivates us for finishing it? If we answer with a vacuous indifference, we will extract nothing from our reading efforts. On the other hand, if we are reading the book with a clear intention and expectation, we will most likely fulfill those intentions and expectations upon arriving at the book's conclusion. Yet, the decision to determine how this book will change our attitude and the difference this book will make on our pre-reading/post-reading life perspectives will ultimately be our own decision.

We are all encouraged to respect this decision-making process on our own terms so that the power of deciding how this book impacts our lives, especially our understanding of our Divine Character in our *personal narrative*, its relationship with the *Sacred Textual Narrative* and their potential impact on the *Grand Historical Narrative*. All of which represent our own unique creations, created with the assistance of the power of *creation*, made manifest and available through the *power* of our decision-making processes.

HOW TO USE THIS BOOK

This book represents an invitation to readers to extract inspiration and other tools to reimagine, revision and reevaluate how their personal and professional decisions can help transform their ordinary existence through finding our *Divine Character* in our *personal narrative* with our knowledge about the *Sacred Textual Narrative* and making an impact on the *Grand Historical Narrative* with our *Divine Character's* own unique purposes and contributions.

The possibility of two people extracting the same tools and lessons from this book should be very small. The book can be read as a complete work from start to end, provided that we have a clearly formulated intention and expectation to improve our attitudes. This clarity means that we identify the major influences negatively affecting our attitudes and understand why and how we need to change our perspectives about these influences. This approach may require multiple readings of this text according to our own schedules and processes for self-awareness. Most importantly, the possibility of multiple readings should remove any stress or anxiety about the first reading bearing anticipated fruit to empower and improve our attitude about our lives and its importance within the *Grand Historical Narrative*.

Alternatively, this book can be utilized for specific questions or affirmations about behavior patterns and perspectives that limit us from accessing an optimal sense of *Self* at various stages within our *personal narrative*. Glance over the individual chapters and consult them for specific instances to gain additional insights to questions and concerns that depress our attitude and impair our ability to achieve contentment. Each chapter title was selected for quick reference when we need an immediate power boost to understand how we can feel empowered and how we can empower and improve our attitude with some imaginative problem-solving.

Whatever the approach, we should always revisit the book with its principle purpose in mind—a *narrative approach* to help direct our thinking and curiosity to empower and to improve our attitudes. As such, we must remember that we are active participants in unpacking the lessons and messages contained within it *if* this book can change our current directions and personal journeys. After all, the book's *narrative approach* will only point a direction out or reveal a path that we may have overlooked in our own hurried lifestyles. Even more compelling, this approach will helps us to refocus our perspective away from external influences, especially commercial media and subversive advertising, that have disempowered our own unique, independent decision-making processes. In this way, we can feel empowered to reassert our own authentic, organic needs, *not wants*, to strengthen our connection with *creation*, not just the superficial consumerism or hyped fades. As a result, we should all experience a positive shift in our attitudes and their need for empowerment and improvement since we will be inspired to think about new ways to access the power of *creation* to attain an optimal perspective on how best to nurture our individual needs and their potential contributions to our collective betterment.

OUTLINE AND OVERVIEW

This book presents our narrative approach around three main themes to discover our "true" *Divine Character*, that is, our *Inner Messiah*. Part 1, entitled *Our Life Stories as Penultimate Narrative*, encourages us to re-think and to revisit our current storytelling and its narrative components in chapter 1. Thereafter, we will evaluate, analyze and strategize ways to obtain the superlative expression for our *personal narrative* and its relationships with the *Sacred Textual Narrative* and the *Grand Historical Narrative* in chapter 2.

Part 2, entitled *Our Empowered and Improved Self as Optimal Narrator*, provides a fascinating and engaging approach to encourage us to assume optimal narrative control over our *personal narratives* through empowering and improving our narrative voice. To conceive of assuming the role of *Optimal Narrator*, we must avoid self-destructive behavior patterns and embrace constructive creative exercises (chapter 3). In addition, we must rely on our natural instincts and intuition to empower our decision-making capacities (chapter 4). Thereafter, we will learn how to formulate and to feel "completeness" within the *Self* through understanding and avoiding the consequences associated with our current "incomplete" *Self* (chapter 5). Moreover, we will work with our doubts as transformative emotions to motivate us to visualize and to attain a superlative reality (chapter 6) and we will appreciate and leverage the value of our current *Self* to maximize our "self-worth" and its potential contributions to our *Self* and others (chapter 7).

Part 3, entitled *Our Inner Messiah as Quintessential Divine Character*, will acquaint us with the most powerful, transformative notions presented within this book (or elsewhere)! We will present the narrative evidence as the foundational defining components of the term *Inner Messiah* and the appropriateness of its application to our own *Divine Character* (chapter 8). Then, we will explore the most direct encounter with our *Inner Messiah* as *Divine Character* through the narrative convergence of our *personal narrative* with the *Grand Historical Narrative* via our *Sacred Textual Narrative* (chapter 9). Finally, we will encounter the power of our *Inner Messiah* to rescue our lives from ordinary existence and to instill an extraordinary perspective between our *Divine Character*, its ability to access the power within all *creation* and its potential to revise our past errors in terms of both an individual and collective narrative exercise (chapter 10).

Chapters' Intent and Structure

The chapters have been drafted to facilitate accessibility and to encourage our creative interpretations related to our personal journeys of empowerment and improvement. No two persons reading this book should reach the same conclusion or interpretation regarding its overall message and its application in their personal lives. Similarly, no two readings of these materials should create the same result since each reading should reveal additional information not formerly revealed. More importantly, the book was crafted with the intent that our thoughts and ideas, which are ever changing, evolving, and adapting to our lives' demands, represent the principle characters in the presentation of this message and its lessons. As a result, the text should operate as a living document itself with ideas, concepts and lessons that can be discerned with repetitive readings within different seasons of our lives.

To unlock the power of our imminent (or immanent) literary undertaking, each chapter has been carefully drafted around a three-point, decision-making strategy. First, the chapter commences with a clearly articulated objective in our transitional thinking toward attitudinal empowerment and improvement. Then, the chapter expounds the most relevant teachings associated with that objective through entertaining and revealing scenarios about why we must achieve that objective to empower and to improve our attitudes. Finally, each scenario concludes with a powerful reflection that helps us to utilize our imagination to extract the most effective lessons to embrace our improved and empowered attitudes.

PART 1

Our Life Stories as the Penultimate Narrative

1

The Narrator, the Narration, and the Character(s)

THIS CHAPTER ENCOURAGES US to ask ourselves what would our current reality look like if we rethink our storytelling perspective and each component of our storytelling tools—the narrator, the narration and the characters? We are sitting in a movie and about to watch the movie of our life. The camera moves in for a close-up of us sitting in our seats to capture each expressive gesture of our face and to accentuate the light from the projected image's reflection expressed within our emotions. How do we feel about seeing our life story unfold before our eyes? Would you add, subtract or leave alone any movie footage? Change certain scenes or settings? Recast the principal characters or supporting roles? Why was the movie made even in the first place? And does it have a particular ending, or just continues on indefinitely through perpetual sequels? How ever we answer the foregoing questions will reflect our unique imaginations and individual perspectives. Recognizing the obvious, our daunting task requires us to look at "us" as an individual and collective storytelling phenomenon. So, as we reconsider our character, and the storytelling phenomenon itself, we must breakdown its essential elemental components to clearly demonstrate and to transcend the boundary between ordinary and extraordinary existence.

To accomplish this chapter's task, we will embark upon a transformative journey of storytelling as we rethink and reimagine our lives as an unfolding story with trials, tribulations, mysteries and other factors that shape our sense and influence our perspective about the *Self* as narrator and principal character in its narration. Through embracing the *narrative* as the ultimate enabling device for our imagination, we can understand our control over destiny through our ability to conjecture about endless possibilities. In particular, we can all conjecture that a superlative existence that can be attained through perceiving growth opportunities within the most ordinary and mundane life experiences. Otherwise, our hopes and dreams may become permanently tainted with an unnecessary, destructive myopia centered on less-than-optimal narrative elements, like hopelessness and despair.

Like with the other fundamental elements of our decision-making, our ordinary, daily routines contain many elements that we might need to reconfigure and rearrange to understand our current emotional state and its manifestation in our present attitudes. Evidently, we have found this particular page in our mutual quest for some form of self-improvement to our lives. This improvement can be readily achieved through evaluating the most prominent factors in our ordinary routines that impact our emotion states and encourage us to seek alternative, superior forms of personal and/or professional contentment. As a result, this chapter must help nurture our ambitions and intentions to *perceive* those sustainable aspects, present within our current situations, that can create opportunities and possibilities to transform depleted dreams and goals into important building blocks for the creation of a full, superlative character, i.e., a sense of the *Self*, within our overall narrative.

The "Certainty Trap"

The threshold matter in achieving this chapter's objective is recognizing our relationship *and* dependence on notions of certainty in our ordinary existence. As reflected in most organized religious thought, we are all searching for some tangible anchor to guide us to a point in the unknowable future. The need for an anchor can be categorized as an innate desire or control over unknowable, yet inevitable, future events. Most telling, the human relationship between the inevitable transition between life and death warrants special consideration as we explore our notions about what an afterlife may or may not consist of. Regardless of our religious or spiritual allegiances, most religious customs and rituals describe the "afterlife" as nothing more than living states between differ-ent dimensions. For example, the Ancient Egyptians provided elaborate instructions within the tomb of their dead for the deceased's soul to travel safely between the living world and "afterlife." Most mainstream Judeo-Christian belief systems expound some notion of life after death or the "world to come," all of which promise believers that the physical death will not constitute an ultimate cessation of life. Rather, physical death can be considered a spiritual right of passage permitting the individual's consciousness to commune with the religion's notion of the Divine on the most intimate and empowering conditions. Similarly, Eastern reli-gious philosophies promulgate ideas about transmigrating souls between lifetimes and human existences that ensures their religious followers an eternal, temporal existence that surpasses the mundane and converges with the Divine in a perpetual worldly pattern.

Regardless of the belief systems, its rituals and its "afterlife" concep-tions, there seems to emerge a singular theme common across cultures and theologies—an individual can conceive and manage its inevitable encounter with death through appreciating its indestructible, enduring soul and its continued, modified existence. This particularized immortal-ity represents a character trait we can identify with the spiritual narrative device, *deus ex machina*, whether in story or character, that somehow can resolve the irresolvable and/or explain the unexplainable without provid-ing a scintilla of evidence for its actual existence. To justify our reliance on such narrative devices, we shift our own creative responsibility and relinquish our role as chief principal narrator to an invisible, unknowable narrative voice that creates the ultimate narration for our *Self* and, de-pending on the scope of the narration, for all creation. Generally speak-ing, certainty that cannot be verified or confirmed in sufficient degree can only be attained in our imagination. But, since we are applying our imagination for a specific purpose, we need some basis to legitimate our observations and conclusions. So, we turn to narratives that have been recognized to contain and/or to be inspired by a sacred, divine narrative source, i.e., a Divine Narrator. We shall classify these narratives as *Sacred Textual Narratives* due to their dependence on sacred texts for their main narrative elements.

The *Sacred Textual Narrative* helps us to see glimpses of certainty in various interim periods of own narrations, especially the events and circumstances we can and cannot control throughout our everyday existence. For example, while most people are pacified and relieved to escape the anxiety about the mysterious period between life and death with strong religious or philosophical convictions, we must analyze the cultural and religious factors behind such convictions. Within our narrative purview, we can discern the narrator's authority and its ability to instill peace and awe in anyone who accepts its authority with absolute certainty can maintain that certainty, *as long as that authority remains unchallenged and unquestioned.* It is the belief in the narrator's authority more than the narrator itself that provides the basis for our convictions and, in turn, the conviction itself becomes superfluous. Benefits from narrative certainty do not only quiet our own anxieties about the infinite possibilities that might exist at the moment of our death, but the certainty instills a living hope that can successfully combat grief, in most incidences, in our loved ones that must endure with loss.

For the purposes of better understanding the narrative elements within our ordinary existences, we must first focus on three critical elemental components of our ordinary existence. Component One (the "Be" element) includes a thoughtful analysis of our current routines and how structuring our daily activities reflect and contain our preferences for certainty over uncertainty. Component Two (the "Beyond" element) encourages us to formulate an honest assessment of our ability to understand our lives, all aspects of ordinary existence and how we apply our narrative creativity to our own character development and its interactions. Component Three (the "Best" element) motivates us to search and to strive to apply the two previous narrative components in an optimal fashion through perceiving and generating extraordinary possibilities within the confines of our daily existence. In this manner, we set forth the two operative narrative structures to contain these components.

THE GRAND HISTORICAL NARRATIVE AND OUR PERSONAL NARRATIVE

The dynamic nature of these three elemental components warrants an appropriate narrative methodology to understand and to appreciate their presence within our daily routines. Through this methodology, we can refine our ability to identify the sources, as well as our reactions, to certainty and uncertainty within narrative thinking processes and to develop an empowering and improving perspective about our character as narrator, our character within narration and our character through other characters.

To accomplish this transformation, we will extrapolate the narrative impetus of the *Sacred Textual Narrative* as a representative narrative construct to describe the mysterious interim period two separate, distinct states of existence and to structure our imagination around a tangible narration and a plausible narrative voice. When we wish to project our narrative voice into a grander narrator beyond the *Self* to express the entirety of creation and to recognize our personal creative capacities within it, we can perceive that grander expression as the *Grand Historical Narrative* and that personal expression as our *personal narrative*. This narrative methodology will help us to start to reposition our own *Self* and its expression through our own *personal narrative* in relation to its expression within and interaction with the much larger, more important overarching historical narrative of all civilization, the *Grand Historical Narrative*.

Grand Historical Narrative

Through reimagining and repositioning our attention on the elongated timeline of the *Grand Historical Narrative*, we may come to understand *why* the "me-against-the-world" mentality has not really placed our society in a position to appreciate our collective roles in helping each other to understand the magic and mystery contained within the *Grand Historical Narrative* and its original claim to the Divine Character at the "absolute beginning" that may be outside the time constraints within our *Sacred Textual Narrative*. As a result, the thought of our lifetime, or any particular moment in our life, having such power and consequence to evoke fear, anxiety, dread or pain becomes somewhat inconsequential when we compare the actual time-quantity of our lifetime and its relative moments within the *Grand Historical Narrative*.

If we were fretting about our boss or spouse for some significant moment of time, then we were squandering significant moments in our own lifetime that only add to our insignificance on the timeline of the *Grand Historical Narrative*. That additional insignificance does not come from the negative feelings and emotions about a particular situation and their dilatory impact on our ability to find happiness. Rather, the disconnectedness originates with our separation from the power of creation and our appreciation of that power to create our superlative existence. It is that very disconnectedness that separates us from enjoying our lives and moments in the time allotted within our own personal timelines and the opportunities to interact with the *Grand Historical Narrative* in various capacities.

Moreover, the term *creation* is a term that requires a deep personal understanding to unlock its creative capacities within our imaginations and our possibilities. Of course, religious-oriented scholars and practitioners and their *Sacred Textual Narratives* have usurped these terms for theological exposition and exploitation to validate their religious agendas. Unfortunately, these terms encapsulate powerful language that must be reclaimed by all individuals, regardless of their religious views and personal prejudices, to reorient the debate toward a "collective" understanding of the Divine and the Divine's presence in the world today. Many self-help and New Age authors, not all, are determined to resurrect the past and to revisit faith practices that challenge modern faith belief systems. Yet, such authors rarely evaluate the inter-relationships between modern faith practices and their predecessors and continue to promulgate an unnecessary contempt that preempts meaningful, contemplative or mutually beneficial exploration.

The rejection of *Sacred Textual Narratives* in this context does not only dilute the authority of the *Grand Historical Narrative* to affirm and to preserve generally accepted narrations, but distracts the narrator's voice in both *Narratives* by imposing an added burden to defend its narration, its characters and even itself. Scholarship appears to be changing this thinking and, hopefully, will eventually redefine the parameters of the debate.[1] More importantly, the ancillary benefits of this scholarship include immeasurable benefits for all creation; provided that we find ways to temper the uncertainty the scholarship creates before such benefits can be obtained.

Personal Narrative

Simply put, our *personal narrative* enables our sense of character, expressed through our own voice, to describe our creative capacity to ourselves and to project that creativity upon others, including interactions with the *Grand Historical Narrative* and *Sacred Textual Narrative*. Our *personal narratives* are complex narrative constructs since they fall under our personal creative dominion and serve various functions within our daily existence (which we will discuss at numerous portions throughout

1. See, generally, Bellah, *Religion in Human Evolution*.

the book). That said, we must recognize that our *personal narrative* requires certainty to flourish and to learn how to react efficiently and effectively to uncertainty. Our *personal narrative* can best be understood defined through understanding its function within the overall narrative scheme.

To concretize our thinking about how our reaction to uncertainty negatively impacts our *personal narratives*, we must think about why are we reading this book. We all share a modicum of expectation that this book will reveal something about our "true" nature and enable us to improve our attitudes about our daily lives. Yet, that expectation itself contains a representative dynamic between the certainty and uncertainty in our daily lives and decision-making processes. For example, some of us may feel very certain that this book will fulfill those expectations, while other readers may have be cynical about this book's overall effectiveness. It would appear that the tension between certainty and uncertainty in our thinking processes reflects, among other things, our personal tolerances for certainty's role in our decision-making process.

Sometimes, skeptical thoughts can help transform an uncertain outcome into a certain outcome since our ability to fulfill *lesser* expectations can be usually achieved. Hence, we must establish a user-friendly construct for "certainty" and understand how our own *personal narrative* operates as a sliding scale to move between labels of uncertainty and certainty. Only after that construct can exist in our personal, professional and spiritual vernacular, we can exercise greater control over our preference for certainty over uncertainty in our decision-making processes.

Ironically, the complex world of quantum mechanics can provide some simple clarity about the role of uncertainty in our decision-making process. In particular, we shall utilize a simplified definition of a complex principle, known as the *Heisenberg Uncertainty principle*, which basically states the better one knows an object's position in a *particular* location at a *particular* moment in time, the less one knows the object's momentum in arriving at that *particular* location.[2] Conversely, the more one knows an object's momentum in traveling to a particular location, the less one knows the object's position at a particular location.[3] Simple enough in articulation, and even more simple in its application to understanding our current and desired attitudinal states.

---

2. Holzner, *Quantum Physics Workbook for Dummies*, 276.
3. Ibid.

Most of us reading this book can vividly describe our current attitudinal state and the more energy we apply to articulate our current attitude, the less vividly we can weigh the influences and their impact on our arrival at that *particular* attitude and *vice versa*. Even if we cannot immediately see the groundbreaking nature of that statement, we should ponder its consequences for the import of certainty of in our decision-making process.

As we read this paragraph think about how certain we are that we are actually reading this *particular* paragraph and how certain we are about the influences that brought us to the conclusion of this *particular* sentence in this *particular* paragraph. Hopefully, we can all appreciate how the more elastic applications of the *Heisenberg Uncertainty principle* outside the realm of quantum mechanics can assist us in the exploration of how we rely on our constructs of certainty and uncertainty in transitioning between different moments along our life paths, traversing between diverse emotions and attitudes and traveling toward an empowered and improved attitude. Our *personal narratives* help remind us about how we have created our ordinary reality and why we have difficulty transitioning into something extraordinary due to our need for certainty. This need for certainty wherever we find ourselves within our *personal narrative* helps us to understand where we are in our life journeys, especially the certainty inherent in our ordinary existence. Thus, the need for us to understand momentum and placement of our dreams and hopes along this trajectory requires us to step outside the ordinary narrative conventions and to deal with the uncertainties associated with shifting and reinventing those conventions. An ordinary existence with ordinary expectations provides ordinary certainties, most of which, we have previously encountered and can manage. On the other hand, an extraordinary existence with extraordinary expectations comports with extraordinary uncertainties, most of which we will have little, or no, familiarity.

Let us clearly set forth a modified version of the *Heisenberg Uncertainty principle* for the purposes of this chapter's objective. We will usurp Heisenberg's main thought that uncertainty is inherent in all attempts to analyze any object that moves and rests through our ordinary reality, that is, the confines of linear time and space and their operations within the dimensions of our ordinary, perceivable existence. Here, we will place an additional layer upon this main thought associated with our objective to extract the extraordinary from the ordinary. Most relevant, uncertainty no longer applies to the object/thing moving through conventional time and space dimensions because our individual perceptions create the actual confines of our trajectories when moving from an ordinary to extraordinary state of existence.

The uncertainty associated with our emotions and their manifestation in a perceptible dimensionality within our own consciousness, as well as their ancillary application to the physical world and our immediate surroundings, warrants the consideration of our modified *Heisenberg Uncertainty principle* in our narrative methodology. Restated thusly, the better we think we understand the decision-making process attempting to improve or to empower our *personal narrative* away from our ordinary, daily existences toward our extraordinary, reasonable aspirations, the less we know about the full impact on how and when that decision-making process will enable us to achieve our reasonable aspirations. Conversely, the better we think we know how and when a decision-making process will enable us to achieve our reasonable aspirations, the less we will understand our attempts to improve and to empower our attitude away from our ordinary, daily existences toward our extraordinary, reasonable aspirations. Many divergent factors converge and confirm the relevance of this modified *Uncertainty* principle as discussed in attaining this chapter's objective.

Our emotional reactions to uncertainty in our lives creates the most powerful issues we may face in transforming our *personal narrative*, our lives and our attitudes toward a superlative incarnation as our decision-making processes may subsume needless fears and anxieties that preempt our efforts to make constructive changes. Applying the modified *Uncertainty* principle to this chapter's objective, our ability to reorder our lives and daily routines requires great discipline and conviction since many of us live fragmented existences to fulfill the multifaceted demands placed upon our personal and professional lives. While we may have a complete sense of wholeness, or at least some semblance of wholeness to the outside world, we may have detrimentally compartmentalized varying and differing aspects of our lives. The *personal narrative* and its character needed for our office life may greatly diverge from the *personal narrative* and its character associated with our romantic life, our family life, and our other roles we have voluntarily and involuntary assumed throughout our life journeys. The presence, even potential presence, of a fragmented *Self* within our *personal narrative* for multiple narrations, characters, and even narrators, requires us to pay close attention to the methods we use to unify and to shift between these different narrative elements, as well as

appreciating the uncertainties associated with unifying and shifting between those aspects of our *personal narrative* as described by our modified *Uncertainty* principle.

STEP-BY-STEP GUIDE TO TRANSFORM OUR PERSONAL NARRATIVE AND ITS IMPACT ON OUR NARRATIVE METHODOLOGY

First, we must determine the force behind our own momentum to empower and to improve our *personal narratives* so that we can maximize
the effectiveness of this book in our overall decision-making processes.
Once we can articulate what is truly compelling us to seek positive, constructive changes in our *personal attitudes* toward our selves and our
lives, then we can undertake the necessary steps to exploit the positive
aspects of those changes for improving and empowering our lives. Most
importantly, a clearly identified force will help us understand how we
are moving toward an extraordinary existence through minimizing the
unnecessary distractions from other uncertainties associated with this
process. As alluded to by our modified *Uncertainty* principle, the presence of uncertainty in our decision-making process can lead us to less
than optimal outcomes and needless expenditures of intellectual and
emotional energies.

Second, we need to address uncertainty within our decision-making
processes with its proper name to understand the relationship between
uncertainty and the emotions such uncertainty evokes in transitioning
between different states of our existence in different moments of time.
As with the variations between fragments of our *Self*, we need to identify
variations with the types of uncertainty we encounter within our decision-making process to understand their emotional consequences and
other related limitations. That can be best accomplished through properly articulating and labeling our uncertainties with appropriate labels
that will facilitate our control over their integration into our decision-
making process *and* our *personal narrative*. Most scientific literature
labels uncertainty as a lack of knowledge, an experimental inaccuracy, an
ambiguous definition, an undefined imprecision or some similar linguistic permutation.[4] Whether it is the indefiniteness or indeterminateness of
the future impact associated with transitioning between an ordinary and

4. See, e.g., Hilgevoord and Uffink, "Uncertainty Principle."

an extraordinary existence, or even our perspective to see that transition's possibility, we must embark on this journey from a strong starting point.

Through properly categorizing the uncertainties we feel about developing and pursuing our personal and professional aspirations, we can understand their linkages to our emotions and feelings and how better to control said emotions and feelings to enable us to evolve passed our current life situations. Any form of uncertainty in our daily routines usually produces a plethora of emotional responses that the singular term *uncertainty* can hardly encapsulate in any meaningful way.

Third, we must consider how any precision in addressing our life's uncertainties will help us better control the application of our modified *Uncertainty* principle and its contribution to helping us achieve a superlative sense of *Self* from extracting something extraordinary from the ordinary character of our *personal narrative* and its interaction with both the *Sacred Textual Narrative* and the *Grand Historical Narrative*! Even if the outcome of our decisions may be uncertain, we can be precise in the formulation of our narrative strategies and the evaluation of potential narrative content. This precision can help us piece together various areas of our lives that impact how we can improve and empower our *personal narratives*, especially our perceptions and attitudes about the ordinary and the extraordinary. Precision provides an excellent safeguard against inefficient and irrational strategies for personal and professional growth. It also enables us to equalize our different states of understanding between achieving something extraordinary and potential consequences from that achievement. Precision further assists us in creating a coherent sense of the *Self* and linkages between permutations of that *Self* in different states of existences across our entire journey from the ordinary to the extraordinary.

Fourth, we should consider that influences on our modified *Uncertainty* principle depend not only on our own generated perceptions about our hopes and aspirations because external cultural forces encourage us to pursue things we may not truly want or even need, i.e., narrative bullying between the *Grand Historical Narrative* and our *personal narrative*. To safeguard against any extraneous uncertainty penetrating our decision-making processes, we must look inward for the source of our motivation to transition between an ordinary and extraordinary label for our daily routine. Without a strong, organic sense of our motivations, our evolution to an empowered and improved attitude will be greatly jeopardized.

External forces can create havoc far easier than they can help us create any positive changes into our ordinary existence.

Think back, we have all undertaken some previous personal growth exercise with variations in success or failure. Were external influences and pressures, especially unrealistic expectations from sources beyond our control, the reason why our previous efforts succeed or failed? Most likely, the outside influences represented another factor that we could not control and intertwined with our motivations. For example, we may see our dreams and aspirations associated with an extraordinary existence within the *Grand Historical Narrative* through cultural myths, such as the "American Dream."[5] That said, such cultural myths have particular limitations when we compare ourselves to those who have more or less than us. We may experience emotional angst or guilt as we place our selves and our dreams within a comparative paradigm. Also, we submit our ability to dream and to perceive beyond the ordinary since we restrict notions about the extraordinary to our comparative perceptions. While we must all interact with outside influences throughout our *personal narratives*, especially cultural phenomena, we must be diligent in our efforts to remain faithful to our current quest to improve and empower our *personal narrative* and overall narrative strategy to extract the extraordinary from the ordinary.

Fifth, the ways we deal with uncertainties and their emotional consequences will become the primary catalyst for ways to transition between our current *personal narrative* and our improved and empowered *personal narrative*. When we evaluate the current patterns in our thinking and decision-making, we can discern practices that help us minimize uncertainty and its emotional consequences. Uncertainty usually operates as a "sword" and a "shield" as we forge our individual identity with its ability to experience a full gamut of emotions and to live in every day reality. The "sword" analogy reflects our need to fight and to forge a path for our self-expression and to persevere along that path when we encounter obstacles along our journey. The "shield" analogy represents how uncertainty enables us to protect our selves from situations or directions that do not particularly reflect our best interests. Applying these analogies to our situations, we can find ways that our modified *Uncertainty* principle helps us separate reason from passion as we pursue ways to improve and to empower our *personal narrative*. Most importantly, uncertainty will

5. Frie, "Culture and Context," 3.

ensure our sense of individuality since no one, but our own *Self*, can fight and protect ourselves from expressing our desires and hopes along our quest to transition between the ordinary and extraordinary. Without a strong sense of our individuality and the power to express that individuality in all aspects of our lives, especially our personal and professional communities,[6] we will face unnecessary difficulties in deploying improved and empowered expressions of our attitudes in many aspects of our lives, especially the unification of our true *Self* and our *personal narratives* related thereto.

To emphasize the power of uncertainty and our modified *Uncertainty* principle in achieving this chapter's objective, we must think about our responses to the most powerful form of uncertainty in our life trajectory, i.e., traumatic experience.[7] Many of us have experienced some form of trauma throughout our lifetime. If we were adequately prepared for that trauma, we may have reacted differently or avoided it all together. Before reading on, we should reflect upon ways we have dealt with unforeseen trauma throughout our lifetime. How did we process those traumatic experiences? Did those experiences change our life perspective? Limit our attitudes? Or impact our ability to find some form of joy and peace in any aspect of lives? Whatever their impact, we can all concur that our *personal narratives* contain some traumatic experiences (even in their minutest form).

Attitude Expression as Power of Our Personal Narrative

Building upon the quasi-scientific nature of our modified *Uncertainty* principle, we should think about the need for scientific thought in explaining phenomena throughout our *personal narrative*, either as connected or disconnected narrative consequences with specific narrative functions and isolated characters. As previously discussed, most of our decision-making processes are made with some relation to the *Grand Historical Narrative* that inspires us to place ourselves within the larger, historical continuum of humanity. The tensions between our *personal narrative* and the *Grand Historical Narrative* are most important to

6. Ibid., 4, 6.

7. See, e.g., Romme and Escher, *Accepting Voices*, 157.

understanding and to mastering our ability to extract something extraordinary from the ordinary.

More importantly, we must retreat from self-defeating notions that our lives and their stories, that is, our *personal narratives*, do not have any discernible place within the *Grand Historical Narrative*. All of our *personal narratives* and their life stories occupy some discernible space within the collective *Grand Historical Narrative*, even if not immediately or clearly discernible to our own perception. That *Grand Historical Narrative*, regardless of our outward relationship with it, dwells within each of us in some form.[8] That indwelling enables us to have a direct impact on that *Grand Historical Narrative* in some form since we consciously recognize its existence and its importance to our lives.

Similarly, the *Grand Historical Narrative* contains some portion of us since *all* of us, no matter how small or insignificant we feel, dwells within that narrative's grandeur and expanse. We may deploy various forms of individuality or other self-centered expressions of our selves to differentiate our ordinary existence from the collective. Despite those futile efforts and limiting effects on our perception, the collective nature of all humanity will always be present within, among, through and in us wherever we go, whatever we do and whoever we were, are or will become!

Think about the time we walked down a street and encountered a homeless person. We may or may not have talked with that homeless person. Yet, the homeless individual's physical experience, or even name, may have been blotted from our memories, but the encounter had some infinitesimal impact on our *personal narrative*. Though we may never see that same homeless person again in our lifetime, we may have an emotional imprint from that encounter that encourages us to be more sympathetic with homeless people or, more likely, to motivate us in some way to safeguard our personal and professional lives from sharing a similar fate. Whatever the impact of that encounter, there was some interaction between homelessness and us that altered our *personal narrative* and, in turn, shifted our relationship with the *Grand Historical Narrative*. The encounter between the homeless person and our selves was an event within the *Grand Historical Narrative* because homelessness and beggars have been a dominant presence in the *Grand Historical Narrative* throughout the ages. Our response to homelessness, even as an isolated encounter with a homeless person, helps us to understand how we can

8. Havens and Bakan, *Psychology and Religion*, 81.

access and influence that *Grand Historical Narrative* in many unassuming ways throughout our own life time and *vice versa*, such as our charitable commitments, our social and political ideologies, and our compassionate gestures and related philanthropic capacities.

The *Grand Historical Narrative* aside, our *personal narrative* and its ability to grow and to evolve over the course of our lifetime provides the most significant lessons to achieve this chapter's objective. The power of story to transform, to improve and to empower our attitudes cannot be underestimated. Regardless of our religious belief systems and their *Sacred Textual Narrative*, or lack thereof, we must remember that our ability to embrace the Divine, our Creator or even the unknowable void, can only be understood through story.[9] As with many theological explorations and literary recordings of religious belief systems throughout time, the Biblical drama reveals God's presence to humanity and presents those individuals within the *Sacred Textual Narrative* as a foundational precursor to the *Grand Historical Narrative* that transitions between our ordinary, everyday reality and the extraordinary, heavenly reality (whether real or imagined). Only religious works, in general, have that ability to take humanity's story from the tangible confines of our reality and peer into a spiritual reality without any scientific or tangible evidence, but for the faith and trust in the power of story.

Regardless of the broader implications of the foregoing statements, which will be explored in some detail throughout this book, we are compelled to see their immediate consequences. The *Sacred Textual Narrative*, which traverses between our ordinary realities and our extraordinary spiritual, cosmic realities, utilizes the *Grand Historical Narrative* for its ability to instill faith, hope and purpose beyond a single individual into an entire community of believers. Our individual spiritual quest (*personal narrative*) and its placement next to our collective evolution (*Grand Historical Narrative*) seem to establish a tangible boundary between the ordinary and extraordinary. In particular, humanity appears best suited to understand its collective historical foibles within the context of a story steeped in spiritual mystery and "other worldliness." This reality might explain the one clear continuity through humanity's historical evolution—the quest for God and an understanding of the origins of all creation.

9. See, e.g., Havens and Bakan, *Psychology and Religion*, 81, discussing how the Biblical drama helps humanity understand God and its implications for the original story as humanity engages in an historical struggle for an identity, faith and collective purpose.

Now, our personal quest to achieve something extraordinary from the ordinary can apply this rationale to recognize how spiritual mystery and other worldliness can help us cross the boundaries in our thinking and decision-making process to empower and improve our attitude, especially our understanding of the interaction between our *personal narrative* and the *Grand Historical narrative*. Meaning, our need for new ways of thinking, perceiving and explaining phenomena within our *personal narrative* is critical if this chapter's objective can be achieved. Never mind, we will need this innovation to ensure that this book can effectively deliver its teachings and lessons to help transform our lives into extraordinary existences.

Our threshold step in this process requires us to evaluate the fragmented nature of *Self*, especially those personality traits we have developed for particular situations in our lives, such as dealing with difficult loved ones, coping with stressful bosses or even comprising our beliefs for many personal and professional relationships. While we can easily perceive situations that motivated us to acquire certain personality traits, we might not have similar facility with our perceptions about the "origins" of such traits. Applying the notion that interaction with the extraordinary requires us to utilize spiritual mystery and "other worldliness," we must depart from conventional thinking, even if for a brief moment, to contemplate other options and possibilities. Infinite options and possibilities abound and comport with your belief system and personal preferences, provided that such options and possibilities have connection with the *Grand Historical Narrative*, either through scholarly research, philosophical support or other historical relevance. Accordingly, we can assume a starting point for our exploration of the extraordinary to safeguard against unnecessary and destructive flights of fancy, as well as encourage constructive dialogue about our personal experiences with others from some sort of rational, reasonable basis without evoking pointless and damaging ridicule.

An example of an extraordinary hypothesis that might explain a personality trait and applies the dynamics set forth above can be found in groundbreaking research from the Department of Perceptual Studies at the University of Virginia Medical School, where Dr. Ian Stevenson and his predecessors have been researching past life memories in children from around the world for over fifty years. Notions of reincarnation and past lives, even within the romantic concept of déjà vu, evoke all types of feelings and reactions, ranging from total skeptic to total believer, just like any other notion about the mysterious Divine and other narrative components from the *Sacred Textual Narrative*. Albeit, negative reactions to the topic can be debunked through sound arguments focused about reincarnation's role in certain religions, like Hinduism and Buddhism, and scientific methods utilized by a world-class, mainstream medical institution, like the University of Virginia Medical School.

Among the thousands of cases within the Department of Perceptual Studies' library, Dr. Stevenson studied children in Myanmar who exhibited past life memories and personality attributes associated with Japanese soldiers who invaded Burma during World War II.[10] Stevenson's research on these particular cases, as with his other research, reflects strong applications of scientific methods to exclude external variables on these children's past life stories, especially their innate preference for Japanese attitudes and customs within their personalities. As Dr. Stevenson so eloquently described,

> Not all unusual behavior can be explained by genetics and environmental influences, alone or together. This seems to be true of the unusual Japanese-like behavior we have described. If we excluded other factors in the development of such behavior, the way is open to consider a possible third component in the development of personality. The word reincarnation is applicable here, although this term is difficult to describe in material terms.[11]

This description nicely fits within our rubric regarding an example of an extraordinary possibility with a direct relationship to the *Grand Historical Narrative* that can help us understand our own personality traits in ways that defy conventional thinking.

From the East Asian religious justification to the Western scientific method and institutional credibility, reincarnation may present us with imaginative and constructive ways to explain and to explore our personality traits. That said, we should always be seeking ways to explore and to develop our *personal narratives* around notions of something extraordinary and ways to help us understand our *personal narrative* in relation to the *Grand Historical Narrative*. Reincarnation, whether or not it is a real possibility or some other form of connective consciousness, provides an immediate link of the *Self* to a larger, mysterious reality. Whether our

10. See, generally, Stevenson and Keil, "Children of Myanmar," 171–83.
11. Ibid., 173.

personal belief systems may or may not be receptive to any past life notions, reincarnation could minimize the uncertainty generated by our
eventual, inevitable transition at our death. In cultures where reincarnation represents the mainstream norm, such as Hinduism, most individuals do not fear death as a victimizing experience and are empowered
because they believe that the soul has the power to choose and to create
its own destiny over various states of physical and spiritual existence.[12]

Imagine, if we all apply just an increment of such thinking to our
own lives as we evaluate the evolution of our lives and how we ended
up here, here at this moment in time on this particular page. Do we believe that we exercised the power to create our destiny and the life events
that led up to this particular moment? Or do we feel that we have been
victimized by fate and circumstance? Whatever we may feel or believe,
we are entitled to our own personal beliefs and justifications. Though,
we may want to reevaluate how much power and agency we actually exercised over the situation and ways we could have exercised control to
reduce uncertainty and other less than optimal feelings, emotions and
consequences.

12. Sharma, "Psychotherapy with Hindus," 359–60.

2

Structure the Superlative

THIS CHAPTER ENCOURAGES US to strategize ways to revisit our current narrative expression to obtain its optimal, superlative expression. Before we apply our *Be Beyond Best* analysis to our objective to extract something extraordinary from the ordinary, we must take careful inventory of our *personal narrative* to understand how attitudes reflect our personal stories as we know and understand them and how others encounter and perceive them. This evaluation will help us understand how we crafted stories and deployed our imaginations till this point in our lives to explain the many different stages and seasons in our attitudes' development. Most importantly, this inventory will help us begin to see how and why and how our *personal narratives* apply the three essential narrative elements, (i) Be, (ii) Beyond and (iii) Best, to avoid expanding needless energy on accommodating different aspects of the *Self* and distracting us from obtaining our superlative existence. To extract something extraordinary from our ordinary routines, we must focus our energies and efforts on a singular purpose to unify our *personal narrative*, even its minor story lines, into a cohesive story to improve and to empower our attitudes according to our rational goals and reasonable desires.

"BE" WITHIN OUR CURRENT AND DESIRED STATES OF BEING

Wherever we are in our current thinking and decision-making process about our lives, dreams, goals and aspirations, we must recognize how to "Be" within our current phase of being before exploring possible personal growth strategies set forth in this chapter. Through some convergence and confluence of circumstances, whether generated by or foisted upon us, we have reached this singular point in our lifetime. This point has encouraged us to undertake our mutual literary odyssey and analyze our lives through reconfiguring our lives from our ordinary, everyday existence to an extraordinary, satisfying existence.

The real boundary between the actual state of being today and the possible state of being today plus some modicum of time is the limitations upon our perception. Specifically, we must think about three critical elements contained within our current perception. The first element enables us to perceive the continuum between the origins of current attitudes and the hopes of our future attitudes. The second element provides us with tools to understand the fractures and fragments within our attitudes that we have knowingly or unknowingly established to accommodate less than optimal situations in our lives. The third element deals with convergences and divergences between our *personal narratives* and the *Grand Historical Narrative* and exploiting these divergences and convergences to understand the implications of our current decisions and their impact on our attitudes.

Element One: Continuity in our thinking and decision-making processes represent an important step in actualizing and concretizing our future hopes and dreams from our current state of being. As expounded by Pierre Janet, the pioneer of psychodynamic psychiatry, the existence of any thing, thought or object that ever existed continues to exist in a dimensionality beyond human understanding.[1] Applying Janet's thought, we must recognize that our current attitudes and the factors and influences that acted upon them in the past still persist in our current existence at this point in time. The important lesson for us, as suggested by Janet, is the need for us to perceive and to understand the bridge from our past to our present states of our thinking processes. Our perception of those previous influences and factors will provide critical information

---

1. Romme and Escher, *Accepting Voices*, 44–45.

to help us understand how the past shaped this current moment, as well as how this current moment will affect our future existence.[2]

Moreover, the past and its influences permeate our psychological reality in many ways that help us and limit us in our realities, individually and collectively. For example our identity, especially our expressions of the *Self*, becomes structured around particular boundaries in our thinking and decision-making processes and their subsequent impact on our own desires and aspirations.[3] Our prior use of language, in particular, greatly influences the descriptions of our identities, our desires and our future possibilities.[4] Even academic disciplines,[5] such as science, medicine, philosophy and religion, help and hinder our ability to discern different modes of communications between the past, present and future as we conceptualize demarcations in our ordinary existence, i.e., our transition between the past and present, and their implications on our perceptions beyond such boundaries. Some scholars, like David Bakan, conjecture the developments in academic disciplines have greatly dampened humanity's conceit over three critical academic areas through demonstrating humanity's inability to control cosmology, biology and psychology.[6]

Whatever the source of the boundaries between different moments in time throughout our life, we cannot allow those boundaries to preempt our own exploration of the components that comprise our current attitudes and their role in our ordinary routines. As we think about and along the many stories and events that comprise our *personal narratives*, we must identify the areas of their interconnectedness to help us understand our current purpose, future aspirations and their former incarnations throughout our narratives' trajectories.[7] This analysis is mission critical to achieving this chapter's objective regarding our revision to our *personal narrative*'s ability to optimize our narrative creativity to overcome our self-limiting perceptions of ourselves as victims of fate and circumstance.

2. Ibid.

3. Bucholtz and Hall, "Theorizing Identity," 479.

4. See, e.g., ibid., alluding to how our concept of identity can be limited by overly structured language and other limiting influences.

5. See, e.g., Sharp, "Commodifications of the Body," 289.

6. Bakan, *Sigmund Freud*, 3, noting three major blows to humanity's narcissism regarding how (i) Copernicus delivered a cosmological blow, (ii) Darwin delivered a biological blow and (iii) Freud delivered a psychological blow.

7. Begg, *Synchronicity*, 50.

Any victim-oriented perception impairs our vision beyond repair since, by its very nature, it encumbers our approach to life with a reactive impetus rather than a proactive impulse. More distressing, most scholarship supports the notion that our thinking influences the impact of intention, desire and fear, i.e., *limiting emotions,* on achieving our future aspirations because those *limiting emotions* are communicated to all aspects of existence and extends behind descriptive words or manifested behaviors.[8] This means, we must be very careful about our thoughts and their impact on our decision-making capacities regarding our ability to create a future life with greater purpose and abundance that better reflects our authentic, organic *Self* and its placement at all moments in time.[9]

Before we can proceed to our next phase of existence and our new understanding of our current circumstances, we must reflect on those previous influences and factors that brought us here. Specifically, whether or not those same influences and factors can enable us to achieve our future goals and this chapter's objective. In undertaking this process, we cannot only strengthen our perceptions, but exercise our creative capacity to craft a coherent, singular story that will empower and improve our *personal narrative* and, in turn, empower and improve our attitudes. The satisfaction from this creative exercise will help us realize our true potential that may have been tainted by previous disappointments and trials.

We all carry some form of this unfortunate taint since we all made some decisions throughout our lifetime that ended up less than optimal, as well as may have undermined our confidence to make future decisions. Through exercising our creative capacities, we can reconnect with our inner courage to share in the creative process present throughout all creation throughout the Universe.[10] Scholars, like Paul Tillich, have opined that our participation in the creative process enables humanity to have courage to be as oneself and courage to be as part of the collective.[11] Similarly, this type of courage enables us to understand the full scope and breadth of our *personal narrative* along the perceivable space-time continuum of our lives, as well as motivates us to appreciate and to interact with the creative power of the *Grand Historical Narrative.* As result, we can begin to unite our thinking and decision-making processes within an

8. Ibid., 47.

9. See, e.g., ibid., 35.

10. See, e.g., Kaya, "Compelled to Create," 28.

11. Ibid.

overall framework of our lifetime to understand how to truly "Be" within the present moment in time with the benefit of how we were and do not want to be again in our future existences.

Element Two: The fragmented nature of our identity and its presence in our attitude further stresses the need for singularity of thought and perception in our overall self-awareness. Without this singularity, we will never be able to assume a singular notion of "being" in a particular moment in time since all aspects of our identity and their impact on our attitude will require different states of "being" in a particular moment in time. As a result, the *Self* and its complete sense of wholeness will never actual just "be" since that *Self*, even when at rest, will constantly strive for some wholeness in its sense of "being."

The implications of a fragmented/fractured *Self* for this chapter's objective are significant because we must learn to be in the most complete sense before extending our sense of *Self* beyond the ordinary to achieve the superlative. Even in reading this sentence, we must think of at least two senses of the *Self* with which we are currently struggling. The first sense of *Self* is our current, unimportant, unimproved and disempowered sense of *Self*. The second sense of *Self* is our future, important, improved and empowered sense of *Self*. Those two conceptions of the *Self* alone demonstrate how we struggle with differing perceptions and notions about a single subject—the *Self*. Imagine how the other personas we have acquired over our lifetimes have contributed to numerous fragmented states of the *Self* in our current *personal narratives*. So, we must not despair when we contemplate our current attitudes and their need for some change.

The importance of recognizing how our identities and attitudes become fragmented through our need to project a *Self* for the benefits of others rather than ourselves cannot be underestimated. Without a strong sense of individuality, we neither will be able to achieve this chapter's objective nor to transform our lives according to this book's objectives. We must believe that our inner identity receives some modicum of personal importance in our daily lives without the need to make compromises or modifications to reflect society's expectations for our sense of *Self*.[12] This lack of individuality in our decision-making process becomes more problematic when we think about our current personal and professional lives and how our lives reflect external expectations at the detriment of our own happiness and contentment.

12. See, e.g., Rosenfels, *Homosexuality*, 3.

Ironically, the more our current circumstances do not provide us with personal and professional satisfaction, the more our current decision-making processes most likely contain some form of trauma and contain additional fragmented, dissociated thinking.[13] If we view our lives as diverging from living our full potential and our anticipated satisfaction from achieving our aspirations, we will experience less cohesiveness and peace in our sense of the *Self*. As a result, we may undertake additional differentiations within our identities and decision-making processes to deal with the growing distance between our current, ordinary existence and our extraordinary, existence.

Regardless of our placement within these scenarios, we should always be mindful as we think about our lives and their contents, especially our physical, psychological and spiritual possessions, what portion of those possessions fulfills our own individuality and what portion fulfills societal/cultural expectations. Some of us may be surprised how our desires to conform to social norms have severely impaired, dehumanized and/or objectified our lives and our sense of *Self*. For example, commercial appearances may have motivated us to undertake drastic endeavors in our life, even cosmetic surgery, as we pursue an idealized existence represented within our commercial culture.[14] A commercially-generated idealized existence appears to exploit weaknesses in our own individuality as we seek to satisfy external benchmarks for success, happiness and other aesthetic appearances through our blatant disregard for our own individual hopes, desires and other notions of the superlative.

More importantly, without a strong sense of an internal, singular sense of *Self*, we become more vulnerable to thinking that we can acquire a wholeness, or some empowered sense of *Self*, through purchasing a product or service or undertaking some other prescription. These external self-help cultural/commercial remedies play upon the weakness in our individual *Self* and our inability to unify our thinking and decision-making process to formulate an appropriate identity that manifests our authentic *Self*. Without an improved and empowered attitude, we will continue to believe we do not have the power within us to unite expressions of the *Self* with our current existence to our dreams and desires. External influences will never unleash the power of our attitudes to help us

13. See, e.g., Romme and Escher, *Accepting Voices*, 157, opining that our personality and thinking processes accommodate a collection of more or less separate sub-personalities with an individual, divergent learning process.

14. See, e.g., Sharp, "Commodifications of the Body and Its Parts," 293.

make the necessary changes to relate each individual experience within us to a coherent sense of *Self* that can act with a singularity of intention to reflect all aspects of our *own* individuality.

In creating a unified notion of the *Self*, we can employ various metaphorical constructs to help us understand the relationships between the many facets of our current individuality and the areas of that individuality that require modification.[15] Metaphorical constructs also provide us with important tools to understand how our *personal narratives* can assist our transition between the ordinary and the extraordinary and eventually reflect the superlative. For example, the individual stories within our *personal narratives* can provide important insights about our thinking and decision-making processes at particular moments in our past and how they contributed to our current circumstances at this time. Moreover, these metaphorical constructs will provide us with the requisite tools to establish robust and meaningful relationships between our *personal narratives* and the *Grand Historical Narrative*.

Element Three: The interconnectedness between our *personal narrative* and the *Grand Historical Narrative* will enable us to understand how we can truly "be" in particular moments in time with appreciating present consequences from past decisions and anticipating future consequences from current decisions. This comparative story paradigm will help us gain insight and strength to deal with difficult events through their relevance for improving our lives and the lessons contained within them.[16]

As discussed above regarding the usefulness of a metaphorical construct, we need to conceptualize certain cultural influences on our identity that do not so much fragment our sense of *Self*, but rather unite us to a collective reality portrayed within the *Grand Historical Narrative*. The tangible and intangible factors weighing on our *personal narratives* and the *Grand Historical Narrative* are unique to different moments in time and, in turn, are dynamic in their impact on our decision-making processes. Looking back to the tragic events of 9/11, for example, we can analyze how our national identity and geographic proximity to New York City influenced our reactions, never mind the impact on our personal preferences and ideologies.[17] Hence, we will articulate the major factors in our *personal narrative* in pencil within the margins of this page. We

---

15. Ibid, 315.

16. See, e.g., Adams, *Fragmented Intimacy*, 213.

17. See, e.g., Schildkraut, "The More Things Change," 511–35.

may want to revisit them at the conclusion of this chapter, the book or sometime thereafter.

Besides these individual factors, we must ponder how past events set forth along the *Grand Historical Narrative* create a "powerful psychological reality"[18] that compels our thoughts, guides motivations and inspires our imaginations. More importantly, our perceptions of the *Self*, our *personal narratives* and their relationship to the *Grand Historical Narrative* determines how the narratives' converge and diverge throughout our thoughts, motivations and imaginations. Regardless of where we are in our lifetime and the pursuit of our deepest, most liberating dreams, we are always reminded that our existence will compare and contrast with the lives of others, both past, present and future, as preserved and portrayed within that *Grand Historical Narrative*. Should we decide to befriend this reality without regret for the deficiencies in our current state of being, we will find important building blocks to improve and to empower the opportunities for beneficial change within our current purview.

To conceptualize the foregoing, we should think about the ownership of our thoughts, motivations and imaginations with a shifting deed and/or title of ownership that varies between our *personal narrative* and the *Grand Historical Narrative*. There are moments in our life when we own them completely, we rent them to others according to the *Grand Historical Narrative* or we rent them from the *Grand Historical Narrative*. Despite the variations in ownership and control over our thoughts, motivations and imaginations, we can safely conclude that when they are filled with hope, they enable us to better relate to future opportunities. Conversely, when they are filled with despair, they require us to relate to past and present failures. Thus, we must consider the constant nature between our thoughts, motivations and imaginations to help us extract something extraordinary from the ordinary, even when the *Grand Historical Narrative* and our *personal narratives* may mislead us elsewhere from that possibility.

An important factor in helping us embrace future possibilities over present limitations is our dependence on *originology* to explain elements of *personal narrative* with the *Grand Historical Narrative*. *Originology* represents our thinking process that reduces every situation within our lifetime to an analogy with an earlier situation,[19] especially previous situations with-

18. See, e.g., Greene, "Search for Identity," 191, noting our focusing on the colonial past rather than the colonial present can significantly impact psychological reality.

19. See, e.g., Erikson, *Young Man Luther*, 18.

in the *Grand Historical Narrative* and their manifestations throughout our *personal narratives*. With *originology*, we are better equipped to understand incomprehensible phenomena with more certainty and more through appreciating how the tools and mechanisms within both narratives enabled our predecessors to persevere and to overcome similar struggles, as well as to achieve and to celebrate similar successes.

Yet, we must mindful of our individual imprint within our own *originology* to provide sufficient explanations for the unique aspects of ourselves, which may or may not have been revealed within either narrative. The comfort that can be derived from this type of reasoning provides us with a tangible reality within which we can grow and evolve with an improved understanding of linkages between our current circumstances and their impact on our future opportunities. Even if the reality diverges with the *Grand Historical Narrative* at a particular moment, we can always identify other moments within our *personal narratives* that demonstrate convergence for peace of mind.

Moving forward, the mindfulness required to exploit the positive aspects of convergences and divergences between these narratives rests upon our receptiveness toward implementing notions of attitude formation and perception within both narratives that extend outside ideological limitations and conventional norms.[20] One possible approach to this mindfulness is the integration of some form of spirituality or religious practice that can provide tranquility and order when comparing the convergences and divergences between these narratives.[21] This approach should be considered since the *Sacred Textual Narrative* as consistently played a major role throughout the *Grand Historical Narrative* in some permutation from the beginning. Moreover, religion provides useful ways to establish useful and helpful boundaries for our thinking and decision-making process when we consider some form of accountability to a mysterious Divine narrator within the *Sacred Textual Narrative*.

Most importantly, religion allows us to surrender our ego to a higher state of being that permits the extraordinary to enter our frame of consciousness. For example, we should not underestimate the power of the *deus ex machina*, i.e., an unexpected plot device that resolves a hopeless situation in a play or novel, to help the development of our *personal narrative* to its highest actualization. Should we find ourselves

20. See, e.g., ibid., 22.
21. See, e.g., Spiegelman, *Judaism and Jungian Psychology*, 5.

unwilling or unable to grasp this line of thinking, let us think of various battles throughout history that could have easily turned out differently with major consequences for all humanity. Throughout any compelling story, there must always exist some unknowable element that inspires us to perceive something extraordinary in an otherwise ordinary storyline. Similarly, our *personal narratives* should not be void of this readily available assistance and the infinite possibilities it possesses as we contemplate how the interaction between our *personal narrative* and the *Grand Historical Narrative* can enable us to extract the extraordinary from the ordinary at this very moment in time and beyond.

MOVING BEYOND THE ORDINARY

Our capacity to perceive the opportunities within our ordinary existence that enable us to attain the possibilities beyond our ordinary routines will determine *when*, not how, we will begin to access the extraordinary within our current living situations. This capacity directly correlates with our emotional reactions to loss and our sensitivities to hope. When we move our thinking and decision-making beyond their current, ordinary states of existence, we will experience an immediate loss—the passing of the ordinary and the comforts associated with the familiar. Some scholars, like Stolorow, argue that any form of loss represents a death of a part of oneself, even an existential death, and will require some recognition and grief associated with that loss.[22] So, we should not be too hard on ourselves if we are finding our efforts to move beyond the ordinary into the extraordinary taking more time than we anticipated.

Furthermore, we must remember that the effort required to improve and to empower our attitude toward our lives will foreclose upon certain possibilities, especially the possibility of remaining within the ordinary, and that foreclosure will evoke similar sentiments of loss and grief.[23] No one strategy for our personal growth will ever provide us with infinite possibilities, just a range of possibilities that will preclude the continued existence of perceived possibilities and will provide their replacement with unperceivable, new possibilities. The momentary loss within our perceptions will require us to rely on new ways to think about certain aspects of lives as we attempt to overcome the limitations of our current *Self*.

22. Stolorow, "Individuality in Context," 66.
23. Ibid.

Reordering our thinking may take us places we never knew possible in our search for the boundary between the ordinary and extraordinary. We may seek something, or even a belief system, that enlivens and enlarges our imaginations to grasp a reality beyond our current state of existence. Certain religious/spiritual groups have undertaken this type of thinking in promulgating notions of a mythical past that imbues an individual with all types of material to transform an ordinary story into an extraordinary *personal narrative*.[24] To demonstrate the foregoing, we will look toward the spiritual practice of therianthropy, i.e., the metamorphosis of humans into animals, to understand how the power of a spirit-infused alternative identity routed in animals and shape shifting can instruct us to embrace new ways of imagining our sense of *Self* and its interaction with an extraordinary existence. As Michele Jamal artfully articulated,

> The awakening of the shape-shifter archetype in our present time is a symbolic marker for the emerging spiritual realization that consciousness and situations are malleable and can be shifted. Individuals are shifting through a myriad of identities, reaching for an integrated, multifaceted self.[25]

While most of us reading this book, myself included, have probably only encountered such notions in fictional settings, like shapeshifters on the HBO Series *TrueBlood*, we appear to have substantial and legitimate scholarship on this phenomena in our present society. Perhaps, we all might learn something new from our relationships with our pets or any animal we encounter as we strive to grasp the extraordinary within our ordinary routines.

Furthermore, the use of animals to provide an outlet for alternative identity indicates that a convergence between *personal narrative, Sacred Textual Narrative* and the *Grand Historical Narrative* has allowed mainstream media, especially the Internet, to present magical, religious and esoteric beliefs in a compelling way to encourage new spiritual identities.[26] These animal identities with mythic powers confirm we are all searching for an outlet to improve and to empower our sense of *Self* and how that

24. See, e.g., Robertson, "Beast Within," 24, discussing the Therianthropy movement and its reliance on the mythical relationship between the animal-to-divine element.

25. Ibid., 25.

26. Ibid.

sense of *Self* is projected to and perceived by others. Regardless of our reaction to any of us who actually may hold and/or practice some form of therianthropy, we should be inspired by the possibilities we may have within our grasp to transform our lives beyond their ordinary existence, even with less magical or esoteric, outcomes.

While the shape-shifter archetype represents an extreme reconfiguration of our ordinary reality, we must seek more realistic and tangible ways to reconfigure that reality to achieve something extraordinary. In particular, we should look for clues in the most basic things around us, like language, to unlock something mysterious that will encourage us to seek beyond conventional boundaries. Through the power of language, we have the ability to express our desires and interests,[27] as well as create a sense of *Self* that can fulfill them with reasonable certainty. Even within conventional spiritual paradigms, Jewish mysticism expounds notions of letter play to extract extraordinary meanings from single words within the Bible.[28] Hence, we need to think about how best we should consider reordering and reconfiguring our vocabulary to express our intentions *and* our abilities to grasp the extraordinary from our current predicaments.

In using negative, self-defeating, self-effacing language to describe ourselves, we will continue to create barriers between the extraordinary and us. However, if we begin to consciously make an effort to reconfigure our vocabulary to reflect our true capacities, the extraordinary will move closer within reach and the ordinary will move away from its current position within our lives. We will never fully understand our true purpose and how attitudes must be empowered and improved to reflect that purpose if we continue to cloak that purpose with extraneous language and disruptive hyperbole that limits our access to the extraordinary.[29]

Moreover, we must recognize our abilities and inabilities to perceive the extraordinary in our existence will be dependent on our attempts to process relevant sensory input and its impact on our sense of *Self* and our attitudes. Researchers have concluded that our perceptions are filled with perceptual inaccuracy or sensory deception just as much as perceptual accuracy.[30] This means we must exercise extreme caution and awareness as we venture into this new territory to ensure we are pursuing an op-

27. Bucholtz and Hall, "Theorizing Identity," 480.

28. See, e.g., Bakan, *Sigmund Freud*, 267.

29. Begg, *Synchronicity*, 49, noting that motivation without intention does not point anywhere and just consumes energy with neither intention nor purpose.

30. Slade and Bentall, *Sensory*, 1.

timal strategy for our overall well-being. Most perceptions that cannot be publicly verified or concretized with some certainty, especially within the *Grand Historical Narrative*, should warrant special concern since our cultural norms will taint them with potentially limiting and destructive labels, e.g., hallucinations, delusions of grandeur, insanity or similar nomenclature.[31]

To minimize our encounters with such unpleasantness, we must recognize that our dreams and other ways to see beyond the ordinary should always have a rational, reasonable basis according to our individual standards that subsume elements of our cultural norms. While indigenous cultures might be more receptive to notions of ordinary and non-ordinary realities as traversed by the village shaman, most of us live in worlds limited by the practical nature of every day reality. No one should be discouraged about the *possibility* of interacting with the "spirit world" or other forms of non-ordinary reality, just be mindful that such interaction may lead to unnecessary ridicule and distraction from achieving an extraordinary superlative for our *personal narrative*.

Without doubt, this book is meant to expose us to possibilities as we search for something beyond the ordinary. We just need to establish some guideposts along this journey to ensure all of us, wherever we reside in relationship to the Divine, to achieve the full benefits presented in this book. Our goal is to establish flexible boundaries to prevent academic disciplines or other influences[32] from compartmentalizing ordinary, everyday paradigms in our quest for an improved and empowered sense of *Self* and attitude. In achieving this task, we should be mindful about the law of human gravity that states a person will gravitate from a condition that appears to contain greater distress to a condition that appears to contain lesser distress, never in reverse.[33]

Applying this law to our decision-making process, we should be able to discern patterns throughout our lifetime that confirm its most basic point—most people are distress-adverse. That said, we must conceptualize our decision to extract something extraordinary from the ordinary as confirming this principle. For example, when the law of human gravity is applied within a clinical paradigm of addiction and recovery, we can

31. See, e.g., ibid., 80.

32. See, e.g., Sharp, "Commodifications of the Body and Its Parts," 314, noting how flexible boundaries preempt academic disciplines from compartmentalizing certain paradigms.

33. Twerski, *Addictive Thinking*, 102.

discern how an addict's perception changes depending on the addiction/ recovery cycle in the addict's *personal narrative*.[34] During the addiction cycle, the active addict perceives abstinence as the state of greater distress rather than the chemical substance. During the recovery cycle, the recovering addict perceives the chemical substance as the state of greater distress rather than the abstinence.[35] This shift in perspective operates as the critical component in recovery. Similarly, we must shift our perspectives about how our ordinary states without change represent a state of greater distress and how our extraordinary states with change represent a state of lesser distress.

To effectuate this shift in our perspectives, we must identify the changes in our lives to help facilitate this process and to empower and improve our sense of *Self*.[36] First, we must change our egos, such as our personalities, behaviors and motivations, which prevent us from accessing some semblance of the extraordinary. Second, we must change the current direction of our personal and professional lives to something that comports with the *Grand Historical Narrative* and our potential *personal narrative* convergence with some aspect of an extraordinary historical occurrence. Third, we must ensure that changes within our *Self* and attitude will enhance our personal and professional relationships. Fourth, and most important, we must ensure that the change can be maintained in all aspects of our improved and empowered *Self*, as well as our optimal *personal narrative* that exemplifies the superlative. With such changes and their potential consequences, we will have new abilities to interact with the extraordinary since our old boundaries and conditioning to their limitations will fade throughout this process.

Notwithstanding the foregoing, we always have the power of our dreams to help us figure out new and innovative ways to reconfigure our ordinary lives to participate in the extraordinary. For example, some researchers have concluded that our dreams reflect the empirical extensions of our lives where continual tensions between motive and contingency plays out in our dream states and enables us to apply certain meanings that defy regular consciousness.[37] These tensions between motive and

34. Ibid., 103.

35. Ibid.

36. See, e.g., Cramer, *Protecting the Self*, 94, discussing the major components of a robust definition of the *Self*.

37. Capps, *Jesus: A Psychological Biography*, 264, commenting on the work of Bert O. States and his analysis of dream narratives.

contingency further amplify divergences and convergences between our *personal narrative* and the *Grand Historical Narrative* in ways only the freedom of our dreams can allow. Hence, sometimes we may need to pay close attention to our dreams, if not for their thematic and dramatic content, but the organizational logic and its potential consequences to reveal something beyond ordinary consciousness that will represent an achievable superlative.

THE ELUSIVE SUPERLATIVE AND OUR QUEST FOR ITS AVOIDANCE

Contentment and satisfaction are the hallmarks for civilized, cultured living in most societies in the modern world. Yet, contentment and satisfaction cannot ensure our happiness or some representation of everything we always wanted because the attainment of our entire dream would only leave us depressed since we cannot anticipate nothing more or better for ourselves in the future.[38] Keeping this in mind, we can recognize that any notion of a superlative should not be considered a final manifested sense of the superlative over the entire course of our lifetime. Rather, all notions of the superlative, in any form, must be considered a dynamic construct that changes and evolves over time according to our psychological, personal, professional and spiritual needs. As the *Grand Historical Narrative* demonstrates, the notion of "best" varies between time and cultures and must operate in the same manner within our *personal narrative*. Without this safeguard, we may become victims of our own best and its limitation on our future development.

As we consider reordering our lives to transition between states of ordinary and extraordinary, we need to appreciate how those states communicate with each other through our perceptions of their similarities and differences.[39] We must understand that the current intersection between the extraordinary and ordinary represents an optimal, superlative state and our task requires us to extract emotional nourishment

---

38. Rosenfels, *Homosexuality*, 9, noting how the personal importance of an individual cannot be tied to the attainment of its wants without dire consequences for its wellbeing and future hopes and aspirations.

39. Bakan, *Sigmund Freud*, 207, discussing the intangible nature of transference in the doctor-patient relationship and its broader spiritual implications outside a clinical setting.

to boost our self-esteem[40] to exploit the possibilities of this current moment. Moreover, that intersection will shift as we move between different moments in our lives with each new intersection providing us greater insights into how best we can discern the extraordinary in our ordinary existence.

Hence, we can only live some permutation of "best" over a particular time period before external and internal influences require us to revisit our definitions and notions of what actually qualifies as "best." This spirited, playful notion of superlative should encourage us to appreciate how the current components of our *personal narratives* may unknowingly represent an optimal, superlative configuration that has been permitting the extraordinary into our everyday existence. More importantly, we must question how the stories and events within our *personal narrative* accurately reflect some aspect of an optimal, superlative configuration (including those areas that have motivated us to seek an improved and empowered attitude). Once we make peace with all aspects of our personal narrative, especially its more trying and challenging pieces, we can begin to focus the most relevant portions of the *Grand Historical Narrative* to order our lives with building blocks for an extraordinary, superlative existence.

This chapter concludes with a simple thought: Does the power to extract something extraordinary from an ordinary experience, event or circumstance rest within the power of our *personal narrative* to perceive its superlative character within its ordinary narrative functions? Smile!

---

40. Twerski, *Addictive Thinking*, 24, noting that most emotional problems originate from low self-esteem.

PART 2

Our Empowered and Improved Self as Optimal Narrator

3

Remove Self-Destructive Behavior Patterns and Their Triggers

THIS CHAPTER'S OBJECTIVE, OUR avoidance of self-destructive behavior patterns, is crucial for our overall well-being and our success in this personal growth endeavor. The existence of self-destructive behaviors exists in all our lives in some capacity. Whether we smoke too much, drink too much, use illicit drugs too much, engage in sexual promiscuity too much, drive recklessly too much, or practice some other high-risk behavior too much, we must clearly identify conduct that tends to reinforce destructive behavior and preempts us from living a constructive existence.

The divide between constructive and destructive can vary depending on particular behaviors and their impact on our physical, psychological, emotional and spiritual well-being. For instance, some of us may consider a glass of wine per day as a constructive behavior since we perceive certain benefits to that one drink, such as the enjoyment derived from its taste and/or the calming effect derived from its alcohol content. Without opining on the medical consequences of that one glass or its potential to establish a gateway to other practices, i.e., hard alcohol, prescription drugs, sexual promiscuity, etc., we must be mindful of the direct consequences of a repetitive ritual within our personal lives. The actual act of pouring and consuming a single glass of wine per day suggests a profound character trait dwells within our identity that operates according to its own needs and wants. That character trait teaches us that certain behaviors have infiltrated our *personal narratives* and have created very compelling repetitive patterns in our ordinary behaviors, even if they initially appear innocuous and mundane.

The real work in achieving this chapter's objective will be identifying the repetitive behavior patterns that comprise our identity that *either* improve and empower our sense of *Self* and our attitudes *or* destroy and disempower our sense of *Self* and our attitudes. The first step in identifying self-destructive behavior practices is considering those practices in relation to our complete sense of *Self*, that is, our identity. Identity, unlike the *Self*, is an elastic term that encapsulates the main adjectives we use to describe our existence within our *personal narrative* and its relation to the *Grand Historical Narrative*.

Generally, an identity is some sense of *Self* that defines us to other people and enables us to feel a sense of internal wholeness. The *Self*, on the other hand, represents an internal, complex enterprise that cannot be readily described through adjectives or other external mechanisms since our emotions play an important role in communicating our sense of *Self* to ourselves without regard to consequences from either our *personal narrative* and/or the *Grand Historical Narrative*. Simply put, our identity formation utilizes many external and internal factors, while our sense of *Self* represents innate feelings and emotions unique to each individual. That said, the interplay between identity and *Self* exposes our vulnerability to certain destructive behavior practices in certain moments in our lives when we experience uncertainty and/or insecurity.[1] We have the power to avoid the pitfalls of destructive behavior practices if we understand how the self-destructive behavior satisfies both the weaknesses in our identity and the inadequacies in our sense of *Self*.

Applying these notions about weakness and inadequacy to our daily glass of wine example, we can discern a potential explanation for that daily consumption pattern—a single glass of wine appears to help us to overcome some weakness and inadequacy within our internal emotional workings. For the purposes of our analysis *and* achieving this chapter's objective, we will consider a repetitive practice, like consuming a glass of wine on a daily basis, as some form of a self-destructive behavior because the practice does not serve any clearly *discernible* benefit to our ordinary existence. We cannot argue that we need that daily glass of wine to live

---

1. Capps, *Understanding Psychosis*, 131, noting how self-destructive behavior patterns correlate to identity uncertainty, especially shifting between identity states that generate confusion and other psychotic disorders.

a full, abundant life because if we assume that position, by default, we admit our dependency on an external substance. This definition becomes more robust when we replace the glass of wine scenario with far more destructive practices, like illicit drugs, sexual promiscuity or other high-risk behaviors. That said, we could only fathom that a daily, repetitive practice serves some *indiscernible* benefit that relates to an unperceivable weakness and inadequacy in our identity and/or our sense of *Self.*

To understand how such weaknesses in our identity and inadequacies in our sense of *Self* can create havoc in our lives, we must look to the psychological implications of such conditions as acute identity confusion and its impact on mental health. For example, acute identity confusion culminates as our weaknesses in our identity prevent us from making and acting out important decisions in our lives, such as relationship commitments, career choices and other self-defining life activities.[2] The consequence of such acute identity confusion usually concludes with a psychotic break, that is, a complete mental breakdown, that requires the patient to sort through identity issues. Moreover, the inadequacies associated with the *Self* generally manifest in deceptive personal developments as ways to rationalize and to deal with weaknesses in identity and, in turn, require relearning and rethinking social and intellectual values to overcome these deficiencies.[3] Just because such identity issues increase the risk of psychotic disorders,[4] we cannot dismiss their less intense impact on our behavior practices without discernible benefits.

Inadequacies in our sense of *Self* and weaknesses in our identity can manifest in many ways that can qualify as destructive behavior. For example, most research studies conclude that confusion over sexual identity correlates with substance abuse and compulsive sexual behaviors, especially among younger adults.[5] Further factors weigh upon this correlation as identity confusion motivates individuals to create lifestyles that sustain their self-destructive behavior patterns, such as avoidance of marriage and parenting commitments and high-pressured professional career choices.[6]

2. See, e.g., ibid., 134.

3. See, e.g., ibid., 135, discussing latent identity crises in the context of fellowship and sexual intimacy.

4. Ibid., 131.

5. McCabe et al., "Sexual Orientation, Substance Use Behaviors and Substance Dependence," 1334, correlating bisexual youth and adults with substance abuse and sexual compulsion behaviors.

6. See, e.g., ibid., 1333.

We can revisit our glass of wine per day example and ask how we structure our daily routine around that consumptive pattern. Certainly, that example does not appear as psychological distressing as substance abuse and sexual compulsion, but we can grapple with our logical justifications for our daily consumption. Addictive thinking, in general, contains a superficial logic that seduces and misleads the addict.[7] Similarly, we can conceptualize a multitude of reasons to justify some of the more destructive aspects of our daily routines, like having a glass of wine. Yet, we would be truly hard-pressed to demonstrate some tangible benefit from engaging in that behavior. The absence of any benefit does not itself qualify the activity as addictive, but the activity's repetitive nature *plus* the absence of a discernible benefit certainly makes the activity suspect.

Another important factor in our analysis of certain behaviors rests with our propensity to engage in behaviors that satisfy only one aspect of our identity or sense of *Self*. We may subscribe to a peculiar behavior pattern to help offset an emotional deficiency in one aspect of our identity, such as a feeling of failure or a sense of inferiority.[8] The fear of failure itself can compel us to engage in destructive behaviors that preempt any attempt, successful or unsuccessful, to pursue our dreams and aspirations. After all, we can be considered a failure if we never even tried to succeed in the first place! This simple thought contains immeasurable consequences for all aspects of our lives.

We become victims to our imaginations when we create all types of unattainable wondrous scenarios for our futures and feel totally inadequate to achieve any semblance of that wonderment in our lifetime.[9] Feeling victimized by circumstances outside our control, we may flirt with destructive behaviors to help us move away from feelings of insurmountable, crushing despair. The piece of identity and sense of *Self* that surrenders to this notion communicates with those feelings of failure and prevents our perspective, as well as other participants in our lives, to see beyond the victimizing feelings of despair.[10] This vicious cycle requires

7. See, e.g., Twerski, *Addictive Thinking*, 7.

8. See, e.g., Rosenfels, *Homosexuality*, 116, discussing how individuals use sadistic mechanisms to avoid the possibility of failure in human attachment and inferior thoughts in their love capacities.

9. Kakar, *Mad and Divine*, 148, commenting on idealist thought among Hindu and Buddhist philosophers that stress the ontological status of our imaginations' omnipotence.

10. Romme and Escher, *Accepting Voices*, 26–27, noting how researchers want an

strict discipline to appreciate how we, along with other influences in our lives, can create future possibilities that replace despair with hope and allow us to escape from destructive behavior practices.

Unlike other self-awareness exercises presented throughout this book, self-destructive behavioral patterns represent more direct, disruptive external influences to our thought and decision-making processes. Such patterns require the intervention of counteractive external influences to break and to revisit the destructive behaviors in our lives. Ranging from the Higher Power in twelve-step programs to our friends and family members, we must remember the power of relationships in creating the addictive behavior and in breaking the addictive cycle. For example, researchers have examined that even in our most addictive/destructive phase, we are engaging in a form of pseudo-creativity that sustains and benefits our compulsive behaviors and their addictive/destructive consequences.[11]

So, despite the other perceived failures or fear of failures in an addictive individual's life, we can appreciate their success to perpetuate and to sustain their destructive behavior patterns against all reason and rationality (even if the addict cannot consciously comprehend this success). This act of destructive creation, no matter how perverse or consequential, still unites everyone that engages in addictive/destructive behaviors to the power of all creation and its infinite possibilities beyond the addiction.[12] Addiction and self-destructive behavior, by themselves, prevent us from seeing the full range of creative possibilities as the satisfaction of the addiction and destructive behavior becomes the primary impetus for creativity. We must think about how the behavior patterns within our life, especially those behaviors that contain no discernible benefit, limit our own ability to access the full power and possibility of creation.

For purposes of this chapter's objective, we will study addictive/destructive behavior-type patterns in our current states of being to understand how such patterns fulfill particular weaknesses in our identity and/or satisfy specific inadequacies in our *Self*. Once we identify those patterns and their contributions to understanding our identity and our sense of *Self*, we will perceive opportunities and possibilities beyond our

---

enlarged clinical perspective to understand how patients cope with the phenomena of inner voices.

11. See, e.g., Rosenfels, *Homosexuality*, 107.

12. Havens and Bakan, *Psychology and Religion*, 83, noting how the possibilities of knowing a larger whole, the possibilities for distortion increase with proportion.

current relationship with those behavioral patterns to replace destructive practices with constructive behaviors. Finally, we will consider how to avoid behaviors and practices that neither represent nor create superlative benefits for all aspects of identity and our sense of *Self*.

INTIMACY—THE ART OF BEING WITH ALL ASPECTS OF OUR IDENTITY AND OUR SENSE OF SELF

The critical component in determining the strength of our identity and our sense of *Self* is how our decision-making processes during its formation utilized intimacy and our ability to act through on our commitments based on that intimacy.[13] Intimacy helps us to make meaningful commitments and healthy attachments to various people and situations within our lifetime. However, some of us may have encountered some trauma in the development of our identity and sense of *Self* that makes us struggle with intimacy in our relationships and other crucial aspects of our lives. Regardless of how we view intimacy in our current states of being, we must be mindful of its role in the various areas of identity and our sense of *Self* that limit our attitudes from achieving their optimal existence. In particular, our own weaknesses in our identities usually create unforeseen harm and confusion as we try to pursue lesser forms of intimacy with less than desirable consequences.

Our pursuit of destructive, or even disruptive, activities to our daily routines could contribute to an "identity decline" with contributions to our identity weaknesses, such as: (i) "time confusion" (when our perception of time regresses to its early infancy state and cannot affect future identity development); (ii) "identity consciousness" (when we recognize the resolved discrepancies between self-esteem, aggrandized self-image and projected self-appearance); and (iii) "work paralysis" (when we perceive inadequacy based on unrealistic ego ideal demands and inability to settle in a societal niche for the employment of our natural talents).[14] As we contemplate the foregoing, we can understand what aspects of our own identities were subject to similar declines along our life journeys and their cumulative impact on our vulnerability to destructive/addictive behaviors.

---

13. See, e.g., Erikson, *Identity, Youth, and Crisis*, 155–57.

14. Ibid., 185.

Considering intimacy deficiencies within our own identity and sense of *Self*, we can appreciate how destructive/addictive behavior patterns can offer a potent, but inferior, intimacy equivalent. Our relationships with repetitive behaviors without discernible benefits, i.e., potentially destructive/addictive behaviors, represent hybrid forms of intimacy—an asymmetrical intimate relationship with the repetitive behavior that contains elements of closeness, compassion, commitment and accord.[15] The question we must ask ourselves is why have we chosen to share intimacy with a repetitive behavior over more constructive intimacy partners and practices and does this intimacy with a repetitive behavior produce beneficial or detrimental effects?[16] Ironically, our intimacy with the repetitive behavior precludes any intimacy with the underlying condition that prompts us to engage in that behavior. For example, addiction / self-destructive behavior usually operates as a form of self-psychology in a vain attempt to resolve feelings of emptiness and depression.[17] As we prefer the intimacy of the addiction / self-destructive behavior over any intimacy with the feelings that instigated it, we become more detached to understanding the less desirable, destructive aspects of our state of being.

Moreover, the intimacy we can generate from addiction / self-destructive behavior patterns provides a certain modicum of comfort in our more distressing moments since it can distract our attentions from doing the work to repair weaknesses in our identity and inadequacies in our sense of *Self*. This distraction might lead to dependence on the addiction / self-destructive behavior, or in more extreme cases, we may come to abuse such behaviors intentionally, and the negative consequences from such dependence and abuse may eventually supersede the underlying instigation.[18]

So, as we contemplate those aspects of our current state of being and its repetitive practices without discernible benefits, we must consider how much intimacy we have invested in those repetitive practices to the detriment of alternative relationships that would have challenged our identity and sense of *Self*, along with our understanding of them at this

15. Adams, *Fragmented Intimacy*, 86, noting how asymmetries exist between four modalities of intimacy.

16. Ibid., 83, commenting that addictions can contain certain intimacies that can be regarded as beneficial or detrimental to the addict.

17. See, e.g., Flores, *Addiction as an Attachment Disorder*, 69.

18. See, e.g., Freimuth, *Hidden Addictions*, 3, expounding the definitions of dependence and abuse and their related treatment codes as set forth in the DSM-IV.

particular moment in time. We should be able to identify what aspects of the repetitive behavior truly qualify as addictive/self-destructive when we analyze what we have forfeited to maintain our repetitive practices without discernible benefits. Thinking back to our daily glass of wine scenario, we might notice how that daily ritual within our *personal narrative* came with greater opportunity cost than originally surmised by our initial assessments.

Through intimacy, we may come to understand better ways to deal with and overcome weaknesses in our identity and inadequacies in our sense of *Self* as we seek new relationships in new ways that modify the conventional aspects of our ordinary existence. These innovations can take place in many areas of our lives. Even something as simple as our speech and certain variations in our speech patterns can enable us to empower our fantasies and imaginations with new modes of communications between our essentialist and nonessentialist identities to present our selves for a variety of purposes and circumstances.[19]

Whatever modifications we make within our personalities and attitudes to accommodate our identity weaknesses, those modifications, like our repetitive behaviors without discernible benefit, may function to keep us from experiencing a true wholeness of the *Self* as we seek to rationalize their divergent existences within our ordinary personal and professional routines.[20] Most importantly, such modifications continue to force us to pursue inferior forms of intimacy with other people and external circumstance that have marginal impact on repairing our identity weaknesses and other inadequacies with the *Self* since they only appear to satisfy specific, isolated aspects of the *Self* rather than addressing the overall *Self*.

Based on the foregoing, we can conjecture that we have an innate need to substitute an artificial form of intimacy for a real form of intimacy when aspects of our identity and our sense of *Self* do not provide sufficient strength in our decision-making process to make a choice and to act through upon its foreseeable and unforeseeable consequences. For example, most individuals who pursue a non-mainstream, conventional existence seek virtual outlets to act upon their interests, such as video

19. See, e.g., Bucholtz and Hall, "Theorizing Identity," 499, discussing how phone sex operators use variations in speech patterns to create fantasies and to monetize certain sexual identities.

20. Romme and Escher, *Accepting Voices*, 157, hypothesizing about how a personality accommodates a collection of more or less separate sub-personalities.

games and special interest websites. The application of a virtual filter, like the Internet, amplifies problems associated with identity weaknesses since like-minded people usually gravitate toward the same special-interest websites and activities, thereby aggravating artificial intimacy and its attitudinal consequences.[21] Our own individual interests in current events can recall numerous tragedies directly linked to various websites over the years, ranging form financial scams, misleading advertisements, relationship horror stories and other sordid tales.

For the purposes of this chapter's objective, we must evaluate how we create our own forms of artificial intimacy to deal with our identity weaknesses in our current state of being. Perhaps, we prefer other modes of virtual expression to house our expressions of artificial intimacy away from the Internet. Certain repetitive behaviors without benefit originate from an impulse control disorder and may significantly disrupt our ability to pursue healthy forms of intimacy.[22] Hoarding, for example, and its dependence on compulsive shopping represent a virtual expression since that activity allows us to create intimacy with inanimate objectives, along with their selling mechanisms, that appears superior to other forms of intimacy in our current lives.[23] Moreover, compulsive consumption provides the perfect outlet for an intimacy-instigated addictive/self-destructive behavior pattern because compulsive shopping distorts our perception to the mundane limitations of our daily existence as we acquire objects neither with regard to their financial consequence nor with regard to their potential benefit to our overall well-being. Regardless, all of us at some point can think back to some purchase, clothing item or other domestic possession, and conclude we did not have a rational or reasonable basis to make that purchase. Hopefully, we have not incurred unnecessary consumer debt that continues to burden us after the emotional satisfaction from the purchase has waned.

In thinking about our intimate relationships with repetitive and/or excessive consumption patterns, one particular consumptive pattern

21. See, e.g., Ross, "Typing, Doing, and Being," 343, noting how young adults are exploring their sexuality through pursuing sex on the Internet. See also Center for Disease Control, "Trends in HIV-Related Risk Behaviors," 971–76, reviewing the impact of sexually oriented websites that facilitate sexual activity, minimize sexual risks and increase the HIV-infection rates.

22. See Freimuth, *Hidden Addictions*, 4, defining impulse control disorders like pathological gambling, kleptomania, etc.

23. Twerski, *Addictive Thinking*, 58.

stands out for special consideration—our vacations. Most of us reading this book have taken at least one vacation in their lifetime, never mind the past twelve months. Wherever we traveled to and whatever we observed there, we have vivid and intimate relationships with our vacations that provide us with important insights regarding intimacy and repetitive behaviors in our states of being. First, the physical act of "taking a vacation" requires us to surrender our permanent routine to a temporary excursion with many uncertainties. Second, we intentionally expose ourselves to rejection and disappointment as we seek the necessary approvals, whether from professional superiors, family members or other dependants, to travel beyond the boundaries of our ordinary existence. Third, we gladly exert the energy and encounter the stress to travel to our vacation destination, which, in most cases, greatly outweighs the familiarity associated with our daily routines. Fourth, we immerse our sights and senses in a temporary environment with the anticipated outcome that such ephemeral immersion will help restore and repair us from the stresses of our daily routine. Fifth, at the inevitable conclusion of our vacation, we return home and resume our daily grind and look forward to planning our next vacation.

According to our definition that categorizes an addictive, self-destructive behavior as a repetitive activity without any discernible benefit, our vacations may not only satisfy that definition, but educate us about other areas of current states of being. While we might be compelled to argue that our vacations enable us to maintain our professional and personal status quo, we cannot completely ignore the fact that vacations, like other compulsive consumptive patterns, require consistent repetition without cessation to experience a temporary discernible benefit, reminiscent of a short-lived, chemically-induced high. We need not only to continue to consume vacations to experience that "high," but we need variations in our vacation destinations and experiences to maintain that "high" to our daily routine. As we contemplate the ramifications of that statement, we might want to consider the areas in our current, ordinary existence that compel us to pursue nourishing intimate relationships with the ephemeral nature of our vacations, rather than our permanent, everyday circumstances. Furthermore, we can better appreciate how the one glass of wine per day example communicates a muted version of this notion that when our lives lack meaningful intimacy to repair our identity weaknesses and inadequacies of the *Self*, we succumb to repetitive practices without readily discernible benefit.

Logically, even if not psychically, spiritually or otherwise justified, the amount of financial and emotional resources we have spent on vacations till this point in our lives could easily have contributed to our early retirements—a non-repetitive activity! Perhaps, we are just wired to engage in repetitive practices even when the discernible benefits from such practices are void of any rational, tangible benefits. That said, our dependence on vacations to help us cope with our daily stresses suggests a similar correlation with other addictive/self-destructive behavior patterns. Vacation junkies, like other addicts, value the closeness with our vacations over our daily routines, favoring mental and emotional engagement with our vacation destinations or experiences rather than our daily routines.[24] While vacations are wonderful, nurturing experiences in many ways unlike true addictive/self-destructive behaviors, their presence in our lives cannot distract us from doing the necessary work to seek meaningful intimacy within our ordinary routines to repair our identity weaknesses and other inadequacies of the *Self* to ensure all repetitive practices within our state of being contain some tangible, discernible benefit.

PERCEPTION—POTENTIAL BENEFITS BEYOND REPETITIVE, SELF-DESTRUCTIVE BEHAVIOR PATTERNS

In actuality, the most powerful tool we possess to qualify various behaviors in our lives is our power to perceive their importance to our every day existence. Unlike our definition of an addictive/self-destructive behavior as repetitive practice without discernible benefit, clinicians define an addiction as an individual's willingness to sacrifice all (even to the point of complete-self-destructiveness) to satisfy an addictive craving.[25] The willingness to sacrifice "all" to satisfy our addictive craving and/or our self-destructive tendency suggests a total impairment within our *perception* to understand and to appreciate the dangers associated with our addiction (as well as any repetitive behavior pattern without discernible benefit).

As set forth above, we may intentionally impair our perception at the detriment of our need for intimacy or other inadequacies in our sense of *Self*. Regardless the cause of the impairment, our perception limits our

24. Adams, *Fragmented Intimacy*, 95.
25. O'Brien et al., *Addictive States*, 18.

possibilities to see beyond addictive/self-destructive behavior and to consider more constructive alternatives. Even the Bible clearly warns us against giving free rein to our desires and the potential harm from actions undertaken with willful blindness to our own peril.[26] Despite the longstanding historical caveats against such behaviors, we still permit our perceptions to become impaired by our intentions and desires, rather than real perils and consequences to our overall well-being.

Perception also influences how we analyze symmetries with our relationships with repetitive practices without tangible benefits to determine if such relationships qualify as addictive/self-destructive. For example, we may view a symmetrical relationship with our vacation-taking activity, that is, our annual vacations may nourish and satisfy us with tangible benefits to justify our financial and emotional sacrifices to make them possible. However, where such relationships can be categorized as asymmetrical because the vacation destination and/or experience did not provide a tangible benefit to satisfy our personal sacrifices, we become vulnerable to extreme irritability and emotional pain.[27] As we contemplate symmetries between repetitive behavior practices and ourselves, we must determine how those symmetries either limit us to perceive possibilities beyond this current moment in time or encourage us to perceive *and* to create new possibilities beyond our ordinary, everyday existence. After all, the true value of repetitive practices in helping us perceive and construct new opportunities beyond the ordinary boundaries of our regular routines rests in their ability to help us avoid distressing emotional states and their delimiting consequences.

As a side note, most addictive/self-destructive behaviors share common symptoms with other medical conditions that may or may not originate with imbalances associated with brain chemistry or other physical symptoms.[28] For purposes of this chapter's objective and the book's potential contribution to our individual self-awareness, we should seek immediate medical attention and intervention if we feel, or have any reason to feel, that any repetitive behavior practice without discernible

---

26. See, e.g., Twerski, *Wisdom Each Day*, 4, citing Prov 1:17 regarding the bird's blindness to the snare as he vainly attempts to capture food at the peril of his freedom and reviewing related rabbinic thought on this subject.

27. See, e.g., Adams, *Fragmented Intimacy*, 97.

28. See, e.g., Twerski, *Addictive Thinking*, 6, enumerating similarities associated with addictive diseases such as delusions, hallucinations, inappropriate moods, and abnormal behaviors.

benefit could adversely affect our mental health and well-being. At the very least, we should consult with a local psychologist or other professional counselor to help us refocus our perception on healthy behavioral practices. An important component of any self-help exercise is the ability to recognize when the "self" itself cannot provide all the "help" we need to transition into the next phase of our lives and to achieve our goals for the exercise.

That said, and provided that we feel comfortable with this undertaking, we need to analyze each element of our addictive/self-destructive behavior patterns to understand their impact on our perceptive abilities to comprehend the full scope of their impairment. Most medical professionals and scholars conclude that behavior disorders that qualify as addictive and/or self-destructive in nature center around seven main components. Each component, for our purposes, represents a different stage in our relationship with an addictive/self-destructive qualifying behavior pattern, i.e., repetitive behavioral pattern without any discernible benefit, especially the degree of impairment on our perception.

Initially, our perceptions become subject to immediate impairment as we adjust our *tolerance* levels to suit particular behavior patterns and their ability to produce a desired effect. Over the course of time, our perceptions about our tolerance level will become increasingly impaired as we focus attention on the desired effect rather than the effort required to sustain that desired effect. Revisiting our vacation scenario, for example, we may find ourselves spending more time way from our daily routines and/or more money on vacation activities to maintain and/or supersede the perceived benefits from our previous vacations. Yet, our desire to maintain and/or supersede previous forms of vacation bliss greatly impair our rational judgment about the "true" costs associated with our vacation dependencies and its real benefit to enhancing our ability to cope with the mundane stresses associated with our daily routines. If we visit a five-star luxury resort last year and pampered ourselves with amazing spa treatments, we must, at least, meet if not surpass that standard of luxury in the subsequent year. Otherwise, we may feel that our leisure activities may be inferior and incapable of delivering the same therapeutic results from our previous vacation adventures. Unfortunately, we may want to regain our perspective on the situation and invest similar time, energy, effort and financial resources to determine why our current routine requires us to take that type of vacation in the first place, or engage in some similar leisure activity, to cope with our daily personal and professional stress.

As "staycations" continue to become more popular in light of recent economic realities, we must consider any *withdrawal* symptoms from our previous vacation habits and how those withdrawal symptoms may add to or subtract from other aspects of our personal and professional dissatisfaction with our daily routines. Even if the absence of a wonderful vacation to an exotic locale does not entirely depress our spirits, we probably perceive the lack of opportunity as a cause itself of some additional stress in our daily routines or another reason to become dissatisfied with our current life circumstances. Rather than perceive the positive aspects of our staycations, e.g., we have a job that pays us to take time off, we perceive the restricted nature of that paid time as a reason to lament the lack of a vacation. Obviously, we would all prefer a wonderful, luxurious vacation over a dull, boring staycation. However, that preference is a direct consequence of our impaired perception preventing us from seeing the underlying conditions within our lives that (a) make us feel entitled to a vacation and (b) discourages us from exploiting the opportunity of the staycation to make positive changes in our personal and professional routines.

Another impairment characteristic indicative of addictive/self-destructive behavior patterns is our ability to perceive the accurate quantity of time, intensity and effort to effectuate the desired effect from the behavior. Our intense focus on extracting something discernible from a repetitive behavior pattern without a discernible benefit makes us vulnerable to regular, conventional standards as we seek to replace those standards with new, self-serving conventions that justify and reinforce our behavior patterns. While some of us may think that the creation of self-serving conventions will enable us to see beyond our addictive/self-destructive behavior patterns, such conventions only reflect the vicious nature of how this perceptual impairment can trap us and prevent us from seeing the true folly of our ways. Through establishing our own conventions and norms that justify and sustain our addictive/self-destructive behavior patterns, we create an altered reality that become impervious to any constructive change from healthy, outside influences.

Adhering to our vacation example, we can all recall some vacations in our personal history that required us to max out the credit cards. Unless financial exigencies in our daily routine warrant fiscal irresponsibility, we would have probably *never* exceeded the credit limit on our credit cards *but for* the impaired fiscal perceptions created by our vacations. With hindsight, could we really say that the exuberant consumer interest rates justified that spending pattern when we resettled into our daily routines and resumed our monthly bill responsibilities? Perhaps, some of us may say it was a vacation of a life time but just make sure that when we perceive "life" and "time" those two notions do not encompass some self-serving definition that justifies a credit score nightmare by normal, mainstream conventions.

Desire that is persistent and controls our behavior creates an additional impairment layer upon our perspective and our ability to see alternate possibilities beyond a repetitive behavior pattern that does not produce a discernible benefit. We can understand how this type of desire creates a vicious, cyclical pattern and extenuates the repetitive nature of the behavior because we might be too stubborn to make any constructive changes in our behavior patterns without the ability to perceive an alternate, superior outcome. Moreover, once we surrender all control over our behavior to an unattainable, unsatisfying desire, we usually do not allow ourselves to recognize and to admit defeat. Rather, we seek out ways to justify additional efforts to pursue our desire even with minimal results.

Think of the times when we booked a special room at a luxury hotel and, upon arrival, we received a room that did not even come close to our expectations (and expense). Even if we demanded a refund on the spot and switched hotels, very few of us probably ever ended our vacations at the moment of disappointment and returned home prematurely to our personal and professional obligations. Instead, as with other behavior patterns controlled by unfulfilled desires, we continued on with our vacation plans and found some way to justify how that crappy room in a fancy hotel was not going to destroy our vacation. Well, the bigger question (or better example of our perceptions' impairment) is why would we ever have to subject our selves and our pursuit of a restorative leisure activity to such unnecessary and damaging disappointment in the first place? As Paulo Coelho so aptly pointed out in *The Alchemist*, the greatest adventure does not require a global adventure to discover everything we require for happiness and contentment can be found at *exactly* where we started.

Perception impairment further distorts our personal concept of time, especially the time allotted to the preparation of, participation in and recovery from the addictive/self-destructive behavior pattern. While we may consider such time allocations minuscule within the ordinary course of daily events, we must consider the opportunity costs associated with such allocations in light of our time investment in an habitual, repetitive behavioral practice that does not produce any discernible benefit. When conceptualized within that framework, we can appreciate how our impaired perception of time and its misallocation on addictive/self-destructive behavior patterns prevents us from grasping new time management methods that could yield far more productive, fruitful results for all our misspent time and energy. Specifically, the opportunity costs associated with our time misallocations for addictive/self-destructive behavior patterns significantly undermine our efforts to derive satisfaction from our occupational and social obligations, as well as dilute healthy benefits from normal recreational activities. Thus, we are left with diminished capacities to repair our perceptions and to overcome this cycle of time myopia.

With regard to understanding this phenomenon in the context of a repetitive behavior pattern with no discernible benefit, we can consider the actual time spent planning and executing our vacation plans in relation to the quantum of enjoyment derived from the vacation itself. Clearly, we will observe a gross imbalance in that comparative exercise that negates any possible justification for our customary, repetitive travel excursions. Despite this rational conclusion, our perceptual impairments tend to weigh those factors differently, even if not rationally, to allow us to plan our next travel getaways without regard to the time misallocations and their related costs on our other ordinary, daily activities. Never mind, the potential loss of leisure and other pleasures we sacrifice from our daily activities to pursue other repetitive behavior patterns without discernible benefit (especially outside a vacation context).

Ultimately, these incremental perceptual impairments culminate in our inability to address the underlying physical, spiritual, emotional or other issue that instigated our initial utilization of the destructive behavior and exacerbate our addictive/self-destructive behavior patterns. Meaning, our perceptions eventually become so impaired that we embrace notions of destructiveness to express our identities and to describe our attitudes without any regard to more constructive possibilities. In turn, we consciously utilize nihilistic perceptions of our identity weaknesses and inadequacies of the *Self* to create exaggerated extremes that make us errantly perceive our addictive/self-destructive behaviors as a creative achievement, rather than as behavior destroying any creative semblance within our identities and our attitudes.[29] So, some critical questions emerge for us to consider, such as: (i) what does our repetitive

29. See, e.g., Kaya, "Compelled to Create," 20, citing Jung and his thinking regarding the unity of the artistic personality in destructiveness to pervert beauty into ugliness and claim a creative achievement.

behavior patterns without discernible benefit mislead us to consider as a creative achievement? (ii) how does our mislabeled creative achievements preempt us from perceiving more constructive possibilities?; and (iii) can we still be indifferent to repetitive patterns without discernible benefits in our lives knowing their impairment upon our perceptive abilities to see beyond the current cyclical behavior patterns in our lives? These thought-provoking questions should have no readily available answers until we can take back full control of our perspective on our addictive/self-destructive behavior practices.

The complete avoidance of addictive/self-destructive behavior patterns may be an unrealistic remedy in helping us break self-generated boundaries associated with these behavior patterns. As clinicians observed in successful adolescent addiction recovery, the complete defeat and control of addictive/self-destructive behavior patterns require the formation and adherence of life goals void of a strong, unmanageable sense of instantaneous gratification *and* the development of a high threshold of tolerance to help us cope with unnecessary delays in the fulfillment of our personal and professional objectives.[30] Accordingly, we must strengthen our perceptive capacities to safeguard against cultivating excessive desires of instant gratification and undermining our tolerance levels for patience with regard to our pursuit of new, constructive behavior patterns with discernible benefits. Otherwise, we may seriously jeopardize new ways that enable us to perceive an ordinary existence beyond our addictive/self-destructive tendencies. We may also undermine the maintenance of constructive behavior patterns that improve and empower our attitudes and their impact on repairing identity weaknesses and inadequacies of the *Self* through misallocating our perceptive capacities on the means to satisfy our immediate impulse rather than the fulfillment of the actual impulse itself.[31] In this way, we can start repositioning our behavioral boundaries beyond their current territory and incorporate new, healthy repetitive practices with discernible benefits into our daily routine.

Shifts in behavior patterns can also occur from where we apply our perceptual capacities to understand weaknesses in our identities and

30. See, e.g., Twerski, *Addictive Thinking*, 16.

31. See, e.g., Bakan, *Duality of Human Existence*, 6, noting Paul Tillich's definition of idolatry as the worship of the means toward the fulfillment of an impulse just as the fulfillment of the impulse itself and its consequential impact on the loss of a sense of existence to the unmanifest impulse.

inadequacies in our sense of *Self*. In doing so, we may recognize how fragmented perceptions satisfy fragmented aspects of the *Self* and increase our vulnerability to addictive/self-destructive behavior patterns in our futile attempts to satisfy the fragmentary *Self*, rather than resolve the underlying fragmentation. Moreover, psychologists have observed how the Internet and its social media outlets create new identity expression opportunities that challenge unitary notions of identity as virtually-nurtured identities enable individuals to transform identity weaknesses and inadequacies of the *Self* into "luminous fantasies" that can exist between different dimensions.[32] This research further emphasizes the importance of shifting our perceptual capacities outside the confines of repetitive behavior practices without discernible benefit to encounter new, innovative ways to deal with our identity difficulties and their impact on our attitude. Specifically, we may devise constructive, healthy behavior patterns that can best deal with assembling fragments and fractures in our sense that unduly encumber our attitudes for their optimal expression. For example, we should appreciate how compulsive behavior patterns result from our inability to find a healthy outlet and receptacle for our excessive emotional investment that, in turn, fuel our obsessive tendencies over our creative powers.[33] Thus, our understanding of such dynamics clearly demonstrates that we will not be able to create constructive, healthy behaviors without focusing our perspective beyond the restrictions of our addictive/self-destructive practices.

Before we conclude this discussion, we must recognize that additional assistance to perceive beyond the repetitive patterns of behavior without discernible benefits can be found with the elements that accompany our perceptual capacities' transformation. Whether we rely upon the presence of a higher power as described in twelve-step programs,[34] the change and fluctuation in our personal circumstances and societal norms,[35] or our own inner voices and intuitive feelings,[36] we must always be mindful that we are not alone in pushing and overcoming the boundaries associated with

---

32. See, e.g., Robertson, "Beast Within," 15, identifying the work of Dr. Sherry Turkle regarding the Therianthrope movement (i.e., shape shifting / metamorphosis of humans into animals) on the Internet and its impact on transforming broken faultness into a luminous fantasy that coexists between different dimensions.

33. Rosenfels, *Homosexuality*, 106.

34. Sigmund, "Spirituality and Trauma," 224.

35. Ibid., 226.

36. Romme and Escher, *Accepting Voices*, 180.

our addictive/self-destructive behavior patterns. We will always have some sort of assistance to reconfigure our behavioral boundaries, provided that we can discern and rely on that assistance beyond the boundaries of our repetitive behavioral practice without discernible benefits. These notions will be explored in later chapters of the book.

AVOIDANCE—WAYS TO NURTURE
CONSTRUCTIVE BEHAVIORS FROM
DESTRUCTIVE BEHAVIOR PATTERNS

To successfully avoid our destructive behavior patterns in improving and empowering our attitudes, we must first recognize the conscious and unconscious existence of "collective shadows and images" that should be eradicated from our current states of being.[37] For example, Carl Jung believed that therapy allowed patients to discover their own dark side and relationship to these collective "shadows and images" that belonged to us all.[38] Jung's belief instructs us that we must not only avoid our own individual destructive behavior patterns, but the influences of similar behaviors present in our encounters with the greater collective and other social interactions.

Challenging circumstances that motivate us to justify our destructive behaviors and to forfeit potential constructive modifications further stress the importance of avoidance in overcoming the limitations of our addictive/self-destructive behavioral patterns. While we may assume that we have the strength to indulge such behaviors and experience their deceptive, vacuous benefits, we cannot continue the same destructive behaviors and the conduct associated with such behaviors and expect they will bring forth any positive or constructive changes within our everyday existence. Never mind, the continuation of destructive behavior practices, in any permutation, will preempt our quest to transition beyond our current ordinary states of existence and to experience superlative expressions of the *Self* and their potential impact on our everyday attitudes.

Our ability to create repetitive behavior patterns with discernible benefits depends on the removal of unnecessary, destructive encumbrances that preempt us from introducing something new and constructive into such behaviors. Hence, the avoidance of prior destructive

37. Spiegelman, *Judaism and Jungian Psychology*, 40.
38. Ibid.

behaviors will purge negative and limiting influences, such as our addictive/self-destructive value judgments and rationales,[39] so we can reorder our realities to accept and to foster superlative behaviors that improve and empower our everyday attitudes. Moreover, we must understand how our addictive/self-destructive behaviors have consumed the creative potential inherent in our emotions, especially our feelings associated with love for others and ourselves, and how we must reclaim that creativity to pursue new constructive behaviors built upon the insights gained from our misspent emotions.[40]

The reclamation of our emotions and execution of our creative capacities further stresses the importance of our avoidance of destructive behavior patterns to avoid feelings of self-deception that distort our reality in which we can cause, control or even cure our addictive/self-destructive behavior patterns.[41] For example, some scholars have pondered that the

> inherent emotional importance of love can give it an exaggerated influence which has fraudulent implications both for the self and for the objects of love, leading to *great and potentially destructive frustrations in human affairs.*[42]

Our acquaintance and/or reacquaintance with such powerful emotions will make us extremely vulnerable to the "fraudulent implications" of our constructive capacities and potentially undermine any potential for reordering our behavior patterns around a superlative alternative.

Furthermore, avoidance of destructive behavior patterns becomes a crucial component when we appreciate the collective nature of our creative capacity, rather than our current selfishness in exercising our creative capacity to sustain repetitive behaviors without any discernible benefits for ourselves, *and* for others.[43] Most importantly, our current addictive/self-destructive behavior practices have made us hypersensitive to dealing with our stress triggers, as well as conflicts between reality

39. See, e.g., Kaya, "Compelled to Create," 19, defining creativity as the ability to bring something new into existence and employing Ayn Rand's definition of art as a "selective recreation of reality according to an artist's metaphysical value-judgments."

40. Rosenfels, *Homosexuality*, 121.

41. See, e.g., Twerski, *Addictive Thinking*, 25.

42. Rosenfels, *Homosexuality*, 107, emphasis added.

43. Ibid, 107, noting how the pseudo-creativity of the compulsive adaptive life only increases self-serving forms of individual validation to maintain false competitive struggles outside the collective.

and our impaired perceptions of reality.[44] As a result, we attach unrealistic importance to our practical accomplishments to shelter our excess psychological capacities and their sensitivities from any criticism or modification resulting from our repetitive behavior patterns, especially those patterns that fuel our compulsive and obsessive natures.[45] In turn, we may employ compulsion and obsession to protect our practical accomplishments from any rational challenges that devalue their self-perceived importance in our lives.[46] So, next time we show off our souvenirs and other purchases from our yearly vacations, we might want to see how our emotional reactions to our friends and family members who challenge the usefulness of those purchases demonstrate the foregoing and can help us avoid future consequences from previous/current repetitive behavior practices without discernible benefits for ourselves, and for others.

To facilitate our avoidance efforts, we must seek a healthy, supportive replacement for the addictive/self-destructive behavior patterns that limit our creative capacities. A potential substitute for such behavior patterns might be new, or modified, relationships with stabilizing influences. For example, some form of spirituality and a relationship with the Divine have consistently proved a potent force in overcoming addictive/self-destructive behavior patterns and in maintaining sobriety for extended periods of time.[47]

Research in this area suggests that traumatic experiences associated with addictive/self-destructive behaviors usually encourage some form of spiritual growth to offset our realistic, sometimes dire, views about life after prolonged periods of self-inflicted suffering.[48] Our sense of an authentic "religious" or "spiritual" experience may directly correlate to our notions about what is right and just in pursuing constructive behavior practices over destructive behavior patterns.[49] For example, we might realize our destructive behavior practices, especially repetitive behavior patterns without discernible benefits, create unjust outcomes as they only satisfy our immediate needs for gratification without regard to what may be right or

---

44. See, e.g., Twerski, *Addictive Thinking*, 58.

45. Rosenfels, *Homosexuality*, 109.

46. Ibid.

47. See, e.g., Sigmund, "Spirituality and Trauma," 224.

48. See, e.g., ibid., 227.

49. See, e.g., Drobin, "Spirituality, the New Opiate," 237.

wrong with the satisfaction of that immediate need.[50] Moreover, the immeasurable need for the instant gratification of our needs and the destructive practices needed to effectuate that gratification removes any possible, constructive relationship with the Divine or some form of spirituality, since the primary relationship with our gratification forecloses all such possibilities.[51] Through integrating a spiritual component in that relational dynamic, we can break away from our repetitive behavior practices that preempt healthy expressions of our creative capacities and the constructive relationships they can help us attain, especially with the Divine.

Avoidance enables us to forge new possibilities in our ordinary reality that can help us manifest superlative expressions of our creative capacities through healthy, constructive relationships. As we move toward the promise of this reality, we must also be mindful of our identity weaknesses and other inadequacies in our sense of *Self* that made us vulnerable to addictive/self-destructive practice in the first place. That said, we might derive some comfort from the fact most spiritual thinking in the Judeo-Christian tradition stresses the unknowableness of God. Yet, despite this unknowableness, many people throughout history still persevere in their efforts to know, at least, some aspect of God. Accordingly, we too must persevere in our own efforts to know the unknowableness of certain aspects of our identity and our sense of *Self*, especially those aspects of our prior addictive/self-destructive behavior patterns that challenge our attainment of future constructive behavior. In so doing, we will begin to see overwhelming changes in our lives with phenomenal consequences in improving and empowering attitudes as we encounter the creative possibilities with our newly acquired constructive behavior patterns with clearly discernible *and* experiential benefits.

50. Bakan, *Duality of Human Existence*, 6.

51. Ibid.

4
Listen to the "Gut"

THIS CHAPTER REMINDS US about the power of our instinct and intuition to acquire information for innovative, decision-making. Different modes of communications offer different possibilities for information acquisition and different interactions with our innate information processing capacities. The value of exploring these alternative communicative modes rests in their ability to strengthen our trust and reliance on our own confidence, especially our emotional reactions to situations that defy conventional rationality. A visceral impetus might facilitate a significant transformation in our decision-making process and our attitudes that could enable us to perceive extraordinary possibilities within our ordinary states of being. This impetus will enable us to hone our communicative abilities beyond mere rational and conventional standards and to conceive superlative outlets for our improved and empowered attitudes.

The act of listening to the "gut" can be characterized as an irrational, yet justifiable, emotional response that provides reasonably reliable information and/or insight about a current or future event. This particular listening experience produces tangible benefits through intangible means that greatly varies between individual listeners and their psychic attunement. Yet, despite our inability to fully understand how our "gut" perceives, processes and communicates intuitive information to our consciousness, we all have had at least one listening experience that enabled us to confirm the reliability of this phenomenon.

Within the context of our *Be Beyond Best* construct, this "gut" phenomenon provides a critical aspect of honing our communicative abilities with unconventional sources to improve and empower our attitudes beyond the confines of their conventional limitations. Communication with our intuitive informational source will enable us to exercise more power and control over our perceptive awareness.[1] Improvement and empowerment to our perceptive awareness instantaneously take place the moment we start *perceiving* the intuitive information from our "gut" as our perception begins to accept this intuitive informational dynamic. In turn, we also revisit and redefine boundaries of communicative capacities as our relationship with intuitive information creates new insights about the possibilities present within ordinary and extraordinary informational sources.[2] Considering the discipline required to confirm and to interact with our "gut," we will have sufficient opportunities to train and to control our intuitive capabilities,[3] such as establishing boundaries and allocating time commitments. Our abilities will also become more attune to the discern common, distinguishable patterns present throughout the informational dynamic, as well as the emotions, circumstances and other factors that influence our intuitive capabilities.

With our new communicative abilities and awareness, we can undertake an important transformational process to improve and to empower our attitudes through comparing how our current states of being represent our reliance, or lack of reliance, on our intuitive capabilities. In order for us to fully experience the notion of how to "Be Beyond Best," we must understand the "gut" and its impact on the "Be" component. For example, our current of state being provides an invaluable proving ground to highlight those areas of our lives where we knew, or had reason to know, that an intended outcome, possibility or result would fulfill our ideal expectations. In those instances where are decision-making capacities reflected reasonable reliance on our intuitive instincts to produce such results, we cannot only confirm its efficacy for better living, but we can appreciate the boost to our confidence to trust ourselves and our "gut" as helpful allies at life's more challenging, indecisive moments. For further validation of the power of our "gut," we can also reflect upon how our current state of being would be improved, or impaired, if we

1. Romme and Escher, *Accepting Voices*, 108.

2. See, e.g., ibid., 21.

3. See, e.g., ibid., 143, commenting about the people who hear voices and ways their interactions change and evolve over time.

had better communicative capacities to understand, to translate and to implement our intuitive instincts. This comparative exercise will further enhance our confidence and our ability to adjust our attitudes to transition beyond our current existence and to perceive the possibilities of the superlative.

Our connection with the "gut" will help further connect us with more esoteric, relational dynamics and appreciate their potential positive impact on our lives. To grasp this concept, we could think back about those moments in our lives when we cried out for help to a higher power, whether God, the Divine or some intangible creative force in the Universe. Regardless of our bravado and machismo in denying our own emotional weaknesses and fears, we all have faced, or will face, an extreme loss in our life that will require us to search out something from outside our own *Self* and its emotional weakness to overcome. Perhaps, some of us may feel that we are immune or better equipped to deal with such loss or pain. Well, if we all listen to our "gut" and its reaction to more trying moments in our lives, we will be loathe to contradict this generality. Even more compelling, the *Grand Historical Narrative* contains many instances of humanity's quest for a higher power, especially God, to overcome extreme injustice, persecution or other forms of sufferings. Drawing upon this historical precedent, we can look to numerous historical writings and sources to help us put things in perspective in relation to the *Grand Historical Narrative*. Biblically speaking, we can observe many accounts where humanity has conjectured that God hides from His creation during times of despair.[4]

This clandestine relationship between the Divine, despair and us provides us with valuable insights to our conceptions about the Divine and/or some higher force. If we always expect that our encounter with the Divine should always produce the highest possible emotional consequences, we always will avoid seeking the Divine or some higher force in our darkest moments. It is our own expectations that preempt us from experiencing and/or accessing the Divine at those particular, dispirited moments. Similarly, we may have limiting expectations and experiences with our "gut" as we allow our passions, intentionally or unintentionally, to impair the value and reliability of our relationship with our intuitive informational sources. More precisely, we negligently focus our creative

---

4. See, e.g., Twerski, *Wisdom Each Day*, 227, citing Isa 40:27 as an example about God being hidden from us during times of despair and mentioning Job and his trials as example of God's injustice resulting from immutable laws of nature.

capacities on the emotional consequences derived from our *desired* outcome, rather than the range of potential and alternative consequences from the *actual* outcome. In so doing, we limit our relational receptivity to various forms of information from our "gut" and other potent, intangible aspects of our own individual belief systems.

Emotional restraint becomes more significant in our evolving relationship with our "gut" as we move beyond our current states of attitudinal formation toward improved and empowered alternatives. Our "gut," by its nature, requires us to have an intimate relationship with our "inner self," especially the workings of our inner emotions. This connection between our "inner self" and the "gut" helps to facilitate our control over our emotions and passions to safeguard our intuitive information from misinterpretation and misapplication. An area where most of us have our deepest, profound struggles can be considered the influence of love and its emotional permutations within our lives.

Some clinicians have categorized love as a deep emotion that focuses the awareness of an individual on an external object that requires us to exercise our awareness and comprehensive capacities to appreciate the object of our love.[5] If we can appreciate this emotional paradigm from an external approach, we will have knowledge to understand how love, especially forms of self-love, figures into our communicative dynamic between our inner *Self* and our "gut." For example, we must understand what we love outside the inner "*Self*" that motivates us to search for intuitive information within "gut." Furthermore, we must appreciate how love figures into our overall emotional scheme and requires us to express forms of self-love through feelings of entitlement to external objects and satisfaction with internal passions. In this regard, love becomes an important catalyst to help us understand the full power, breadth and range of our emotional capacities and their internal workings.

Through mastery of our own intangible intuitive communicative capacities, we will empower and improve our attitudes with refined emotional reactions to our "gut" and intuitive information. Rather than limiting ourselves to allowing our personal and professional environments to create negative consequences to our digestive tracks, like acid reflux and indigestion, we can nurture our "gut" with healthy reactions to numerous emotional provocations in our current environment and prepare ourselves to transition beyond our current circumstances. Most importantly,

5. See, e.g., Rosenfels, *Homosexuality*, 10.

we will be better equipped to deal with disappointments as we hone our abilities to anticipate less than ideal situations and to implement constructive avoidance strategies of such situations and their negative impact on our attitudes. Hopefully, we will realize and appreciate ways to utilize our "gut" and intuitive informational capacities to see beyond the less constructive factors weighing upon our attitude formation.

Finally, the link between our "gut" and our capability to achieve the superlative in life cannot be underestimated in its importance to help us connect with the best possibilities beyond our present realities. This link is most obvious in helping us to rely on our own, individual benchmarks related to personalized definitions and manifestations of the superlative in our lives. For example, our intuitive informational source, our "gut," and its contributions to our decision-making processes encourage our awareness of a sort of metaphysical consciousness. This metaphysical consciousness permits us to redefine the conventional limitations of our daily reality and to satisfy the emotional needs of "inner *Self.*" In turn, we become more open to possibilities about how intuitive actions and thoughts might actually shape our physical realities that reflect the superlative outcomes from this metaphysical decision-making perspective.[6]

The satisfaction of our deep-seated intuition also facilitates the attainment of the superlative through our decision-making processes and their subsequent impact on our attitudes about our reality, whether real, perceived or even metaphysical. Otherwise, we will further disconnect and disenfranchise our intuitive capabilities from healthy and helpful meaningful expressions and their potential impact on our attitudes.

Specifically, we may become victims to less constructive emotions at critical moments in our lives that perpetuate inferior outcomes as we erroneously rely on self-serving definitions and other forms of self-deception about particular situations, rather than our intuitive instincts.[7] For example, we might accept a job offer to satisfy our own definitions of personal success and professional satisfaction. Yet, during the interview, we may have had a strong intuitive sense ("informational exchange") that

6. See, e.g., Robertson, "Beast Within," 14, noting how some religious groups view metaphysical exercises, such as metaphysical shape shifting thoughts from human to animal spirit possession, to help increase our control over physical reality, even producing physiological changes that defy ordinary reality.

7. See, e.g., Freimuth, *Hidden Addictions*, 48–49, describing self-denial patterns in addiction patients and their reinforcing behavior patterns to satisfy both their self-esteem and addiction.

our potential supervisor, work culture or other office dynamic did not entirely comport with our own definition of personal and professional satisfaction. Most of us would disregard our intuitive instinct to the detriment of our personal satisfaction as we deceive ourselves that the professional satisfaction would more than outweigh any personal dissatisfaction, especially since the intangible basis of our instinct might reflect our irrational fears or other hesitancies. Inevitably, such compromises that make us ignore our intuitive instincts usually end up with dire consequences to our selves and our attitudes as our self-deceptions eventually give way to the harsh realities about a less desirable, but avoidable situation. Hopefully, our encounter with this book and our achievement of this chapter's objective will help us avoid these types of inferior outcomes and their consequences on our attitudes.

THE DYNAMIC BOND WITH OUR "GUT"

As with effective relational dynamics between therapists and their patients in clinical settings, we must establish a "therapeutic alliance" or "attachment bond" between our rational *Self* and our intuitive *Self*. This alliance or bond provides a similar function to hone our intuitive instincts and to integrate them into our decision-making processes. For our purposes, we should conceptualize this "alliance" or "bond" as the attachment between patient and doctor through the process of transference, i.e., the process by which patients distort reality to accept a beneficial relationship with their doctors.[8] Similarly, we must establish this type of bond between our conscious thinking and our intuitive informational sources to help us communicate more effectively between these two disparate intellectual modalities.[9] This modified communication modality will improve and empower our capacity to perceive extraordinary possibilities within our ordinary states of being through being more receptive to less conventional information, more internal informational sources. In turn, our attitudes will become transformed through our newfound internal reliance mechanisms and reflect this empowerment and improvement through

8. See, generally, Horvath and Luborsky, "Role of the Therapeutic Alliance in Psychotherapy," 561–73.

9. See, e.g., Kuhar, *Addicted Brain*, 177, discussing how the beginning phases requires the establishment of a therapeutic alliance and/or an attachment bond to promote an effective doctor-patient relationship.

filtering extraneous influences as we exercise confidence in our decision-making processes.

An important consequence of bonding with our "gut" will be our access to almost limitless internal informational sources as we ascribe new interpretations to our emotions and feelings to help us make better, more informed decisions. Knowing that our "gut" will become an essential copilot in traversing our lives' more turbulent moments, we will further empower and improve our attitudes to seek more constructive connections with less conventional informational sources. As some of us might have observed through our life travels, we always encounter individuals with alleged, serene souls who might have offered us a massage, a yoga class, a meditation exercise or some cosmic wisdom in our quest for peace from our personal and/or professional stress. Somewhere in our recollections, those encounters present us with important life lessons because they remind us about how the *decisions* we make about our lives *directly* affects our attitudes with (and about) others. After all, if we possessed that inner peacefulness and pleasant dispositional attitude, we might have never needed that expansive luxury vacation or spa treatment in the first place. Yet, we can take inventory of our current existence and examine those life areas where we can effectuate important changes to our attitudes, especially how they reflect the comfort derived from our "gut's" protective function in many basic life decisions. Researchers have concretized potential benefits from communicating with internal information sources that can be summarized as follows:

> (i) clearer recognition of patterns; (ii) easing of anxieties; (iii) discovery of alternative theoretical perspectives; (iv) improved acceptance of internal informational sources; (v) clearer recognition of the meaning behind the internal intuitive information; (vi) appreciation of potentially positive aspects; (vii) better structuring of the contact with our intuitive impulses; (viii) more effective use of therapeutic intervention to remedy unhealthy reactions to irrational intuitive impulses; (ix) improved tolerance and understanding within the family or professional relational dynamics; and (x) overall personal growth.[10]

These potential benefits appear to have many elements in common but their shared mention of improved and empowered clarity requires special consideration for us to achieve this chapter's objective. Evidently, a

---

10. See, e.g., Romme and Escher, *Accepting Voices*, 50–51.

strong, healthy bond with our "gut" provides us with an effective tool to recognize how our inner power guided our lives and all our life choices to our current circumstance and how we can access that power to transition into a future with an empowered and improved attitude.

More interestingly, this bond with our "gut" might help us revisit our relationship with the Divine, especially our curiosity about spirituality and religion, and its potential contribution to our future plans. Whether or not spirituality and/or religion will provide any beneficial effects on the evolution of current attitudes is questionable. Research about the role of religion in overcoming certain psychological conditions, such as addiction and anxiety, is inconclusive as researchers have focused on religion's impact on an individual's mental health and found no correlation.[11] That said, researchers have stated that such inconclusiveness may be a result of the research methods themselves since patients' reactions to religion might be too subjective to measure in terms of religion's own value-added contributions to a patient's recovery.[12] The problem, according to some researchers, is the unique nature of our spiritual journeys (or lack of them in some cases) in comparison to psychological models that are designed around generalized, average individuals and usually view spiritual/mystical experiences as "pathological deviations."[13]

So, the evidence of absence does not necessarily mean an absence of evidence regarding God, faith and other religious expressions in empowering and improving our attitudes to help our daily existence. Like with our unique communicative tools with our "gut," we must also develop individual benchmarks to determine if a spiritual/religious component would benefit our overall attitudinal development. Even more important, we must become attune to changes in our perception of the mysterious and esoteric as our bond with the "gut" may create ancillary communicative capacities that extend beyond the *Self* and our current state of being.[14] A direct attitudinal consequence from this revised relationship with the Divine might be our access to more religious-theme books and commentaries to help broaden our thinking processes about the potential

11. See, e.g., Belzen, "Spirituality, Culture, and Mental Health," 297.

12. Ibid., 299.

13. See, e.g., ibid., 309.

14. See, e.g., Romme and Escher, *Accepting Voices*, 55, commenting about the beneficial effects of controlling internal auditory dialogues to understand their sources and to improve the overall quality of life.

contributions from intuitive informational sources on our overall emotional well-being.

Many of us deal with much stress and anxiety in our daily life and our reaction to those disruptive feelings usually cause us to make less than optimal decisions, never mind preempt us from communicating with or seeking guidance from a "Divine perspective." For example, we are reminded from ancient Jewish texts, like the Talmud, about how our emotions can dampen our abilities to act with reason and rationality when faced with heightened emotions. Rabbinic thought summarizes many examples of this phenomenon and warns us that our wisdom will leave us when we act in rage because our actions will only satisfy our rage and not accomplish any other constructive objective.[15]

Other faith traditions have similar writings and warnings against allowing our emotions to become unfettered and running our amuck with our reason, such as Christian and Islamic teachings about humility and Buddhists teachings about contemplative meditation. Whatever the tradition or the writing, we must learn how the emotions generated by our current circumstances could impair or enhance the bond with "gut," as well as our ability to process the intuitive information derived from that bond. Through keeping our emotions under appropriate control, we will better access our perceptive gifts and experience a windfall in intuitive information regarding how we can exploit our "gut" to help us move beyond the informational processing limitations of our current existence.

OUR INTERPRETATION OF INTUITION AND ITS CAPACITY TO CREATE CHANGE

The ability to transform our current state of being and to move beyond the limitations within our daily routines rests within our brain to communicate with our intuition and to visualize and to pursue the revelations from our intuition.[16] Harnessing the power of our emotions to create quasi-hallucinatory states of power, we can hone our brain's creative capacity to utilize our intuitive instincts to identify liberating dreams and ambitions within our subconscious psyche that tantalize our imagination and inspire our motivation to succeed beyond their current possibilities.

15. See, e.g., Twerski, *Wisdom Each Day*, 77, citing Pesachim 66b and Kiddushin 41a from the Talmud.

16. See, e.g., Slade and Bentall, *Sensory Deception*, 8.

The intangible nature of our intuitive capabilities makes us receptive to other intangible modes of communication and expression, especially those elements of our brain function that allow us to explore our imagination without limitation. That exploration itself will help us understand communicative linkages between our intuition, its ability to create visual images in the brain and our ability to transform intangible thoughts into tangible realities. This process works best when we ground our communicative capabilities between our intuition and our imagination in reasonable, rational and healthy expectations so that we can avoid unhealthy emotions and the diversions they create. Thereafter, we can map our feelings and emotions onto our intangible thinking process and help to manifest them within our tangible decision-making process as we contemplate choices that will allow us to bring those abstract thoughts and desires into our physical realities. The overall effect will be improved communication our intuition as we improve and empower our understanding of its potential contributions to the ultimate achievement of our dreams and desires.

In addition to empowering our communicative capabilities with our intuition beyond their current states of existence, we must also contemplate new ways to describe our feelings and their manifestation within our imaginations. Specifically, our need for new terminology arises from the metaphysical nature of our intuitive communications and our intra-psychic reliance on their value for our lives.[17] The linkage between a descriptive term and its impact on our *Self* cannot be underestimated here since our power to identify the intuitive notion of desire will help us understand the emotional influences on our *Self* and its reaction on our imaginations. For example, our desires form a substantial basis of our identity and expression of our *Self* that can easily be seen through our personal relationships, professional ambitions or other behavioral interests.[18] Through our intuitive instincts, we can understand and appreciate our desires from within our organic *Self*. We can also employ our intuitive instincts to better interpret how our emotions manifest within our *Self* and compel us to express our selves in pursuit of those desires. As a result, we will further refine our communicative abilities with our "gut" and enhance the impact of our desires on the development of the *Self* and its expression in all aspects of our lives.

17. See, e.g., Bucholtz and Hall, "Theorizing Identity," 472.

18. See, e.g., ibid., discussing how sexual desires form the basis of individual identity and other uses of linguistic descriptions.

Another benefit from evaluating the link between our desire and our intuitive information source is recognizing its dynamic nature and its ability to adapt to change without unnecessary emotional and intellectual lag. When we reflect upon the moments in our lives where our "gut" influenced our decision-making, we can think about the instantaneous nature of the intuitive information's impact on changing our emotional states. For example, situations and circumstances that have triggered our reliance on our "gut" usually produce a direct, instantaneous emotional consequence upon which we formulate decisions with minimal reflection. The absence of an emotional lag between our decision-making and intuitive informational input increases our adaptability to those situations and circumstances and, in turn, provides an additional benefit from listening to our "gut." With this adaptability, we can strengthen our *Self* and our will to move beyond our current, limited information sources. We can further analyze how our emotions can be better harnessed to bring us to optimal expressions of our *Self* and the achievement of its desires as expressed through our empowered and improved attitudes.

The pursuit of our desires based on intuitive instigations/hunches will help also refine our transitions toward our empowered and improved attitudes through enabling us to appreciate the intangible nature of our tangible pursuits and to purge destructive emotions that cloud this pursuit. This means, we make choices that are geared to assist us in achieving our desires based on a string of our intuitive instincts/hunches starting with the desire's formation based on our unique preference for a particular object or thing. We really cannot definitively say where the origin of our desire truly emanates but we can observe where that desire takes us throughout our life journey. An intangible, kernel of desire, formed within the unreal reality of our "gut," provides us with a life altering reality that constantly changes and evolves in various phases of our lives. As with spiritual quests, our desires motivate us to search for things that we wish we had, and, in that process, require us to purge our former desires and reasoning skills to make way to undertake the quest and to make room for the personal and spiritual growth from the entire exercise.[19] Recognizing our desire's dynamic nature, we can reinforce our attitudes with a flexible optimism to shield us against submitting to despair because distressing emotions will eventually cease, even if not on our preferential time schedule.

19. Drobin, "Spirituality, the New Opiate," 233.

In moving beyond our current state of existence, our "gut" will guide us between emotional realities that inspire us to bring our desires from their intangible gestation to their tangible manifestation. Our "gut" projects our internal psychic realities into our intellectual thoughts and enables us to make decisions with unexplainable insights. If we could create a philosophical approach to our "gut" and its proper role in helping us achieve beyond our current limitations, we might all call this approach a form of "transcendental idealism."[20] That is, we can understand that our internal ideal creative potential is only constrained by our submission to the limitations present in our external realities.[21] Desire, within this philosophical construct, operates to propel our idealism beyond its limitations, whether internally perceived or externally juxtaposed, to find an appropriate outlet for its expression and its attainment. Hence, we must truly appreciate the complexity of our desires to understand how best to achieve them, especially when we establish and submit the limitations that we deceive ourselves into believing that keep us from their fulfillment.

Now, the real value in this philosophical approach is its ability to unleash our true creative potential as we recognize its applications in all aspects of our lives. For example, the notion of "transcendental idealism" permits us to recognize that the external physical world as, *we perceive it,* is nothing more than a "part of our mind that is projected outside."[22] Think about that statement and read it a few times aloud to yourself. Regardless of its profundity and esoteric ambiguity, "transcendental idealism" tells us we are not only living in the conditions and circumstances we perceive ourselves in at this current moment, but we are living in a situation, *a complete episode of our personal narrative and every episode before and after in that narrative,* that we birthed within us, just like a mother births her child!

The power to create a living situation, whether personal or professional, first must come from within our inner *Self* where our "gut" has its dominant influence. The connection between our "gut" and our mind is simple—our "gut" feels something and our mind translates those feelings into a communicative reality that we can process within our thinking.

20. Aleman et al., *Hallucinations*, 21, discussing Behrendt and Young's philosophical approach known as "transcendental idealism" and its perspective on how we perceive the world around us and its physical limitations.

21. Ibid.

22. Ibid.

As a result, our "gut" is the engine of the creative component within our *personal narratives,* whether or not we are consciously deciding to listen or to ignore it. So, we should think about and reflect upon those moments in our lives when we not disconnected to our "gut" and how much we actually created new circumstances and situations within our *personal narratives.* It would seem most of us when we become disconnected with our "gut" could not really access the full power of our creative capacities, especially for their useful and/or beneficial deployment. So, if nothing else we take away from the import of this chapter's objective in the development of our empowered and improved attitudes, we must recognize without efficient communications with the "gut," we will become unnecessarily inefficient in birthing our external realities and their need for constant modification toward their superlative formations.

An interesting implication of this "philosophical approach" requires us to examine its consequences on our collective interactions, that is, our relationships with others and how those relationships form the characters within the settings of our *personal narratives.* Indeed, we have ultimate dominion over the settings and plots within our *personal narratives* but they also require some flexibility and openness to allow the participation of others in living in our daily realities. "Transcendental idealism" allows us to experience a sense of "otherness" in the sense of riding the journey of our desires from conception to attainment (even if some modified, limited form of those desires). We cannot actually observe any tangible aspect of the boundaries between our dreams, desires and realities that preempt us from transporting any notion of our *Self* between those different states. Yet, we can harness the power of those states and experience the ramifications of indulging our *Self* in each individual state to understand their contribution to our current reality. Even this statement itself contains a degree of intellectual intangibility since we can sort of grasp its intention but its actual meaning is elusive.

Intangibilities encourage us to apply labels or reasoning constructs upon them to help us exchange ideas that unite others around common thinking patterns, especially our shared contributions beyond our *Self,* i.e., the collective. For example, our internal creative capacities are common among and within all us, despite external differences in the formation and development of our *Self* and our attitudes. This common creativity can be a considered a fundamental element of most institutional religions since the power to create and its relationship to the Divine provides a cohesive explanation of this phenomenon. Specifically, most religions relate our creative capacities to God's creative capacities through a celestial construct known as "soul" that was created by God beyond the confines of any earthly reality and beyond our physical perception.[23] This construct operates as an important tool in relating our *Self* to something beyond and above the *Self*, along with any physical limitations on our *Self*. It also provides us with a critically important and invisible character in our *personal narratives*—the silent soul. Yet, the religious among us will argue that we all have a soul. For the purposes of this chapter, we should simply conceptualize the soul as a common communicative construct that allows us to communicate (passively) with each other's souls and with the source of our personal creation (how ever we chose to identify and to label that creative, eternal source). In this way, we can better relate to the characters within our *personal narratives*, even though we may never fully understand our interaction with them on any discernible intellectual level. Unlike déjà vu moments, we can honestly say that variations in levels of our communications with others may originate from something beyond ordinary understanding, especially when we allow characters/individuals within one phase of our *personal narratives* and we eradicate or entrench them quickly within our overall narratives.

So, as we think about achieving something from within our deepest desires beyond our current state of possibilities, we should think about how effectively we are communicating with our "gut" and listening to its insights. Otherwise, we will be unnecessarily encumbered in our quest to understand what we cannot understand regarding why we feel such great distance between our *Self* and our dreams, desires and other possibilities.

The Superlative Relationship between Our "Gut" and Creation

When considering the power of our "gut," we must remember its connection to the sublime and esoteric, especially the entirety to creation. Some scholars, like John Muir,[24] have opined that all the particles present at the beginning of creation and throughout the entire cosmos dwell within us. These same particles allow us to interact and to connect with our environment in non-traditional ways when we allow our internal sense of

---

23. Kuhar, *Addicted Brain*, 23–24, discussing relationship between fantasy and reality as a form of relationship with the Divine through the soul.

24. See, generally, Muir, *My First Summer in the Sierra*.

Self, i.e., our intuitive abilities, to guide us along our life journeys. Within us, we can perceive and communicate with the building blocks of all creation and, in turn, create our own sense of reality as we strive toward its superlative manifestation in our life. The "gut" represents the superlative tool in our quest to manifest an optimal existence for our lives because it enables direct communication with "stuff of creation" without the clutter of our external environment and the pressure of outside expectations. As a result, we can refine and refocus our decision-making processes around our internal sense of *Self* and its reliance on our intuitive informational source to formulate and to achieve our desires that will manifest our superlative *Self* as we empower and improve our attitudes.

Due to its connection with all creation, our "gut" provides us with an opportunity to apply our creative capacities in a superlative manner to help us commandeer through our desires and to achieve our potential. As history and research teach, our desires that spur our creative endeavors motivate us to seek ways to possess them.[25] However, our quest to possess our desires usually ends up with our desires possessing us in some capacity. Think about this statement—what we really seek to control in the end ultimately controls us! We have exercised our creative capacities to create a situation or circumstance that limits our full potential through entrapping us by our very own devices.

This phenomenon is very common among people who are seeking their desires without regard to the consequences of their fulfillment. For example, the pursuit of our desire becomes all consuming that we actually ignore its source, our "gut," and its important intuitive lessons about how best to achieve that desire within the grand scheme of our *personal narrative*. Rather, most of us ignore our internal safeguards and disregard our intuitive sense as we rely on the *Grand Historical Narrative* to inform us about the nuances of our desires, especially our comparative successes regarding their achievement and enjoyment. With the *Grand Historical Narrative*, we can compare our personal histories within the context of the historical collective and receive affirmation, confirmation and/or motivation related to the value of achieving our desires and their overall importance to connecting our *personal narrative* with the *Grand Historical Narrative*.

Ironically, the true measure of success related to achieve our desires, along with the important strategies to facilitate their achievement, dwell

25. See, e.g., Romme and Escher, *Accepting Voices*, 82.

within us without the distractive influence of the *Grand Historical Narrative*. As long as we turn inward for answers and guidance, we will have better control over desires and their achievement, rather than them controlling us. The moment we shift our gaze to an outside source, like at the *Grand Historical Narrative*, we allow our desires to cut free from our "gut" and its invaluable communicative support and perspective. Without that anchor, our desires run amok and take control over our thoughts, cloud our decision-making process and, eventually, consume us.

While we must exercise extreme caution and restrain in preventing our desires from controlling us, we cannot avoid the positive aspects of passion and love throughout our lives and their ability to connect us with our environment. In addition to grounding our desires with our "gut," we should also ground them with the environment so that we can better understand their placement within our *personal narrative* and its relationship to the *Grand Historical Narrative*. More importantly, this connection with the environment will enhance the communicative capabilities of our "gut," especially since some clinicians have opined that love is the development of our biological capacity to receive information from our environments over which we can exercise personal power to control.[26] Love of our *Self* will safeguard our desires from their connection with the "gut" since the "gut" will not only provide us with more insights about the achievement of our desires, but will facilitate communication with the environment to maximize our information access and our optimal decision-making processes.

The true superlative power of our "gut" beyond its intuitive instincts is its contribution to our understanding of our purpose, as expressed in our *personal narrative*, and its role in all creation, as understood in the *Grand Historical Narrative*. In some ways, our "gut" reminds us about our mysterious relationship with the Divine or other awe-inspiring, mysterium since it allows us to observe events and conditions within our *personal narrative* without clearly revealing itself and the nature of its interpretative origins.[27] Recognizing its sublime nature, our "gut" provides us with the requisite tools to transform ordinary possibilities into extraordinary opportunities through allowing us to achieve the superlative manifestation of our deepest desires via maximum informa-

26. See, e.g., Rosenfels, *Homosexuality*, 11.

27. See, e.g., Spiegelman, *Judaism and Jungian Psychology*, 23, discussing Jung's interpretation of the word *religion* as allowing us to interpret life as a numinous and awe-inspiring event.

tion and optimal decision-making. Most importantly, our "gut" is our only inherent mechanism that can organically link our *personal narrative* with the *Grand Historical Narrative* without exercising any active rational decision-making process subject to external factors and considerations beyond our *complete* control. In the end, our "gut" provides a constructive outlet for our desires and our ability to control them without them becoming leviathans that eventually devour us.

Regardless of the words written on these pages, we must step back as we conclude this chapter and revisit its objective regarding strengthening our connection to intuitive information to empower our decision-making so as to achieve superlative outcomes. After reading these words and flipping through these pages, we must ask ourselves what does our "gut" tell us about this chapter and its value to our overall attitude empowerment and improvement? Do our "guts" make us feel content we have adequately extracted all the relevant information from this chapter? Do our "guts" tell us that this information is too convoluted or academic without practical application? Or do our "guts" say we should reread certain portions of this chapter now or read the entire book first and revisit this chapter? Or do our "guts" say that we should stop reading at this point and put down the book until it summons us to continue reading? Whatever our "guts" instruct us to do at this point, our "guts" have a definitive position on this chapter and this book.

Let us take a moment and carefully listen to what the "gut" is trying to tell us, especially what we are trying to create from reading these pages. Whatever we heard or sensed, we should write in the margins of this chapter and revisit throughout our reading of this book to determine how effective and valuable this "listening to the 'gut'" can really be in creating and achieving the superlative forms of our desires as conceived within our "gut." Go forth and birth great creativity so that our *personal narratives* can put a big dent into the *Grand Historical Narrative* to ensure we have lived up to our fullest potential through utilizing our intuitive, creative instincts.

5

Complete the Sense of "Self"

THIS CHAPTER WILL INSTRUCT us how to empower our *personal narratives* to help form a complete *Self*. To understand why our attitudes may reflect less than optimal emotions within our current states of being, we must understand the *Self* and evaluate those areas of our *Self* that reflect fragmented or disconnected manifestations between who we are in our relationships, how we are perceived by others and what we want from our achievements. For purposes of this chapter's objective, we can use an elastic definition of *Self* that represents (i) a central authority of the soul and its creative capacity in relation to its Divine origins[1] and (ii) an animating force behind our dreams and ambitions that enables us to function within the linear development of our *personal narrative*. In this way, our *Self* can be defined as our individual sense of emotional satisfaction with an experiential selfhood that enables us to feel complete in any situation or circumstance[2] and propels us to seek additional manifestations of that sense of completeness throughout our personal narratives' evolutions.

We can conceptualize this process as a simple exercise. For example, is there an aspect of our *Self* that motivates us to read this book, i.e., a desire to change our attitude, to overcome a self-destructive behavior pattern or to understand failed ambitions? Or, perhaps, our general curiosity compels us to read through these pages with a confident self-assurance

1. Spiegelman, *Judaism and Jungian Psychology*, 22.
2. See, e.g., Frie and Coburn, *Persons in Context*, 62, noting that experiential selfhood is more a mindfulness of the emotional life rather than an entity or thing.

that our *Self* is a complete entity and we are seeking to affirm that completeness, i.e., a curiosity to confirm our sense of *Self* and its perceivable perfections? Whatever our ultimate reasons, we must increase our awareness of what aspects of the *Self* are reflected within and throughout our *personal narratives*. Particularly, whether those reflections are accurate representations of our complete *Self* or our fragmented *Self* and the bases for that differentiation.

Unlike more clinical definitions that encapsulate identity, personality and character trait, our definition of the *Self* provides us with a working construct to help us understand and to relate to external influences that impact the *Self* and its sense of wholeness. After all, we are looking to develop a therapeutic remedy of sorts within the storehouses of our imagination to give birth to a complete *Self* that will enable us to experience personal and professional satisfaction at various moments throughout our *personal narrative*. Our definition permits us to evaluate how, where, when and in what capacities we deploy either a complete *Self* or a fragmented *Self* at different times in our *personal narrative* through isolating moments in our *Self*'s evolutions throughout our personal history. Moreover, we can relate to our own individual experiences of the *Self* as a motivational force that helped shaped our dreams and ambitions as ancillary expressions of our fragmented *Self* that seeks to come together to form a complete *Self*. Hence, the pursuit and fulfillment of our dreams and ambitions will enable us to improve our self-awareness about our need for a complete *Self* and its presence throughout our *personal narrative*.

With this self-awareness, we will begin to formulate new empowered and improved attitudes to allow our complete *Self* an opportunity to interact with all the relationships in our current state of being, especially the relationship between our complete *Self* and our fragmented *Self*.[3] We also will become more receptive to see how the complete *Self* can move us beyond our current state of being and help us overcome obstacles created by the fragmented *Self*. Finally, the complete *Self* will enhance our control over emotions and feelings and, in turn, permit the attainment of the superlative in various aspects of our lives, especially our attitude formation and expression. Through mastering esoteric knowledge about our *Self* and possibilities presented by the complete *Self* and challenges offered by

---

3. See, e.g., Cramer, *Protecting the Self*, 93, reviewing how our capacity to differentiate between the *Self* and the other involved differentiation and modification of the ego and ego structures to help us identify appropriate representations of the *Self*.

the fragmented *Self*,[4] we will be able to extract therapeutic benefits from achieving this chapter's objective to empower and improve our attitudes.

Before we commence our discussion about our search for the complete *Self*, we must differentiate our *Self* from our identity for purposes of this chapter's objective and the analysis presented throughout this book. For example, we must appreciate how the *Self* operates as a mechanism to express our identity. Our identity, unlike our *Self*, requires much more clinical analysis and research to describe in its formation and development since it represents a foundational component, rather than an evolutionary component, of our *personal narratives*. Most importantly, our *Self*, whether complete or incomplete, allows us to exercise control and dominion over our own self-expression and permits us to relate our abstract dreams and hopes within the context of our reality as created by and experienced in our *personal narratives*.[5] So, please keep this variation in mind when we revisit theses notions below since the boundaries between our identity and our *Self* may be more amorphous than we think and, in turn, demonstrate more incompleteness in our *Self* than we originally thought.

CONSEQUENCES OF AN INCOMPLETE SELF IN OUR CURRENT STATE OF BEING (PART I)

The various forces on the development and evolution of the *Self* that influence our identity development from childhood throughout early adulthood could preempt us from nurturing our natural proclivities in our personal and professional interactions. In particular, the dedication to acquire knowledge of self-expression and its application to our *personal narrative*, especially specific career choices, may result from external expectations outside of our natural psyche and may drastically impact what we identify as our complete *Self*. This identification phenomenon and its impact on our search for the complete *Self* can be observed in something psychologists call a "moratorium dynamic." This dynamic can have either a positive or negative impact on us as we seek a "niche for [our special]

---

4. See, e.g., Bakan, *Sigmund Freud*, xi, noting the import of knowledge about esoteric notions of Jewish mysticism helps to unlock therapeutic effects of psychoanalysis.

5. See, e.g., Stolorow, "Individuality in Context," 256.

gifts" as we revisit aspects of our incomplete *Self* within a "re-ritualized" version of our complete *Self*.[6]

"Re-ritualization" encourages us to accommodate, recognize and process our personal weaknesses and their impediments for the formation of our complete *Self*.[7] To help us achieve this chapter's objective, we will consider how our personal and professional lives may currently reflect these moratorium dynamics and their ability to explain our successes and failures in our attempts to create a complete *Self*.[8] We will also suggest why these moratorium dynamics might not always explain our need to transition from a fragmented to complete sense of *Self* since other factors, like psychosexual issues, require additional considerations in considering the most prescient impetus for our "re-ritualization."[9]

Moratorium Phenomenon: Erik Erickson, the pioneering developmental psychologist who researched psychosocial development and identity formation, describes the *moratorium phenomenon* as a sort of identity crisis that compels some of us to seek out a niche for our special gifts.[10] In particular the major moratorium dynamics require us to re-evaluate aspects of our perceivable *Self* (most likely, our fragmented *Self*) and to undertake a re-ritualization of the identity between that *Self*'s immediate engagements, whether personal or professional commitments, to acquire new skills to transition to an optimal, complete sense of *Self*. This moratorium, according to Erickson, is defined as a period of delay granted that we grant to ourselves when we are not ready to fulfill an obligation *or* who are forced to undertake an obligation outside our own preferential timing.[11]

Various tensions emerge during this period that Erickson postulates creates a "latency period" that resembles a "combination of prolonged maturity and provoked precocity."[12] Perhaps, we can instantly recall those

6. Erikson, *Identity, Youth, and Crisis*, 184–85.

7. Erikson, *Childhood and Society*, 184–85, discussing the ego's need to master various areas of life, especially those areas in which an individual finds himself, his body, and his social role wanting and trailing.

8. See, e.g., Erickson, *Identity, Youth, and Crisis*, 156, noting how a sexually mature individual is more or less retarded in psychosexual capacity for intimacy and psychological readiness for parenthood.

9. Ibid.

10. Ibid., 185–85.

11. Ibid., 157.

12. Ibid., 156.

moments in our lives when we were faced with excessive stress or tension from a job situation or family squabble that trigged an emotional awareness reminiscent of Erikson's descriptions.

Erickson also identifies two components within the moratorium phenomenon to describe how and when we may chose to reform our sense of *Self* within a moratorium period. The first is classified as a psychosexual moratorium that enables a fragmented *Self* to participate in a "latency period" after puberty and to learn "technical and social rudiments" for a "work situation."[13] Erickson cautions against too much reliance on this component, also known as "libido theory," since that component does not adequately explain the period of "prolonged adolescence" during which some of us may not acquire sufficient psychosexual capacity for any healthy and/or appropriate form of intimacy.[14] Intimacy's function and its contribution to the formation of our complete sense of *Self* become crucial as we interact with a community and assume, as well as transition into and out of, personal and professional identities. According to Erickson, intimacy operates as a conditioning agent to help us to undertake serious commitments and to focus "free role" experimentation into a particular niche (that is defined by society and yet liberates our unique talent).[15]

The dynamic nature of the moratorium phenomenon reminds us that the more unique gifts and talents we possess, the more moratoria we may undertake to integrate them into our complete *Self.*[16] Erickson also identifies various societal values and their influences on these moratoria, ranging from apprenticeships and adventures to psychiatric care.[17] Regardless of the moratorium and its effectiveness for defining a complete sense of *Self,* multiple moratoria may help us to avoid the pitfalls of an incomplete *Self* that has been fragmented to satisfy various "social pockets" through either personal circumstances or professional ambitions.[18]

Childhood Influences: How can any serious self-help-oriented book not make some gratuitous reference to our childhoods? Fortuitously, the moratorium phenomena induces a longing for our childhood, especially

13. Ibid.
14. Ibid.
15. Ibid.
16. Ibid, 157.
17. Ibid.
18. Ibid., 158.

how we revisit the earlier portions of our *personal narrative*. This revisitation allows us to interact and to manipulate our memories to help us better understand differences between the fulfillment and relinquishment of childhood dreams and their consequences, direct or indirect, on our *personal narratives.*

According to Erikson, any serious consideration about our contemplation/execution of a moratorium period requires us to revisit our roles within society and their historical evolution from our childhoods. As Erikson opines, the moratorium period is characterized by "selective permissiveness on the part of society and of the provocative playfulness on the part of youth."[19] The interplay between our youthful identity and its projected *Self* in society is a complex process that requires us to revisit the completion of our adolescent phase and absorb new "identifications" to assimilate into society.[20] During the acquisition of these new "identifications" and the assemblage of fragments from the incomplete *Self*, we learn from our transitions away from childhood playfulness and youthful experimental zest to the gravitas of young adulthood.[21]

As poignantly described by Erikson, the transitory phase interjects our young adulthood with a profound decision-making process that utilizes increasing intimacy and commitments.[22] Through positioning our notions of a complete *Self* between the known conclusion of adolescence and the unknown unfolding of adulthood, we can reposition our *Self* at a prior moment in time that will enable us to appreciate our own highly unique enterprise of self-awareness and identity development in our *personal narratives* and to understand how variations in social circles, durations, intensities, and ritualized exercises affected, and continue to affect, this enterprise.[23]

Erikson further opines that childhood perspectives on other roles of family and friends play a major role our sense of *Self*.[24] These perspectives, according to Erikson, help us to establish respect for "a kind of hierarchy of expectations" against which we can compare and "verify" our

19. Ibid., 157.

20. Ibid., 155.

21. Ibid., noting Erickson's description of this processing of the adolescent "absorbing sociability" and "subordinating" his childhood identifications.

22. Ibid.

23. Ibid.

24. Ibid., 159.

Self, both complete and incomplete, in later life stages.[25] This childhood hierarchical identity comparison process depends on our childhood interactions with "trustworthy representatives" from meaningful roles who fostered and nourished the youthful component of the *Self*.[26] The crucial moment in Erikson's analysis takes place when "identity formation" begins and identification ends.[27] Our identities and their acceptance by the community are important since if the community rejected or disproved our youthful identities and other childhood constructions of our *Self*, we would have needed to modify them to something other than their original permutation.[28] Throughout this process, Erikson emphasizes how our self-certainty in its sense on our *Self* becomes challenged in the developmental process and becomes prone to discontinuities and crises in the crucial stage in the life cycle.[29]

Our ability to converge identity elements, per Erikson's conceptualization, takes place at the end of childhood within the "normative crisis," known as adolescence.[30] Erikson claims that our adolescent *Self* suffers most deeply at the final stages of identity development and, in that process, becomes acquainted with the confusion associated with contemplating and processing a plethora of identity roles.[31] In this process, our individual identity and ego development, along with their impact on our sense of a complete *Self*, are most engaged based on their interaction and experimentation with fantasy and introspection.[32] The overall impact on our eventual identity and complete *Self* can be compartmentalized through these experiences and how they helped us become aware of the *Self* within a societal setting. These tensions appear most manifest in intimacy and its function in helping us embrace a sense of a healthy *Self* and its impact on identity expression.[33]

In considering identity development from childhood to young adulthood and its impact on the moratorium phenomenon, intimacy appears

---

25. Ibid.

26. Ibid.

27. Ibid.

28. Ibid., 160.

29. Ibid.

30. Ibid., 163.

31. Ibid., 163–64.

32. Ibid, 164.

33. See, generally, ibid., 168.

to become a critical factor in instigating and shaping the moratorium's trajectory on our need for identity modification, especially fragmentation of our *Self*. Erikson discusses a notion of "mutuality" that becomes present in sexual excitement, but seems to have application within our *Self*'s identity development. For example, Erikson identifies the counterpart of intimacy as "distantiation," i.e., the readiness to repudiate, ignore, or destroy those forces and people whose essence seems dangerous to our own.[34] Accordingly, the moratorium phenomenon in an individual suggests a direct application of distantiation whereby we seek to destroy the pre-moratorium *Self*, especially the incomplete *Self* and feelings associated with that incompleteness, as we perceive them to be a threat to the attainment of our complete *Self*.

As we can learn from the two case studies below, the successfulness of the moratorium phenomenon on identity development appears to depend on (i) pre-moratorium reasons for exploration of our incomplete *Self*, (ii) post-moratorium acceptance of the our more complete *Self*, and (iii) our newfound comfort with intimacy to accept our *Self*'s evolution. If our moratorium is successful, e.g., produces some positive improvement in self-perception, hopeful attitude, and circumstantial adjustment, then we know that we have successfully maneuvered through the symptoms of the minefield of the fragmented *Self* that precipitated the moratorium. On the other hand, our emergence from our moratorium period could demonstrate a decline where the post-moratorium *Self* contains aspects of "time confusion" (when our perception of time regresses to its early infancy state and did not impact our *Self* at this current moment),[35] "identity consciousness" (unresolved discrepancies between self-esteem, aggrandized self-image, and projected self-appearance as manifested in an amplified fragmented *Self*),[36] and "work paralysis" (perceived inadequacy based on unrealistic ego ideal demands and our inability to settle in a societal niche for our natural talents / "true gifts").[37] Even if these aspects were present in our pre-moratorium sense of *Self*, their presence alone does not appear to negate the possibility of post-moratorium identity improvements.

34. Ibid.
35. Ibid., 181.
36. Ibid., 183.
37. Ibid., 185.

We will *briefly* examine two historical personalities, George Bernard Shaw (famous playwright) and John Nash (Nobel laureate mathematician) to illuminate and to concretize the foregoing observations. While much has been and will continue to be written about both personalities and their historical relevance, our interest is strictly limited to their interaction with the moratorium phenomenon in the specific context of this chapter's objective to empower our *personal narratives* in our search for a complete sense of *Self*.

Case Study #1—Shaw's Moratorium

We can learn from studying Shaw's moratorium that our search for a complete *Self* requires us to have an honest dialogue with our *personal narratives* to determine our current human capital and our heartfelt desires to apply that capital in our quest for a complete *Self*. Shaw appears to have applied the moratorium phenomenon to complete his notions of *Self* as demonstrated by his transition to a professional identity away from a self-serving businessman to a creative/socially-conscious artist. Erikson specifically focuses on Shaw's description of "breaking loose" and his moving away from his friends, family and home.[38] As Erikson summarizes, Shaw granted himself a prolonged interval between youth and adulthood in which he attempted to find "a place in ordinary society for an extraordinary individual."[39] Erikson also noted that Shaw was suffering under a "false success" since he felt his success in the business world trapped him and prevented him from achieving a more authentic sense of *Self* without looming imposter neurosis.[40] How do these factors about Shaw's life resonate with our current feelings and emotions about our professional predicaments and their impact on our personal satisfaction?

Although Shaw did undertake a radical schism with his previous personal and professional life, he did transport some positive identity attributes with his new sense of *Self*. For example, Shaw applied his work habit that compelled him to write five pages per day so as to produce some work product over this prolonged interval.[41] That said, Erikson does provide an important description about Shaw's reaction to his father's

38. Ibid.
39. Ibid., 142.
40. Ibid.
41. Ibid., 144.

"drink neurosis" that played an important role in Shaw's "psychosexual aspect" of his sense of identity.[42] Shaw described his father's situation as either a "family tragedy" or "family joke" and his adjective choice and creative, self-deprecatory approach to family problems intimates an important component for his fragmented sense of *Self* and his subsequent moratorium.[43]

We can learn from Shaw's manipulation of his *personal narrative* how we can employ language to enhance our reactions to schisms between notions of our complete and incomplete *Self*. For example, Shaw appears to have drawn upon his family dynamic throughout the execution of his moratorium period, especially revisiting his family lineage and its aristocratic roots (i.e., ancestry related to the Earl of Fife),[44] applying his family propensity for noisemaking through instruments (i.e., Shaw's writing),[45] and embracing dramatic elements from the arts to create diabolical imaginary friends (i.e., Gounod's *Faust*).[46] These family components appear to have assisted Shaw in assembling a more complete *Self* that emerged after his moratorium period. Shaw, through his writing and other creative and social endeavors, secured an occupation that allowed his professional identity to apply his "dominant faculties" and to receive nourishment from his pursuits. It further appears Shaw's willingness to embrace his past and family dynamics assisted his achievement in adopting a healthy, complete *Self* that could be reinforced by social norms and liberated by its creative impulses defined by societal norms and expectations. Clearly, Shaw successfully managed the moratorium phenomenon to achieve a niche for his personal gifts that were well-received by his society and subsequent literary history.

We should carefully consider the aspects of our own family dynamics and their contributions to the completeness or incompleteness of our *Self*, especially if we want to undertake a moratorium in the vein of Shaw and emulate his successful strategy and outcome.

42. Ibid., 145.

43. See, e.g., ibid., quoting Shaw's comment that "to say my father could not afford to give me a university education is like saying that he could not afford to drink, or that I could not afford to become an author. Both statements are true; but he drank and I became an author all the same."

44. Ibid., 147.

45. Ibid., 148.

46. Ibid., 149.

Case Study #2—Nash's Moratorium

We can further learn from studying Nash's moratorium that our sense of an incomplete *Self* might instigate a moratorium period to accommodate a self-generated incompleteness that originated from irresolvable disequilibria between personal, professional and societal expectations. Moreover, our study of Nash's moratorium will also allow us to include a gratuitous mention of sexuality to fulfill our Freudian obligation to include a sex-related variable in our self-help analysis in the fulfillment of this chapter's objective.

Unlike Shaw, Nash suffered from an "acute identity crisis" that appears to have erupted from suffering through a tortured homosexual awareness process. First, Nash's scientific precociousness and its manifestation in dangerous scientific experiments that led to the death of his childhood friend.[47] Second, his social awkwardness was present in his attempts to act upon his homosexual desires as an undergraduate at Carnegie Tech and earned him the name "Nash-Mo" to represent his rejected "homo" tendencies.[48] Third, Nash constantly vacillated between sexual preferences and compartmentalized his activities as extensions of his intellectual prowess and identified them as "experiments,"[49] even including his arrest in a public restroom.[50] These three events demonstrate the origins of Nash's incomplete *Self* and its manifestation in an acute identity crises as he utilized his occupational niche to justify his sexual proclivities through engaging physical intimacy, occupational decision-making, competition, and psychosocial self-definition.[51]

Nash's behavior, both his personal and professional attitudes, appears to contain a destructive bent that, despite his subsequent delusions and psychiatric diagnoses, would support the rejection of his natural, complete *Self*.[52] As Erikson might opine, Nash's rejection of a homosexual identity in the development phase, especially the death of Nash's childhood friend (and perhaps potential boyhood crush), suggests a destructiveness of the *Self* and his natural identity[53] throughout his personal and

47. Capps, "John Nash's Delusional Decade," 365.
48. Ibid., 369.
49. See, generally, ibid, 366–77.
50. Ibid., 371.
51. See, e.g., ibid., 377.
52. Erikson, *Toys and Reasons*, 59.
53. See, e.g., ibid.

professional life, such as fathering a child out of wedlock[54] and destroying his professorial prospects.[55]

Nash, in contrast to Shaw, appears to have crafted an existence that reflected his desire to avoid maturation and to commit to an identity to reflect his true, authentic *Self*.[56] In particular, Nash's delusions prevented him from committing to any personal or professional complete *Self* and the obligations associated therewith. Moreover, Nash's behavior intimates that whether or not he intentionally lost himself in his delusions to find himself, Nash was searching for some transcendent reality to deploy his game theory and related mathematical brilliance to avoid finding his "true" homosexual self.[57] Most importantly, Nash's sexual conquests significantly prevented him from finding his "personhood" since Nash's relationships did not help fortify his complete sense of *Self*.[58] Nash's lack of connection to his love interests and peers may have fed his narcissistic tendencies that fueled Nash's delusions of self-admiration, depreciation of others, and obsessive projection of "genius."[59] As a result of the foregoing, Nash appears to have engaged in a search for the "rock bottom"[60] in which he induced, whether intentionally or unintentionally, his psychotic breaks, to undertake an identity transition within the *de minimis* to avoid dealing with his homosexual identity and its ability to complete his sense of *Self*.[61] Thus, Nash, his rejection of a homosexual identity, and his inability to find social acceptance of anything other than his perceived

54. Capps, "John Nash's Predelusional Phase," 375–76.

55. Ibid, 383, discussing rejecting a prestigious departmental chair at University of Chicago.

56. Dittes, *Mitigated Self*, 81, discussing Isaac Singer and his ability to create a self that centered around his New York City theatrical interests and his childhood memories to become a successful professional storyteller.

57. See, e.g., ibid, 83–84. See also, generally, Capps, "John Nash, Game Theory," 145–62.

58. See, e.g., Kepnes, "Buber's Ark," 104.

59. See, e.g., Capps, "John Nash's Postdelusional Period," 301. See also Capps, "John Nash: Three Phases," 370–71, reviewing Nash's delusions in light of his homoerotic conflict.

60. Capps, "John Nash's Delusional Decade," 201, noting that "rock bottom" represents a devolved form identity from which another self can emerge after extreme self-deprecation.

61. Capps, *Understanding Psychosis*, 150–51, noting how Nash's homosexual relations never progressed beyond the adolescent phase and stunted his sexual development and its impact on his overall need for regression and avoidance of adulthood.

ego ideal was preempted from exploiting the moratorium phenomenon for any individual betterment.

Nash's moratorium reminds us that we may want to undertake a moratorium exercise in searching for a complete *Self* to overcome certain weaknesses and self-destructive behavior patterns that have masqueraded as an inferior form of "completeness" in working through our incomplete notions and their influence on our feelings and emotions, as well as their presence in all aspects of our lives, like our attitudes.

Case Study Observations

These two cases studies, along with the moratorium phenomenon, demonstrate some of the essential building blocks and pitfalls in assembling a complete sense of our *Self*. For example, the moratorium phenomenon represents an important aspect of our effort to attain an optimal *Self* for our personhood and its societal role. When we suffer a socially unacceptable trauma or self-awareness, the moratorium phenomenon may lead us to undesirable results because the circumstances that instigated the moratorium may negate any beneficial effects from its undertaking. As both Shaw and Nash clearly indicate, the stronger our complete sense of *Self* at our moratorium's starting point, the stronger its effectiveness for helping us transition away from an incomplete sense of *Self* and its potentially negative consequences on other aspects of our lives.

CONSEQUENCES OF AN INCOMPLETE SELF IN OUR CURRENT STATE OF BEING (PART II)

As eloquently described by Robert Stolorow, the "narrative self," like our *personal narrative*, is

> assumed to be an interpretative construction, an evolving narrative or story about one's life and personality that reflects one's developmental and relational history and one's values, ideals, aims and aspirations. One might say that, whereas the Kantian self is the inferred subject or agent of reflection, the narrative self is an object or product of reflection.[62]

---

62. Stolorow, "Individuality in Context," 60.

Stolorow's categorization suggests we can control our *personal narratives* through understanding their evolution and their contribution to our objectified, complete sense of *Self* that can be pulled and pushed in various directions based on our sense of incompleteness. As Jung's dictum suggests, our ultimate goal (even extending beyond this chapter's objective) is our realization of our complete *Self*.[63] For us, we should take Jung's identification of this goal as a rallying call to think about ways we can organize the circumstances in our current state of being to allow us to conceptualize our complete *Self*, as well as to identify challenges and obstacles presented by our incomplete *Self*.[64]

Many sources can help us form a complete sense of *Self* from our current states of being, but very few will be as authentic and organic as our own efforts in identifying the causes for our incompleteness and assembling a complete sense of *Self*. The exercise alone will provide valuable insights about the inter-relationships between stories along our *personal narratives* and their impact on overall development and sense of completeness. Remember, if we did not feel as if our attitudes were 100 percent connected with their optimal expressions, we would have pursued alternative activities other than the words contained on these pages. More tellingly, we are using this book as a catalyst to help us undertake these valuable exercises to gain insight and knowledge about key areas in our lives that are ripe for self-improvement and self-development in our road to a complete sense of *Self*.

While nothing in this book should prevent us from seeking professional psychological assistance or pursuing other formal counseling outlets, we must consider the dynamics involved when revising and reviewing our *personal narratives* and why we *ourselves* must undertake the heavy lifting work associated with attaining a complete sense of *Self*. Most professional psychology can be considered a transactions-based business where money, not love, measures the effectiveness and value of counseling services in our development of a complete *Self*.[65] This monetary benchmark might be helpful in facilitating the provision and acquisition of valuable insights into our incomplete *Self*, but the transactional dynamic between provider and consumer in the psychological self-betterment paradigm may contain

---

63. See, e.g., Huskinson, *Dreaming the Myth Onwards*, 46.
64. Ibid.
65. See, e.g., Rosenfels, *Homosexuality*, iv.

an unfortunate myopia.[66] In particular, this myopia may limit the provider from investigating how our *personal narratives* interact and intersect with the *Grand Historical Narrative*. After all, our current state of being and most senses of incompleteness contained therein have derived from some disequilibria between these two narratives as our dreams and ambitions developed by our interaction with the *Grand Historical Narrative* become less attainable within our *personal narratives*.

Another example of why we must undertake the burden of work in seeking a complete sense of *Self* can be analogized to the role of multiculturalism in dealing with multiple oppressions in educational institutions.[67] In that setting, we can discern how previously disenfranchised groups who were denied access to the cultural norms that were perpetuated by institutional structures and media were finally allowed an opportunity to study themselves within the context of the *Grand Historical Narrative*.[68] Here, we must appreciate how our own self-study of our *personal narratives* can reveal the source of own sense of incompleteness, especially in our interpretation of and relationship with the *Grand Historical Narrative*. Without our own identification of inadequacies between these two key narratives, we will not be able to attain a complete *Self* since fragments of our incomplete *Self* will individually relate to either narrative and preempt us from attaining a sense of completeness.

Moreover, our psychologists and counselors may not have access to the fundamental information related to the disequilibria between these two narratives and, in turn, fall back upon more dominant, less individualistic, clinical modes of interpreting our incompleteness. Indeed, we are engaged in that transactional dynamic for their clinical expertise and sometimes that expertise, due to a plethora of our emotional or physical conditions, may be priceless. However, where we have the capacity to make rational and reasonable judgments regarding events within our *personal narratives*, we alone will know where, how and why events in our *personal narratives* coincide or conflict with our hopes and dreams from the *Grand Historical Narrative*, as well as the true scope of their impact on helping or hurting our efforts to attain a complete sense of *Self* in our current state of being.

66. Ibid.

67. See, e.g., Salyers and Wiggan, "Hidden Curriculum in Education," 77, 79.

68. See, e.g., ibid., 79, 81, citing Michael Foucault and post-structuralist arguments on the exclusiveness of education for the purpose of legitimizing a dominant discourse.

Besides transactional relationships creating an external influence on our personal sense of *Self*, we can identify other external forces that could preempt our individual efforts from completing our *Self*. The first major external threat is drug use or other forms of destructive behavior that create artificial emotions and feelings that deceive us into believing a momentary blissful state can be an adequate/acceptable substitute from the emotional satisfaction derived from a complete *Self*.[69] Another external threat with less physical, but more emotional, consequences is our over-visualization of reality to accommodate mental and physical disturbances and their impact on exposing weaknesses in our incomplete *Self*.[70] Usually, we ascribe something akin to "magical powers" to ritual practices that we claim can operate as gateways into or generators of alternate realities, in which we can neutralize negative influences upon our perceptions of reality and can avoid dealing with weaknesses in our incomplete *Self*.[71] Some psychological researchers, like Spiegelman, also note how we use religious or spiritual beliefs to fashion an ideal world that we use to establish our relationship with the real world.[72] Without delving into religious customs, practices and denominational affiliations, we must consider our own expressions of faith in any external force or construct (from the Divine to a molecule and everything in between) and how that faith could potentially enhance or impair our attainment of a complete *Self*. Once again, we alone can only be the correct arbiters of that assessment.

Finally, we must remember that our incomplete *Self* may have been used to help us cope with diverging drives and impulses originating from each facet of our incompleteness.[73] These divergences may help us understand our current emotions and their influences from our current environments.[74] They could also help us understand how we might have warehoused some of our unacceptable impulses and desires within

69. See, e.g., Kuhar, *Addicted Brain*, 150–51, noting the biochemical effects of club drugs and our need to create a self-generated blissful state to avoid drugs' allure.

70. See, e.g., Kakar, *Mad and Divine*, 133.

71. See, e.g., ibid.

72. See, e.g., Spiegelman, *Judaism and Jungian Psychology*, 4–5, opining how Judaism allows the "Halakhic man" to create a reality between his Torah from Sinai and its application to his real life in the modern life.

73. See, e.g., Cramer, *Protecting the Self*, 7.

74. Ibid.

differing fragments originating from our incomplete *Self*.[75] These impulses and desires will be instrumental in helping us form a complete sense of *Self* as we take better inventory of our current environment and its impact on fostering less desirable aspects of our incomplete *Self* and its impediment in assembling our fragmented emotions, dreams and ambitions into a complete *Self*.

TRANSITIONING BEYOND THE INCOMPLETE SELF

To transition beyond our current state of being, we need to consider the subconscious weights that have impaired our reactions and responses to our incompleteness and have prevented us from developing a conscious sense of completeness.[76] The appropriateness of our reactions is imperative since they will determine how we can evolve to a complete sense of *Self*. Most importantly, the ways we perceive our reactions will provide us with additional insights about our subconscious relationships to the incomplete *Self*. We shall refer to these relationships as residing in our subconscious because if they were housed within our consciousness, we would have better control over them and their impact on completing our sense of *Self*. Once we access our consciousness to evaluate and to monitor manifestations of our incomplete *Self*, we will enhance our perceptive capacities to compel fundamental changes in the attainment of our complete *Self*.[77] We will also understand the full effects of how subliminal stimuli reflect our personal histories and unconscious conflicts that prevent us from formulating successful strategies to transition toward our complete *Self*.[78] In turn, we can hone our ability to perceive unconscious influences that extend beyond our current circumstances and prevent us from seeing new possibilities for our new, complete *Self*.

A fundamental change that must take place in all us to move beyond our current states of incompleteness is the unification between our authentic inner *Self* and our projected outer *Self* and how that unification

---

75. Ibid.

76. See, e.g., Fisher and Shevrin, *Subliminal Explorations*, 13.

77. See, e.g., Fisher and Shevrin, *Subliminal Explorations*, 21, citing Reiser's work on the physiological implications of expanding perspective, neural impulses and other perceptive characteristics.

78. See, e.g., ibid.

can help us attain a sense of completeness.[79] For example, our current environments might provide an educational foundation to help engage our inner *Self* with our outer *Self* as we understand why we are residing in a particular professional and personal location and how our locative coordinates nurture aspects of our incomplete *Self* and motivate us to seek a complete *Self*.[80] The tensions between these two expressions of *Self* within our current state of being *alone* motivates us to move beyond our current incompleteness as the prospects of our complete *Self* threaten our incomplete *Self* and its inabilities to contain our ego and other related emotions.[81] Eventually, we will become more aware about the beneficial possibilities associated with removing such tensions from our current state of existence and embracing a complete sense of *Self* that will help to resolve our incomplete, fragmented nature.

Another potential area of change we will experience as we transition between an incomplete to complete *Self* is the emotional strength gained from experiencing control over all our emotions and feelings within a self-contained completeness, rather than projecting those sentiments onto fragments within our incomplete *Self*.[82] This exercise will help our emotional resolve to accept, rather than eject and/or project, disruptive emotions and unacceptable feelings that we can use to help us attain a sense of completeness.[83] For example, most scholars conclude that projection dynamics infiltrate our sense of *Self* as we allocate positive reactions to our internal *Self* and negative reactions to our external *Self*.[84] Through this compartmentalization, we can cope with the dissonance between our internal and external emotional objectives and can prevent us from pursuing a complete *Self* with unnecessary anxiety and angst.

The process to attain our complete *Self* is not without extreme emotional disruption or discomfort because our completeness would have been previously achieved if the process was simple without strife. Some of us may need to engage professional counselors where the emotional distress from our transition to completeness triggers either destructive

79. See, e.g., Romme and Escher, *Accepting Voices*, 25, commenting about patients who hear voices and how those inner voices combine with patients' outer voices to understand their impact on patients' lives.

80. See, e.g., Salyers and Wiggan, "Hidden Curriculum in Education," 81.

81. See Huskinson, *Dreaming the Myth Onwards*, 46.

82. Cramer, *Protecting the Self*, 70.

83. See, e.g., ibid.

84. See ibid., 71.

behaviors or need for therapeutic medicines.[85] Our need for clinical and/or therapeutic intervention may result from the removal of our external defense mechanisms and our *direct* encounters with less than optimal feelings as we evolve toward a complete *Self*.[86] Thus, we must consider these factors as we shift beyond our current state of being and its incompleteness with great care as we achieve a sense of completeness and its implications for a potential, superlative *Self*.

ACHIEVING THE SUPERLATIVE COMPLETE SELF AS REVEALED IN OUR DREAMS

The attainment of the complete *Self* will help us achieve a superlative existence through enabling us to get in touch with our "real *Self*" and exercising our creative capacities to discover our superlative, complete *Self*.[87] We have the power to create within our *Self*, especially our complete *Self*. The more we exercise our creative capacities, the more we can experience assembling our complete *Self* and connecting with higher, esoteric notions about all creations. Some researchers believe that we get closer to the "Universe" when we pin down our complete *Self* and access its creativity in transitioning to a complete *Self*.[88] This creativity will also help us conceptualize and concretize the elements of our complete *Self* that will contribute to our empowered and improved attitudinal development.

When considering how to transition from an incomplete to complete *Self* and its potential optimality impact on our existence, we must undertake extensive creative exercises to understand our ownership of the complete *Self* and its manifestation in our *personal narratives*. For example, we can consider the incompleteness of our *Self* as resulting from our inability to create a *Self* that harmonizes our fears and concerns regarding our mortality and inevitable death. Some philosophers, like Heidegger, believe that our authentic being emerges as we contemplate our reactions to our relationship with death and how those reactions demonstrate an exercise in extreme uniqueness and individuality.[89] As

85. See, e.g., O'Brien et al., *Addictive States*, 5.

86. See, e.g., Cramer, *Protecting the Self*, viii.

87. Kaya, "Compelled to Create," 23, stressing that only in being creative we can discover the real, complete self.

88. See, e.g., ibid.

89. Stolorow, "Individuality in Context," 63.

a result, we can consider the superlative associated with our complete *Self* as a direct consequence from the ownership of our *Self* and taking responsibility for our own existence.

Further expressions of creativity and its impact on our superlative, complete *Self* can be found in our dreams where we encounter the unfettered power of the Divine and can reveal our deepest intentions without self-criticism or external judgment.[90] Dream formation cannot be underestimated in how we define and relate to the superlative and its presence in the potential completion of our *Self,* especially the revelation of unconscious wishes and their importance on completing our *personal narrative.*[91] We should always strive to be aware of our dreams to ensure that we can connect with our unconscious wishes. Otherwise, we might miss a crucial informational source for our *Self*'s evolution and an opportunity for our ability to attain the superlative. The unconscious dreams and wishes provide us with invaluable emotions that help guide us along the acquisition of components of the *Self* and our need to express that completeness through empowered and improved attitudes. No doubt, satisfaction with our complete *Self* will directly correlate with satisfaction expressed in our empowered and improved attitudes through feeling secure and confident in our emotional capacities and their expressiveness in various aspects of our everyday life.

Moreover, we must understand how the superlative formation and application of our complete *Self* can be transported from our dreams into our realities to ensure we can properly empower and improve our attitudes. Jung concluded that we can only access our true creative, superlative consciousness when we truly know the complete *Self* and its relationship to the "larger totality" of which we are part.[92] We can begin to grasp and to appreciate that "larger totality" as we can experience the intermingling of our *personal narratives* with the *Grand Historical narrative* in our dream states. For the purposes of this chapter's objective, we must better understand our dreams and what they are communicating about our incomplete *Self* and its limitations on our creative abilities to attain both a complete *Self* and a superlative expression of that complete *Self.* As we compare our unfulfilled dreams and desires within our *personal narratives* and their influences from the *Grand Historical Narrative,* we

90. Fisher and Shevrin, *Subliminal Explorations,* 17.

91. Ibid, 19.

92. See Spiegelman, *Judaism and Jungian Psychology,* 81.

can begin to strategize ways to fulfill them as we strive for a complete *Self* and a superlative existence from which we attained such completeness.

Furthermore, we must come to appreciate how images, desires and expressions from our dreams help us to formulate and to manifest our superlative, complete *Self*. In particular, we must master how our *personal narratives* distort and transform images influenced by the *Grand Historical Narrative* that operate as an arbiter in determining our sense of ultimate completeness and satisfaction of our *Self* within our daily existence.[93] As we strive to meet the standards set forth within *Grand Historical Narrative* and apply them to our own accomplishments within our *personal narratives*, we begin to see disconnects that do not properly account for our own individual variations and *sui generis* standards of satisfaction, completeness and achievement.

Rather than allowing such variations to amplify our incompleteness and our distance from a superlative existence, we must embrace and employ those differences to complete our *Self* according to our terms and conditions regarding the achievement of our personal and professional goals. Without placing our uniqueness at the forefront of this process, we propound our incompleteness and other dissatisfactions away from the complete, superlative *Self* with unnecessary and unproductive distractions. Recall the many moments throughout our *personal narratives* where we allowed the standards of success set forth on the *Grand Historical Narrative* to extinguish any celebration of our *Self* (complete or incomplete) and our personal accomplishment.

FINAL CHAPTER REFLECTIONS ON THE SELF

Fragments from our incomplete *Self* are included in the images from our dreams, which we must gather and analyze to develop our complete *Self*.[94] These fragments and their manifestation in our dream images allow us to have valuable insights to understand why we have not previously attained a superlative, complete sense of *Self* and how we can maintain that improved and empowered state of existence in all aspects of our lives, especially our attitudes. Hence, we must remember where our incomplete *Self* originated and its influences on directing lives away from

93. See, e.g., Fisher and Shevrin, *Subliminal Explorations*, 131.

94. See, e.g., ibid., 74, noting how day residues provide perceptual materials for the visual and auditory images that manifest in our dreams.

this superlative, complete sense of *Self* to avoid revisiting and reigniting those inferior feelings and emotional consequences. In this regard, we can harness the power of our dream states to help us create, manifest and assemble a sense of *Self* that we can transport and launch our superlative, complete *Self* equipped with unique attributes that enhance our own ordinary reality with a sense of extraordinary satisfaction.

6

Transform Doubt into Conviction

HOPEFULLY, AFTER WE READ this chapter, we will better understand how we can grow from the emotions associated with our insecurities. Arguably, this chapter represents the most important turning point in our attitudinal transformations, as we understand why we all grapple with inner weaknesses that amplify our perception of extreme emotions and, in turn, blind us from recognizing their moderate, manageable nature. Somehow, we all find ourselves with an inescapable feeling of dread as we face life's more daunting tasks regarding our personal relationships, family conundrums and professional ambitions.

Whatever our decision-making processes, we surrender any sense of control and/or manageability about a situation when our doubt causes us to disregard our intellectual capacity to solve any problem. Doubt, unlike most of other emotions, has the capacity to immobilize us completely and leave us stranded upon on our own ever-shrinking islands of despair. Unfortunately, we do not only have one island of despair but we create many islands of despairs throughout our lifetime as we struggle with basic mundane tasks and as we aspire to achieve beyond the superlative. Somehow, we examine the task at hand, step back and just collapse into our own vacuous sense of nothingness without hope of ever having an opportunity to step back up and out from our deep doubt and conquer new possibilities.

As our descriptive metaphors indicate, doubt encompasses an extreme emotion within our psyches that require us to exercise awareness of our *Self* as presented within our *personal narratives* and as compared to the *Grand Historical Narrative*. If we construct a notion of "doubt" as an irrational reaction to an unrealistic emotional challenge, we begin to understand the absurdity associated with doubt and its paralyzing consequences. Why should one emotion, doubt, wield such power over-and-over, in and throughout our *personal narratives*? Recall the times in our lives when we made particular decisions, especially less than optimal decisions, based on a sense of doubt that a better alternative or a preferable strategy would eventually be presented to us. Most of those decisions probably did not end up particularly well. We all have friends that have been in long-term committed relationships for many years and eventually married their partners since they hit a certain age and *doubted* that they could find a better-suited partner at their mid-life. We wish those friends the best but we all know those types of relationships usually end up riddled with self-destructive behaviors, like alcoholism, Internet porn addiction and infidelity. While marriage may present itself as an extreme example, we all have some personal decisions that were made from the same type of *doubt* that neither we could eventually find something better nor we were capable to achieve our ideal.

This chapter conceptualizes doubt as an extreme emotional phenomenon that originates from our failure to place our *Self* and our ambitions within their proper context in relation to their importance within our *personal narratives* and their significance compared to the *Grand Historical Narrative*. This phenomenon occurs when we miscalculate the importance of particular circumstances, situations and/or individuals and, in turn, we misperceive our intellectual and emotional capacity to deal with them. Basically, we ascribe an irrational and unfounded superiority to the source of our doubt that encumbers us with an unnecessary, unproductive feeling of inferiority. We imbue that particular inferiority with special powers that obliterate any modicum of confidence, hope or intelligence to combat those daunting challenges in our lives. The "true" enemy in all this is our own ignorance to misperceive the power dynamic between what we want out of a particular circumstance or situation and what we believe our monumental obstacles are in achieving that want. After all, we must recall everything in our reality, no matter how extraordinary we may believe that reality is, contains flaws and considered an imperfect representation of our perfect dreams or, as in the case with doubt, our worst nightmares. Let us reconfigure the power dynamic between our ambitions, doubts and obstacles and develop a powerful strategy to not only enhance our strategic thinking processes, but to acquire an empowered and improved attitude to safeguard our ambitions from the ravages of doubt and unfair victories of that emotion's origins within our psyches.

In the past, we have always looked at doubt and ambition as two, polarized emotions that create tension between what we have, what we want and how we go about getting what we want (especially without regard to some of the absurdity associated with our desires). A universal example of this phenomenon can be found in our work environments (even during our academic careers) when we were gifted with an insurmountable workload and complete exhaustion. During those times, we may have felt *totally* overwhelmed and did not think it was humanly possible to complete our assignments. We also might have fumed over our boss and prayed for a miraculous escape from our responsibilities. Most of us experience similar escape desires in various aspects of our daily lives when confronted with extreme, anxiety-provoking situations. Yet, somehow, whether by Divine grace, miraculous intervention or sheer industry, we all have survived those situations and may consider them personal and professional triumphs within our *personal narratives.*

For the purposes of this chapter, we must revisit our personal triumphs over our insecurities and identify the common thread in all of them regarding how they have helped shaped us and strengthened our resolve against a plethora of emotional adversities. That said, we must better understand how to evaluate the power dynamic in transitioning from complete and utter despair (i.e., doubt) to victory and total triumph (i.e., success). These extremes help us understand the depths of our personal power to transform our thoughts and to focus our energies to survive a less than optimal situation.

Besides survival, these extremes clearly demonstrate the power of our misperception when we permit doubt to undermine our abilities to work through a problematic situation and to overestimate the direness of our circumstances. The major lesson from this overall conundrum is that we have the power to transform our vulnerability and weakness into extraordinary strength. We all wield similar transformative power. The issue may be our access to that power, especially our ability to apply that inner power, when our emotions become unnerved through doubt. This chapter sets forth how doubt usurps our rational sensibilities and leads us into an extreme state of hypersensitivity. This hypersensitivity creates a unique opportunity for us to regain control over our emotions through acknowledging the absurdity of our doubt and its exemplification of weaknesses within the *Self*. Thereafter, we can assert great control of those areas in our current state of existence that make us vulnerable to the pejorative effects of doubt, we can move beyond the emotional weaknesses in our decision-making processes, and we can embrace conviction—the superlative correlative of doubt—for all aspects of our thoughts and attitudes.

DOUBT AS YEAST TO OUR INSECURITIES AND ITS POLARIZING EMOTIONAL CONSEQUENCES

Our preliminary concern must be the identification of the origins of our insecurities and how we have traditionally allowed doubt to foster those insecurities in immobilizing our decision-making processes. No matter how positive we come across in our attitudes in dealing with others, our lack of confidence will always be a breeding ground for doubt, related emotions and pessimistic attitudes. For most of us, doubt keeps us grounded to the present moment and anchors us to a point in our *personal narratives* from which we struggle to move pass. In distorting our sense of purpose at a particular moment, doubt suffocates our imagination and perception to create and to exploit new possibilities beyond this isolated hiccup in our constructive bravado. Yet, we cannot surmise ways to overcome our doubt and transform it into a motivating emotion that can nurture our confidence and reinforce our positive convictions toward achieving our own superlative emotional forms of self-reliance and self-confidence.

To accomplish this task, we need to reorient the emotional components of our doubts to understand the linkage between our own insecurities and their unhealthy codependence on our doubts. Most of this unhealthy codependence between doubt, insecurity and self-fulfilling failure in our *personal narratives* has an important commonality—vanity. Indeed, the proverbial phrase from the King James Version of Ecclesiastes, "vanity of vanities; all is vanity," provides an important, but simple, framework to understand how our perception of our *Self* and its unrealistic, impaired sense of importance makes us vulnerable to the negative consequences of doubt. We usually find ourselves not measuring up to our own sense of capability or desired posture in particular situation or circumstance that fuels our doubt beyond unhealthy, tolerable emotional levels. Without the specter of our vanity haunting our emotional insecurities, we could be conceptualize and control the situation to transform our doubt in a positive conviction to eradicate our emotional weaknesses and to achieve our desired goals. Imagination appears to be an emotional ally in this undertaking.[1]

Because our vanities are mostly grounded within this world, especially the standards set forth in the *Grand Historical Narrative*, such vanities must be removed from our decision-making processes to unleash the full power of our imaginations. Otherwise, we will be limited by the burdens of the world and standards lauded and praised within the *Grand Historical Narrative* and, in turn, we will be preempted to find ways to apply our doubts to elevate our own special talents into emotional motivators to overcome our personal and professional insecurities. Thus, our imagination will help us combat doubt through creating new possibilities in which doubt can be transformed into conviction, as we perceive new ways to offset doubt with our own unique strengths and talents developed within our *personal narratives* independent from unnecessary influences from the *Grand Historical Narrative*.

From a practical point, we must think about our own personal coping mechanisms when we become seized by doubt when it unleashes a tsunami of emotional insecurities throughout periods in our *personal narratives*. Visualizing the circumstances and conditions that inflate our insecurities, we can think about our process of descent from stable confidence to unstable doubt and identify our personal triggers. Once we grasp the sequential nature of our emotional unraveling, we can begin to exert control over our doubt through our imagination. For example, we can conceptualize that these emotional disturbances allow us to better understand our limitations, our emotional needs and our overall *Self*. Perhaps, we can embrace the potential, intangible benefits from the anxiety associated with feeling less than optimal if we believe that doubt operates as a ritual process that moves us away from our emotional weaknesses and provides an opportunity for empowerment and improvement. In this way, we can exploit the vitality and psychological benefits of ritualizing our emotional trajectory between doubt and confidence.[2] This process is highly individualistic, as variations within and between our imaginations

---

1. Bakan, *Sigmund Freud* (Free Association), 78.

2. Kakar, *Mad and Divine*, 133, discussing the psychic benefits of visualizing our universe and the power of rituals as providing tangible psychological benefits when connected with constructive visualization exercises.

will provide the structural foundation for our private emotional rituals and the benefits we anticipate to extract. We will visit some techniques in the following sections below regarding potential emotional rituals that can move us beyond our current feelings of doubt toward confidence and self-assurance.

After all, one of the most valuable attributes of our doubt is its experiential quality regarding our interactions with other individuals, our environments, our circumstances and our realities.[3] We are all engaging in some emotional expression between our desires to portray a confident, self-assured human and to avoid projecting a doubting, self-questioning ne'er-do-well. The tension between these two disparate emotional states not only feeds our insecurities, but creates unproductive anxieties as we attempt to reconcile the irreconcilable. Without appreciating the nuances between these two emotional states, we become limited by an emotional myopia that prevents us from unpacking the strength within our *Self*. Furthermore, we become so harried in our thinking that we forget about our previous victories over doubt throughout our *personal narratives*.

Our decision-making process becomes jammed and we either panic or distract our attention away from analyzing the sequential nature of our emotional rituals that allow our doubt, rather than our confidence, to become our primary focus.[4] When we experience the foregoing, we apparently consider expressions of confidence, strength and self-assurances as foreign constructs to our emotional repertoires in dealing with disturbing and/or challenging situations. To achieve this chapter's objective, we must revisit and refine our feelings, as well as our perceptions of such feelings, to ensure we can avail ourselves of the confident, self-assured natures within our *Self*. Otherwise, the potential benefits of this book and its ability to empower and improve our attitudes will be thwarted by our own doubts in any current and future self-improvement undertaking!

Before we commence this chapter's important exposition of its objective, we must fully understand and appreciate the origins of our doubt within our thinking and decision-making processes. Specifically, we must become friendly with this persnickety emotional state so that we do not blame our current personal, professional, spiritual or attitudinal stalemates on our inability to overcome our doubt and to encounter our optimal *Self*. Doubt, in some significant ways, can be considered an

---

3. See, e.g., Belzen, "Spirituality, Culture, and Mental Health," 301.

4. See, e.g., Slade and Bentall, *Sensory Deception*, 75, discussing how task demands and task motivating instructions impact the reality of suggested stimuli.

amicable emotional state with a beneficial purpose in preserving our self-esteem when we are faced with a particularly difficult situation or circumstance. Usually, doubt generates its psychological turmoil when something deeply disrupts the solidity of our personal identity and undermines the *Self*.

Rather than that something causing us to separate completely from our *Self*, doubt operates as a defense mechanism to preserve any remnant of our self-esteem as it distracts us from consciously acknowledging any imminent failure against a formidable circumstance, situation and/or individual.[5] Hence, doubt enables us to preserve our own reality and our sense of self-esteem, regardless of its fragility or limitations. Hopefully, this chapter will instruct us on how best we can transform the illusion of doubt's self-preservation function into actual confidence with real benefits for all aspects of our decision-making and thinking processes.

DISCOVER STRENGTH WITHIN CURRENT STATES OF WEAKNESSES

While we all aspire to the notion of the perfect, actualized *Self* without worry or doubt, we all know our own personal weaknesses and faults. These weaknesses can grow into insurmountable stumbling blocks along the course our *personal narratives* as we tend to other matters and circumstances in our lives that distract our attention and effort away from remedying those weaknesses. Rather than engaging in this type of benign neglect with our insecurities, we must assume an active posture in converting our weaknesses and doubts into something nourishing and sustaining. The *Grand Historical Narrative* contains numerous examples of this phenomenon, such as the legendary author, Sir Arthur Conan Doyle, who utilized his personal experience with Asperger's syndrome to create Sherlock Holmes. Some scholars conjecture the famous literary character, Sherlock Holmes, was an "autistic creation from an autistic mind."[6] Though we may not personally suffer from a clinical diagnosable condition, we can appreciate Doyle's ability to exercise his imagination within his current impaired condition to create something that allowed him to move beyond his limitations and to achieve literary greatness.

---

5. See, e.g., Cramer, *Protecting the Self*, 152, enumerating the structure and operation of defense mechanisms.

6. See, e.g., Fitzgerald, *Genesis of Artistic Creativity*, 83.

We can remind our *Self*, as we will do later in this chapter, that many important historical figures within the *Grand Historical Narrative* applied their inner, private weaknesses to achieve an indelible mark on humanity's collective historical evolution. Hence, regardless of the source of our present paralysis, its origins from our doubt and its consequences upon our emotional sufferings, we can take comfort in the fact that doubt unites all of us in our present moment in time and provides all of us with an opportunity to achieve greatness.

In considering doubt's role in our current states of being, we must step back from our usual relationships with our emotions, if any, and approach doubt with its own *sui generis* analytical framework. First, we must surrender our ego to label our emotions from regular compartmentalization and control mechanisms as we appreciate doubt's far-reaching consequences on all aspects of our current realities. Specifically, the power of doubt is its amorphous nature to erupt from disparate types of situations and circumstances, as well as personal and professional encounters. So, some of us might look at doubt in a more favorable light as a regulating emotion regarding the establishment and maintenance of healthy boundaries between our *Self* and the trigger of our doubting emotions.

Some of us, though, may have a less than favorable view of doubt as we view that emotion as the ultimate source of personal disappointments and professional failures (among other pejorative sentiments). That said, our actual emotional bond with the emotion of doubt itself becomes critical in understanding doubt's preconscious and conscious components and their impact on our behavior patterns, self-representations and attitudes.[7] We may embrace doubt as an important, endearing emotional component of our everyday persona to protect us from confrontation or to control us from frivolous expression. Even more illuminating, doubt may keep our happiness emotions in check so that we can avoid feelings of anxiety about losing our successes or other states of ephemeral contentment. Regardless, our intimate relationship with doubt and its various manifestations in various aspects of our lives must be fully understood and appreciated before we can commence any transformative exercise to convert doubt into a principle motivator for constructive change.

Second, doubt has a major impact on how we perceive our situations, our circumstances and our encounters with others as we deceive

7. See, e.g., Cramer, *Protecting the Self*, 94.

our *Self* into the self-acceptance and self-perpetuating state of weakness. In other words, we detach from any sense of strength and constructive creativity as we deny, rationalize and project a distortion of current reality[8] that deceives us into believing why we lack the requisite ability to overcome our doubt and pursue our desires with determination and conviction. Our doubts further distort our perception and continue to trap us in a less than optimal state where our anxieties, fears and insecurities preempt us from perceiving possibilities void of our doubts. We deny ourselves future possibilities with freedom from doubt and insecurities as we rationalize why our insecurities will always plague us and we project how our doubts will impact our future possibilities.[9] As a result, we accept and perpetuate the prominence of doubt in our decision-making processes and, in some instances; we even restructure our lives in ways to avoid encountering that emotion.

Third, doubt must be conceptualized within a cultural construct to understand its psychological phenomenological impact on our attitudes, motives, perceptions, outlooks, reasoning abilities, memory recollections and other emotions[10] in our immediate state of being. Through understanding doubt as a result of our own cultural beliefs, moral values and community roles, we can exercise better control over our beliefs and desires and how they figure into episodes within our *personal narratives* and interactions with the *Grand Historical Narrative*. We become vulnerable to our doubts when we feel our insecurities prevent us from successfully fulfilling an assumed role or function within our personal and/ or professional social circles. We also become desperate when we underestimate our capacity to cope with the possibility of failure and potential feelings of inferiority associated with others recognizing and affirming such feelings.[11] The consequence from premature, perceived failure creates an unstable emotional situation in which we become less equipped to deal with any form of doubt in a productive way, thereby descending

---

8. See, e.g., Twerski, *Addictive Thinking*, 42, discussing truth distortions in addictive cycle of denial, rationalization and projection.

9. Ibid., 42–45.

10. See, e.g., Belzen, "Spirituality, Culture, and Mental Health," 301, discussing stress psychological phenomena and the importance of grounding that phenomena with cultural interactions.

11. See, e.g., Rosenfels, *Homosexuality*, 116, discussing the role of sadistic tendencies to avoid the possibility of failure in connecting with a partner and being recognized by that partner for a failure in love capacity.

into ever increasing destructive, unhealthy behaviors that isolate us from encountering doubt in the first place. As a result, we must avoid any form of distraction from encountering and overcoming our own triggers of doubt to access that emotion's constructive potential.

Finally, we must imbue our doubt with its own emotional language to understand how doubt mutilates our reasoning skills about particular situations and circumstances and obliterates any type of optimism from our decision-making processes. Unlike our other emotions, doubt communicates through stripping us of our intellectual armor and exposing our raw vulnerabilities. Doubt greatly impairs the mental connections we make between circumstances and outcomes since our rational emotions usually get displaced by insecurities and anxieties. Hence, we cannot properly order the emotional tensions between doubt and other feelings that disrupt our usual decision-making capacities to help us create an effective strategy to contain doubt and to bring us to our desired outcome in relation to the source of our doubt. We just ruminate about our inadequacies and our decision-making processes become tainted with our overall disgust at a particular moment in the development of our *personal narratives*.

Rather, doubt completely reorders our current realities to accommodate the emotion's disempowering influences on our *Self*, our cultural context and our potential contributions. Freud, for example, considered speeches within our dreams to evolve from auditory percepts that occurred throughout our wake state and were arbitrarily reassembled within our dreams to provide new insights about our everyday realities.[12] The arbitrariness commonly shared between doubt and our dream state requires us to ponder what factors and influences invite doubt to enter our emotional well-being, especially considering that most of us cannot easily identify the *how*, the *what* and the *why* doubt creates such havoc at particularized moments within our *personal narratives*. Thus, we have need to refine our communicative skills with our emotions to ensure we are properly isolating doubt from our other emotions and we can better interpret its interaction with our circumstances, environments and other emotions.

In essence, doubt operates like an emotional fulcrum between various states of security related to our identity between different episodes within our *personal narrative*s, as well as our interactions with the *Grand*

12. See, e.g., Fisher and Shevrin, *Subliminal Explorations*, 73.

Historical Narrative. All of us experience some form of identity crisis and/or confusion, no matter how miniscule, related to certain activities, such as fellowship, sexual intimacy or competition.[13] Various aspects of our identity may not always perfectly fit within the rubric of our *Self* that we generally accept and we project to others in performing our daily routines. Those aspects of our identity that are outside the *Self* generate unique tensions that expose the *Self* as a sort of imposter that we generated to overcompensate for the rejected notions of our identity that create disease and discomfort in forming and accepting the complete *Self*. When we encounter something that feeds our doubts, we are basically encountering a destabilizing aspect of the *Self* that can equate to a form of identity confusion. Whether it can be categorized as our inability to cope with failure, our desire to avoid confrontation or our general dislike of rejection, our identity confusion and its impact on the *Self* crumbles the moment we permit our doubt to prevent us from experiencing the fullness of our *Self*. To counteract the ramifications from this paradigm, we need to reinforce the completeness of our *Self* and to remedy any insecurity within the sense of our own identity through direct confrontation with the *Self* with the same type of conviction we will apply to the pursuit of our goals and dreams beyond the current moment in our quest for the superlative.

Moving beyond Doubt toward Confidence and Self-Assurance

If we are suffering from any type of doubt, even doubt about the efficacy of this book or this chapter to change our lives, we must determine the "distance" of our emotional dislocation from any offsetting confidence and/or self-assurance. Does that distance become shorter or longer when we consider past failures as an indicator of future failures? Or do we prefer to have our emotions control us rather than controlling them and doubt provides us with an arresting emotional state from achieving our goals? Perhaps, some of us empower our doubt, rather than more constructive emotions, to create a false sense of despair with relevant justifications for our lack of trying to improve our current realities. Whatever our personal reasoning to maintain unhealthy doubts with immobilizing

---

13. See, e.g., Capps, *Understanding Psychosis*, 135, noting activities that reveal latent identity crises.

consequences for our dreams and ambitions, we need to help ourselves to identify and to rely on more inspiring emotions to move beyond our doubts and their ability to anchor us in less than optimal emotional states.

As a preliminary matter, we must recognize what type of change we are trying to create in moving beyond the emotional restrictions of our doubts. Otherwise, this exercise may be futile for any of us who rebel and reject coerced motivations for personal change. In the extreme case, certain individuals may have so inculcated doubt as a fundamental component of their identity and sense of *Self* that any modification to that emotion could create destabilizing psychological conditions. For example, clinicians have noticed that acute identity confusion correlates with a restriction in decisions, choices and commitments as individuals become vulnerable to forms of psychosis in deciding on fulfilling psychosocial definitions related to their personal decisions.[14] When we are confronted with the choice to purge unhealthy forms of doubt within our decision-making process, we may have a similar panic-type reaction as we begin to confront opportunities with new emotional dynamics. Instead of being limited by our doubt and anticipated self-defeating outcomes, we will face new unknowable possibilities that will test our insights and understandings about our *Self* and its relationship to its ambitions, dreams and aspirations. The potential for constructive change is infinite as we move beyond the confines of our doubt, but we must remember our choice in undertaking this movement and our free will in determining how far we will move beyond our doubts. Otherwise, we may become prematurely frustrated before real, transformative changes can be achieved.

Categorizing our psychological shift beyond doubt toward confidence and self-assurance, we should not limit our descriptions and/or measurements of our success (or failure) to traditional emotional demarcations. Rather, we need to conceptualize this shift within at least two parallel emotional conditions. First, we must recognize the requisite mental shift to bring about the transformation in our decision-making process and our perceptive abilities to exude sufficient confidence to negate the ravages of our former doubt. Second, and more importantly, we need to recognize a "phantom" shift that permits us to visualize our *Self* and our new found confidence interacting with circumstances, conditions and personal and professional encounters that would usually fuel our doubts.[15]

14. Capps, *Understanding Psychosis*, 134.

15. See, e.g., Robertson, "Beast Within," 20, reviewing the role of the mental and phantom shift in Therians and their animal religious practices.

Together, these two shifts will bring the process for transformation, not transformation itself, as we work through our unique mental, spiritual, psychic, relational and professional needs and develop our own mode of communication between doubt and confidence. This mode of communication helps us extract the psychological insights we need to evaluate the void between our doubt and our confidence so as to cross that void with minimal disruptive impact to our overall *Self* and our ability to function within our current realities. With our new confidence and self-assurance, we will not only enhance our ability to function within our current realities, we will have access to our creative capacities to change those aspects of our current realities that prevent us from experiencing the success we need to confirm our confidence!

So, what do some of us do if we feel that we cannot escape from the prison of our doubts? Or, we believe that we are so psychologically distant from any emotion of confidence that should just close this book and engage in another distractive intellectual enterprise? Besides throwing our *Self* that proverbial pity party with all its emotional accoutrements, we need to socialize (figuratively speaking) with characters from our *personal narratives*, as well as historical figures from the *Grand Historical Narrative*, to break away from the weight of our doubts and to seize our confidence and the power that confidence possess to transform our doubt into conviction! First, and foremost, we must vividly recall the various episodes in our *personal narratives* in which we believed our doubts would prevent us from progressing to a future phase within our *narratives*. All of us can remember at least one episode within our *personal narratives* where we really believed that "we could not go on" and felt utter and total despair! Guess what, we all went on and overcame that arresting emotional perception. We are even reading this book as further confirmation of our ability to overcome self-defeating emotions, especially our doubt. In a nutshell, we should never fear that any prison created by our doubts is inescapable without sufficient determination, assistance and *conviction* to move beyond the ungrounded basis for the psychological limitations associated with our doubts.

Whenever we feel the power of doubt overcome us, we need to revisit prior doubt-ridden episodes within our *personal narratives* that can remind us about our past victories over our doubts and the certainty of success in overcoming our current malaise. Once we doubt the possibility of anything or anyone, especially our *Self*, we surrender our power to create new opportunities and to exploit new possibilities from less than optimal circumstances (especially the psychological void from our perceived lack of confidence and self-assurance). Let us deconstruct the emotional components of doubt as they manifest within our *personal narratives* to appreciate the connection between our current realities and their accommodations for our lack of confidence.

We should be able to identify at least five emotions that correlate with our feelings related to doubt. These emotions enable us to carve out an aspect within our current realities that permit us to move beyond the emotional boundaries our doubts create since these "micro-realities" permit us to avoid or to overcome our doubts outside our ordinary, daily routines. Let's say, we work in a job that we detest and we carve out an office reality, i.e., a "mirco-reality," with fellow coworkers with similar disdain for their careers. We engage in a "bitch-and-moan" mode of communication with our like-minded coworkers who make us find humor in distressing work situations and provide us comfort in light of professional dissatisfactions. Through these types of communications, we suffer through the unpleasantness in our everyday realities and create "mirco-realities" to cope with our doubts and other defeating emotions. Some of our micro-realities might entail shopping at our favorite stores, traveling to far-off destinations, partying with friends or other distractive endeavors. Regardless of the activity and its immediate emotional im-pact, we never remedy the underlying emotional condition that required us to create our micro-realities in the first place. Without understanding our emotional discontent that requires us to compartmentalize our reali-ties within our daily routines, we will consistently have a need to carve out micro-realities without ever empowering and improving our attitude to embrace the entirety and uniformity of our current reality and our desired future reality. In essence, we permit our doubt to blind us from seeing our emotional contentment and happiness within any singular reality that permits us to interact with any circumstance, condition, situ-ation, or individual. Have we identified at least five emotions that cause us to retreat within a subset of our everyday reality? Let us ponder some of them below.

Doubt, being the opposite of conviction, creates *hesitation* in our decision-making processes. Hesitation makes us gasp for thought and reason as we question our ability to deal with a stressful situation. As a result, most of us will retreat from the factors and situations contributing to our hesitation. Rather, we will intellectually hobble to a self-generated micro-reality, in which we can suspend the regular pressures associated with time and other restrictive performance constraints. We might even hesitate in creating this micro-reality since our minds might be locked in a perpetual state of doubt, incapable from doing anything. The opportunity costs associated with hesitancy emanating from our doubts are vast and include forfeited opportunities that could move us beyond the limitations of our doubt and improve our connectedness with our current and future realities.

Another emotion that feeds doubt is *uncertainty*. Uncertainty, in particular, drives our need to create a sub-reality over which we can exercise heightened control and minimize the emotional distresses associated with uncertainty. Doubt requires uncertainty to dominate our emotional landscapes so our decision-making processes cannot reach any conclusions with even a modicum of conviction. This vicious cycle of uncertainty amplifies our doubts and isolates our relationships with rationality and reason within our daily realities. The constant questioning of our *Self*, our actions and our thoughts motivates our need to carve out a micro-reality with restricted boundaries that allow us to manage our uncertainty within a limited, "controllable" environment. Our retreat into our micro-realities to avoid the disease associated with uncertainty in our thinking processes continues to empower our doubt and to disenfranchise us from our conviction. As we become less adept at dealing with uncertainty in our ordinary reality, we will further condition our doubt to direct us to situations, circumstances, or encounters that permit us to control the outcome within a limited emotional context. Eventually, we may move so far away from any type of constructive self-assurance that our micro-realities will overshadow our daily realities to create an artificial sense of certainty without the requisite conviction to move beyond doubt's charade as uncertainty.

A more nuance emotional manifestation of doubt is *insincerity* and its insidious nature to pervade our decision-making processes without allowing us to improve or to empower our attitudes with any sort of conviction and/or self-assurance. Insincerity operates as a defense mechanism since it permits us to engage in an activity without emotionally investing in the activity. That is, insincerity permits us to do something without conviction to any "real" emotions since our doubt preempts any meaningful emotional attachment. We carve out a micro-reality in which we can assign different emotional weights to accommodate our doubts about successfully completing a project, encountering a certain person, or performing a certain task.

The variations assigned to emotional weights within micro-realities outside of ordinary realities pervade all aspects of our *Self*, especially the patina of propriety that creates artificiality within our attitudes to cope with our reservations about expressing our doubt-free *Self*. For example, we may encounter an individual who strikes a nerve with a particular ideology or disposition with which we vehemently disagree. Rather than allowing our attitudes to empower an authentic response, we grin and bear it with an insincere aplomb that eventually becomes our standard mode of communication. Here, our doubt prevents us from speaking our truth and causes us to employ an insincere response to avoid confrontation or other emotional unrest. While our false smiles may have never really created any harm, fake smiles have caused tremendous damage to our attitudes. In these instances, we have allowed feigned pleasantness to reinforce our doubt and to replace our efforts in finding and nurturing our conviction to improve and empower our attitudes. As a result, we can easily become imprisoned by our insincerity to move beyond our comfort zones to achieve and to exercise our confidence and the attitudinal consequences associated with that confidence.

Through reviewing the emotional underpinnings of our doubts, we can all agree that a common foundational component is *fear*. Doubt heightens our fear against failure or, in some cases, success. This fear prevents us from discerning possibilities within our ordinary realities that can arise when we directly confront our fears. Instead, we avoid our fears through carving out our micro-realities that can preempt any encounters with our fears. As an extreme example, some of us may suffer from travel-related fears, such as fears of flying or driving. Our feelings of doubt related to having an uneventful trip in a particular mode of transportation literally drive us to reorder our lives to accommodate our fears. We may never visit a destination that requires us to travel within an airplane. We may restrict our driving radius to a particular, comfort zone that minimizes our fears and anxieties. However we allow our fears to impact our lives, fear permits doubt to have a physical impact on our current realities that we reshape and reconfigure to cope with doubt and its restrictive consequences. More troublesome, fear precludes our interaction with constructive emotions that can help us move beyond the restrictive boundaries of our micro-realities. Specifically, we will not have access to any conviction or self-assurance to combat our fears as the comfort derived from our restrictive boundaries entrap us within our doubt to move beyond our comfort zone and to fully function within the fullness of our ordinary realities.

Within the litany of emotions comprising our doubt, we can pinpoint how doubt keeps us from hope and other constructive emotions through fostering our feelings of despair rather than developing more healthy forms of confidence and self-assurance. Indeed, doubt enlivens our despair till the point we cannot conceptualize any alternative possibilities. Unlike our other micro-realities, the micro-realities created by despair are most problematic. Despair can be considered the ultimate, darkest manifestation of doubt since it completely forecloses any positive expectations from occupying our current realities. In turn, our micro-realities are generally structured to comport with our complete surrender to doubt and our disbelief in future attitudinal empowerment or improvement. Rather than structuring micro-realities to help us cope with our doubts, we create micro-realities that console us and permit us to mourn our inability to perceive other possibilities beyond the current morass. In such circumstances, despair creates static throughout our complete emotional range as everything we think about automatically encompasses the worst-case scenario. We eventually doubt that anything "good" or "positive" can ever happen in our ordinary realities so we give up trying to embrace positive thoughts. As a result, we can appreciate the effort it will take to pierce our doubts with self-assurance. More importantly, we will need to develop a sense of conviction to destroy those micro-realities created by our despair that can potentially pollute every aspect of our current realities.

Regardless of the emotional underpinnings that resonate with our own doubts, we can comprehend how each emotional component prevents us from moving beyond our current realities to achieve empowered and improved attitudes to overcome our doubt. Conviction, unlike doubt, can be acquired through positioning our thoughts and ambitions on confronting our undesirable emotions within our ordinary realities and through avoiding avoidance of situations, circumstances, or encounters that provoke our doubts and its emotional components.

VISUALIZING AND ACTUALIZING A SUPERLATIVE REALITY WITHOUT DOUBT

When we consider what our lives would consist of without doubt, we can only imagine what our confidence and conviction can help us achieve. Rather than being restricted by doubt to overcome obstacles, we would begin to feel empowered in our decision-making capabilities. Doubt can become marginalized as we exercise greater creative capacities within our current realities to generate potential superlative outcomes in our thinking. Visualizing and actualizing superlative, doubt-free possibilities minimizes doubt's emotional components from manifesting in less than optimal micro-realities. Unfortunately, we have already established pre-existing emotional structures within our decision-making processes that have been greatly influenced by doubt and are susceptible to doubt's emotional triggers. We cannot underestimate the power of certain stressors from unleashing our doubts, especially even the avoidance of encountering and overcoming our doubts in various aspects of our current realities.[16] To help us better deal with these stresses, we should focus our attention and effort on achieving superlative emotional states with persistent conviction and healthy confidence to improve our chances at overcoming distractive doubts.

To derive some strength in our quest to achieve a superlative sense of conviction and its emotional benefits within our ordinary realities, we must be mindful of the commonality of our quest. Wherever we look within the *Grand Historical narrative* (or even our own *personal narrative*), we can discern that each individual we encounter or each situation we create shares a common finitude. This finitude is a mandatory part of existence since everything will eventually cease, even the prominence of our doubt and its emotional consequences in our decision-making process.[17] So, when doubt prevents us from visualizing and actualizing an existence without any doubts, we must conceptualize a superlative ordinary reality, not a micro-reality, without the emotional restrictions of doubt. Doubt, like the circumstances, situations and individuals, will have particular finitude that we all have experienced and will continue to experience throughout our *personal narratives*.

16. See, e.g., Kuhar, *Addicted Brain*, 118, reviewing stress factors in addiction relapses post-recovery and treatment scenarios.

17. See, e.g., Stolorow, "Individuality in Context," 63.

The ultimate question for us is what will we do to ensure that we have the conviction and confidence to extract all forms of unhealthy doubt from our decision-making processes. For certain, we neither can feed our insecurities nor avoid our doubts and their emotional components within our ordinary realities. Rather, we need to visualize a superlative sense of personal and professional reality to actualize the healthy confidence needed to attain that reality.

Among the many ways to transform doubt into conviction, we just need to make the preliminary decision with conviction and how the decision fulfills our expectations and invites us to make additional decisions with modified forms of conviction. Provided that we keep searching and trying to achieve an emotional existence without the burdens, especially debilitating emotions, associated with doubt, we will eventually attain dominion over our insecurities and achieve freedom from our doubts. To actualize the foregoing, we must never forget we have intellectual, spiritual and psychic power to doubt the power of doubt and make decisions that only doubt the lack of our conviction to move beyond our emotional limitations and to bring about superlative, healthy confidence and self-assurance.

7
Revalue "Self Worth" with "Humane Capital"

THIS CHAPTER IS INTENDED to set forth a valuation methodology for our *Self* and our interaction with *all* humanity. Transactional paradigms pervade our daily existence and help us define, prioritize, and value our personal and professional relationships. Within this *quid pro quo* framework, we develop and complete a sense of our *Self* that we use to project the *Self* into our daily realities and relationships. The value derived from others and other external influences may or may not be helpful for us to appreciate our own self-worth and agency within this valuation process. It is as if we severely discount the lessons and experiences contained within our *personal narratives* and we elevate our quest for place and purpose within the *Grand Historical Narrative* as the *sine qua non* of our existence. Besides the strategic Latin terms, these sentiments are most complex and require us to reshape our perspective about every aspect of our lives. Daunting in scope and empowering in exercise, we must peel back the artificial patchwork of externalities that help us contain our *Self* and prevent us from empowering the *Self*. So, take a deep breath, formulate a hopeful intention and open your mind and heart to new ways to value our value!

The difference between "our" *Self* and "the" *Self* becomes the initial analysis in auditing our current self-worth methodologies. When we think about "our" *Self*, we generally refer to a *Self* that we create and embrace to express and to interact with our emotions independent of external influences and/or judgments. On the other hand, we all utilize term "the" *Self* to refer to how we project, and desire to project, our "*Self*" to others in everyday circumstances, situations, relationships, and encounters. Some of us, for example, may be extremely shy and insecure and our "*Self*" deeply reflects these emotional conditions. However, we do not permit "the" *Self* to reveal those emotions in our daily routines for any number of personal and/or professional reasons. Abstractly speaking, "our" *Self* can be considered an organic expression of our interior thoughts and emotions that have not been refined or packaged for public consumption, while "the" *Self* can be conceptualized as a manufactured expression of those thoughts and emotions that can be promoted and projected within public discourse throughout our ordinary realities. The differential between "our" *Self* and "the" *Self* becomes the foundation of our self-valuation analysis as we begin to understand how and why we ascribe varying valuation methodologies to each particular expression of the *Self*. For example, many of us ascribe a fragile valuation to "our" *Self* since we believe exposing "our" *Self* for public consumption will devalue that *Self*. With "the" *Self*, we assign a more robust valuation methodology that is not vulnerable to external fluctuations since "the" *Self* operates within full view of every aspect of ordinary realities. Unless we can strongly assign common values to every aspect of the *Self*, both the "our" and "the" versions, we will never fully appreciate our "real" self-worth independent of outside circumstances, conditions or encounters.

This chapter's objective will help us identify why we fragment our self-worth, how this fragmentation prevents us from reaching our "real" valuation of our self-worth and what we can accomplish with a unified self-worth methodology. Overall, this chapter will enable us to ascertain key emotional variables that we can employ with our valuation methodologies to appreciate and to *celebrate* our "real" self-worth!

To further unpack this transactional paradigm, we should apply an intellectual property legal construct from the entertainment world known as *life rights*. Every time we watch a movie, see a television show, or read a book based on a biography of an individual's life story, the individual received a monetary payment from the producers for the *life rights* associated with that person's life events depicted in the entertainment project. Depending on the historical significance and celebrity-status of the individual, producers and creative management teams can spend any where from a few thousand to a few million dollars to acquire an individual's life rights. Sometimes, the acquisition is limited to a small portion of the individual's life. In other instances, the entire lifespan will be acquired. There are many economic and artistic variables related to life rights transactions. Regardless of the legal technicalities, *life rights*-related transactions can provide us with a constructive valuation methodology to understand how expressions of *our Self* in our *personal narratives* might become valued for public consumption through *the Self* we could place within the *Grand Historical Narrative*.

Disbeliefs aside, we all look for some external valuation mechanism or, at least, an external confirmation for what we consider our self-worth. A helpful framework to ponder the effectiveness of our valuation methodologies is our own life rights transactional model in which we determine how much we would "pay" to acquire various portions of our *personal narratives*. However, our transactional life rights model will not have the benefit of a simple unit of currency, like money. Instead, we will need to develop a complex currency that communicates value through intangible units, like emotional well-being, that enable us to promote "our" *Self* and to engage others with "the" *Self*. For purposes of this chapter's objective, we will consider how our *life rights* increase or decrease in value to "our" *Self* and "the" *Self* with regards to particular emotions. Specifically, we will focus on the emotion of *hope* as the ultimate factor to determine how much *hope* "our" *Self* can generate in transitioning between different episodes in our *personal narratives*, as well as how much *hope* "the" *Self* can instill in circumstances, situations, and encounters associated with interactions between our *personal narratives* and the *Grand Historical Narrative*.

Unlike other emotions, *hope* helps us recognize our intrinsic value to empower and to improve our current realities and seek beyond our current limitations as our hopefulness enables us to enhance our self-worth through our quest for the superlative. To prove why *hope* should be the definitive unit of currency in our self-valuation exercise, we can identify the antithetical emotion that drives down our self-worth to zero—*despair*! Without *hope*, we will have no desire to move beyond our current states of realities to appreciate and to enhance the value of "our" *Self*. Rather, *despair* operates to deceive us from our "true" self-worth since it causes us to devalue "our" *Self* and to minimize the accomplishments of "the" *Self*. When we suffer from the full effects of *despair*, we bankrupt our creative capacities to draw from the wealth of our "self-worth" to move beyond our current malaise and obsession with worse case scenarios. We have all experienced some manifestation of despair at some point in our *personal narratives*.

Our familiarity with that emotion clearly demonstrates its power to obliterate any sense of value in either "our" *Self* or "the" *Self* regarding the value of what we have achieved and the value of what we can potentially achieve in the future. In some of our darkest encounters with that emotion, despair can cause us to forget so many aspects of "our" *Self* that we consciously depress any valuation of self-worth to zero! Hence, without the beneficial aspects of *hope*, we would be victims to various episodes of *despair* throughout our *personal narratives* and eventually surrender our fortune of self-worth to absolute nothingness. This extreme conceptualization helps us appreciate the currency of *hope* in valuing our life rights for personal acquisition and, in some ways, public exhibition.

To begin a meaningful valuation process for our self-worth, we will need to think about new ways to value the experiences within our *personal narratives*. This process will require us to purge our personal prejudices and self-serving motivations to inflate every experience within the context of the *Grand Historical Narrative*, rather than our *personal narratives*. For example, we may artificially inflate our valuations as we allow our original motivations to justify unsupportable valuation methods[1] and lead us into a self-deluded sense of self-worth. On the other hand, we could also permit our disappointments to grossly underestimate our valuation as despair deprives us from extracting any value from the bleaker moments of *personal narratives* and their potential value-added contributions to our interactions with the *Grand Historical Narrative*. Thus, we will need to develop a dynamic valuation methodology that will help us find an adequate, informative self-worth whose valuation components include our internal emotions and their interconnectivity with the greater collective beyond "the" *Self*.

Through understanding current perceptions of our self-worth and future possible valuations beyond their current limitations, we can find a superlative valuation model to help us maximize our individual valuation, as contained within our *personal narratives*. More importantly, we will optimize our potential value to the overall collective social landscape, as pertaining to the *Grand Historical Narrative* and our extraordinary potential roles contained therein.

1. Bucholtz and Hall, "Theorizing Identity in Language," 475, noting how identity research scholarship can be tainted by descriptive language meant to affirm the quest/prejudice of the researchers more than objectively communicate research findings.

THE REVALUATION OF OUR CURRENT PERCEPTIONS AND IDEAS

Evidently, we have questions about our current self-worth and its impact on our attitudes. Otherwise, why would we have read till to this point in the book? While self-worth and the value of "the" *Self* and its function within greater society is important for our personal awareness, they usually have been relegated to the background of our general perceptions of our current realities. Unfortunately, their present *de minimis* status does not provide us with the necessary tools to empower and to improve our attitudes for many reasons. Our self-worth and the value we derived from functioning within / contributing to society, even if it is limited to our salary or professional titles, greatly influence how we perceive everything taking place in our current realities. The greater our sense of self-worth and value to our society, the more likely our perceptions will reflect a greater degree of optimism. The lesser our sense of self-worth and value to our society, the more likely our perceptions will reflect a degree of pessimism. This suggests that self-worth and social value are critical for perceiving opportunities in our current realities that can increase these variables and provide positive attitudinal changes. To understand how we can best work within our current realities to maximize our sense of self-worth and societal value, we must confront the individual variables, especially emotions and circumstances, comprising our individual valuation processes.

As a preliminary matter, we must dispel esoteric, spiritual, or psychic thinking from our basic valuation methodologies. Indeed, those factors can help empower and improve our attitudinal formation but not from the self-worth/societal value perspective. Rather, valuation methodologies should be grounded by our own tangible realities without potential influence from imaginary forces, convoluted fears, or needless perplexities.[2] Sometimes, the obvious factors impinging on our self-worth and societal value become the most compelling elements in our valuation methodologies. We make the valuation unnecessarily difficult when we seek special meaning outside the ordinary flow of our consciousness for purposes of valuing "our" *Self* in relation to "the" *Self* and for others. For

2. See, e.g., Bakan et al., *Maimonides' Cure of Souls*, 62, discussing Maimonides' approach to scriptures as being comprised by philosophers and requiring interpretation within a philosophical context without need for the reader's personal prejudice and imaginary exploration of secret meaning beyond the plain meaning of the text.

example, some of us may be prone to receiving "signs" or interpreting Jungian synchronicities within a hyper-spiritual context. While we all love to feel some extraordinary sense of specialness, we usually derive little benefit from such magical thinking in light of our need for rational solutions to ordinary problems. Analyzing the situation from an extraordinary perspective, we cloud our ordinary perspective with superfluous distraction and speculative conjecture. Hence, we should steal a moment from this chapter and reflect on how we might have searched for extraordinary meaning from ordinary life events and how that search may have impaired our current valuation methodologies to the point of reading this book. Certainly, we can all identify *at least* one occurrence where the surrender of our rational thinking processes to our magical thinking processes caused some minor calamities within our *personal narratives*. Sometimes, the most magical moments are those that remain within our imaginations and are preserved from the ravages of reality and other non-magical consequences.

Another aspect of our valuation methodologies that warrants special caution is the relationship between "our" *Self* and "the" *Self* that prevents us from an objective evaluation of our self-worth and societal value. As set forth above, "our" *Self* is basically comprised of internal emotions and feelings independent of external influences, while "the" *Self* operates as an emotion-manifesting avatar with the outside world. Rather than evaluating their respective emotional variables for calculating self-worth and societal value, we must prevent "our" *Self* from calculating its self-worth and societal value from "the" *Self* and *vice versa*. Otherwise, the psychological dimensions of closeness between "our" *Self* and "the" *Self* will challenge any valuation methodology because those two categories will create both positive and negative friction between them and further complicate our development of an effective valuation methodology.[3] Juxtaposing "our" *Self* and "the" *Self* together for valuation purposes, we will need to be mindful of emotional attachments associated with each *Self* that may cause us to miscalculate our self-worth and societal value as we limit our methodologies to our manufactured myopia.

Overcoming this myopia, we will be able to derive some inspiration from this book's linguistic temperament to inspire more effective communication between our thinking process, emotional awareness, and

3. See, e.g., Adams, *Fragmented Intimacy*, 87, noting the psychological closeness dimensions in an addictive substance/process paradigms and emotional extremes related thereto.

creative capacity. While some of us may be questioning the efficacy of this chapter's objective and verbiage to bring about an increase in our self-worth and societal value, we must remember that we ultimately hold the power to effectuate positive valuation enhancements. Each of us has a unique contribution to make to the *Grand Historical Narrative* regardless of the current valuations associated with our *personal narratives*. Some clinicians have opined that our individuality can only be developed by our "psychological surplus," that is, our unique patterns of giving to other people form the basis of our individuality with its yielding and/or assertive identity attributes.[4] That said, most of us seek opportunities, even if only on an intermittent basis, to express our individuality outside conventional social expressions of "our" *Self* to benefit "the" *Self* and its interaction with others. For example, some researchers claim that children will identify with the opposite sex parent, i.e., son relating to his mother or daughter relating to her father, to accelerate independent character development through avoiding conventional social roles for the family dynamic.[5] Through challenging conventional norms within the intimate family dynamics, we may have acquired unique expressions for "the" *Self* that help facilitate interaction with others. These expressions may help facilitate productive interactions with our professional relationships, may make us more, or less, emotionally vulnerable in our personal relationship or may contribute to our unconventional decision-making processes.

Whatever the manifestation, we must understand that any unique expression of "our" *Self* by "the" *Self* significantly impacts our self-worth. We should value our uniqueness as one of most precious attributes. After all, that uniqueness makes us irreplaceable in so many of our current relational settings. It also enables us to approach future possibilities beyond our current realities with a relative superlativeness that ensures we can maximize our self-value through our self-assurance in any activity that permits us to exercise our uniqueness. As some of us may have already pondered, we cannot glorify our unique individuality to the point where it becomes unhealthy and precludes opportunity for future growth and personal awareness. We may all feel a special sense of "our" *Self* and how others receive "the" *Self* in our professional and personal circumstances. Audience reaction does provide an important measurement mechanism

4. See, e.g., Rosenfels, *Homosexuality*, 12.
5. Ibid., 24.

regarding our self-value and human value, but it forecloses upon our fundamental need to maximize our "humane" value. That is, we cannot just rely on measurements of self-worth that requires us to present "the" *Self*, independent of "our" *Self*, for public consumption. In that context, we are unduly narrowing the transactional dynamic between "our" *Self*, "the" *Self* and others for the strict purpose of finding value in exercising our creative capacity to exploit this incestuous transactional dynamic. Rather than allowing "our" *Self* to develop "the" *Self* independent of *anticipated* audience reaction, we somehow elevate our expectations about the general acceptance of others to dictate our own self-acceptance. Pause here for a second and reflect on the multiple meanings of that state: *our expectations about the general acceptance of others dictate our own self-acceptance process*! Though maybe not profound at first glance, when we intensely reflect on the ways we allow others to determine our self-worth and to affect our self-assuredness, we can perceive a direct correlation between those expectations and our underestimated self-worth valuations.

In order to achieve this chapter's objective with minimal exertion on our intellect (since we want to preserve our intellectual energies to empower and to improve our attitudes), we must translate the creative capacity of our unique individuality within the greater context of society. Unlike previous interactions between our *personal narratives* and the *Grand Historical Narrative*, this particular exercise requires a highly-focused concentration on maximizing our self-worth through optimizing our potential contributions to humanity. This is especially true where such contributions cannot be perceived within the *Grand Historical Narrative* during immediate portions of our current realities throughout our *personal narratives*. For example, we may pursue an exercise, like the empowerment and improvement of our attitudes that appears to satisfy only self-oriented objectives. However, the results of that exercise will probably have far-reaching consequences as the modifications in our attitudes expand outward and affect our personal and professional relationships beyond our own immediate goal.

Similarly, we cannot exclusively exercise our creative capacities for our own individual self-betterment without thought and acknowledgement about the consequences beyond our present realities and our self-contained perceptions. Instead, we must understand that our failure to consider the value of "humane" capital in maximizing our human capital will prevent us from fulfilling our creative mandate to maximize the quality of *all* life as we seek innovative ways to optimize our own self-worth.

In the end, we cannot truly formulate an effective valuation methodology without appreciating the interdependent nature of the individual and society.

Most of us can attribute an impaired estimation about our self-worth, self-confidence, and/or self-assuredness related to our need to empower and to improve our attitudes. Attitudinal formation, after all, requires a psychological awareness of self-worth to determine the appropriateness of our desires and longings within the context of adding to our self-confidence and self-assuredness for optimization purposes. Otherwise, we will experience an inflated sense of self-worth as we turn our valuation methodologies inward on "our" *Self* for "the" *Self* as we become more susceptible to compulsive and obsessive mechanisms that cause us to offset underestimations of our self-worth with excessive gratifications of our longings and desires.[6] All of us, at some moment within our *personal narratives*, have experienced some form of this phenomenon. A universal example could be professional stress and/or dissatisfaction, ranging from a pernicious boss to unfair job loss, that has sent us into a compulsive spiral of overeating, overreacting, over-worrying, or similar obsessive behavior as a coping mechanism to offset the decrease in our perceived self-valuation caused by the professional incident.

Unfortunately, we have all encountered some type of professional (or even personal) disappointment that stunted our enthusiasm and inspiration to find new value for our self-worth or to pursue new opportunities to maximize our self-assurance. This scenario provides an excellent example to the pitfalls associated with a singular variable approach to maximizing our self-worth, i.e., we are only concerned about *our* professional disappointment. Rather, our valuation model should be conceptualized as a multivariate problem that requires us to optimize *at least* two variables. Variable One, "the" *Self*, requires us to formulate a solution to ensure we can project an optimal self-worth in our interaction with others within and beyond our current realities. Variable Two, "humanity," requires us to recognize the interdependence between the individual and its place within *its* society to optimize its self-worth valuation. Without Variable Two, we become even more susceptible to suboptimal valuations through gratifying obsessive and compulsive urges as we detach ourselves from our proper social contexts. Furthermore, we forget that an

6. See, e.g., Rosenfels, *Homosexuality*, 105, advising against applying our creative capacities within an emotional marketplace of buying and selling that pejoratively impacts our judgments and inspirations.

optimal valuation requires an appropriate measuring plane upon which to perceive and to express its tangible value.

Without optimizing the "humane" capital within our social settings, we will be unable to express our optimized valuations without a proper societal context. Removing this notion from the abstract, we can revisit our professional disappointment scenario with this multivariate solution strategy. In a singular variable context, the decrease in our self-valuation occurs due to our self-absorption about being disenfranchised from extracting joy and contentment from our livelihood that comprises the majority of our existence in our realities. However, a multivariate approach to our professional satisfaction will help us understand the implications of our professional dissatisfaction on a larger scale. The fact that we are suffering in a profession that does not maximize our self-worth or enhance our self-confidence could have far-broader implications. As with George Bernard Shaw and his career transaction described in chapter 5, we may be willingly entrapping ourselves to professional situations that are depriving us from accessing our full creative capacities and depriving the world from enjoying our potential creative contributions. While few of us may actually possess the hidden literary talent of Shaw, we all have special unique talents, just as unique and variable as our self-worth and our valuation methodologies, which should receive adequate recognition in maximizing our self-worth and self-confidence. Without contemplating our potential contributions to the greater good of others, i.e., society, humanity et al., our self-worth valuation models will contain an inherent defect and will continue to produce less than optimal valuations. As a result, we need to consider how we pursue self-worth valuation strategies that not only contemplate factors beyond our current realities, but *beyond the implications of our own selves.*

BENEFITS OF AN EXPANSIVE "SELF" IN SELF-WORTH

The arduous task of maximizing our self-worth can be assuaged through an expansion of the "self" in self-worth. We can enhance our understanding of our individual valuation methodologies through recognizing that "the" *Self* is not just a construct of "our" *Self*, but also an amalgam of our personal, professional, spiritual, and social interactions with others. Recognizing the benefits from contextualizing the self in self-worth within a larger group, we can begin to extract benefits from this inter-connectivity. First, we have an effective oversight mechanism to compare our valuation activities related to our *personal narratives* within a larger framework to improve our relationship with the *Grand Historical Narrative* and its lessons for our current self-worth valuation strategies and measurement techniques. As with other communal treatment modalities, our collective stumbling toward an optimal self-worth will help us identify circumstances, situations, and conditions that we alone cannot perceive or factor into our self-worth maximizing strategies.[7] Hence, the opportunity to engage with others will help move us away from the quantitative myopia affiliated with "our" *Self* and its impact on "the" *Self* as we expand our definitional "self" in self-worth.

Second, we must understand how an expanded "self" in the development of our self-worth valuation methodologies empowers our valuation strategies with a collaborative perspective. For those of us with prolonged periods of depressed self-worth and self-confidence valuations within our *personal narratives*, the potential contributions from a collaborative perspective are critical. We may have conditioned our minds, thoughts, and decision-making processes to operate with a suboptimal self-worth for an extended period of time. Such *lumpen* optimality distorts our creative capacities as it forces us to accept less than favorable situations and circumstances, thereby creating an artificial optimality in our quest to maximize our self-worth and self-assurance.[8] Pursuing these false solutions based on unreliable emotional data, we will find ourselves perpetually questioning and searching for an optimal sense of self-worth in all our personal and professional endeavors. However, the presence of an expanded "self" in self-worth can safeguard against the corruption of our emotional data as we formulate a robust valuation model to appreciate our worth within a greater societal context.

Third, we may have incorporated unnecessary impediments to our current valuation models that prevent us from successfully implementing their optimization functions with our current self-absorbed, narrow construct of self-worth, self-confidence or self-assuredness. Without the

---

7. See, e.g., Freimuth, *Hidden Addictions*, 139, noting how group membership facilitates recovery among substance-based addictions because it facilitates identifying unrecognized addictions and improves treatment screening tools.

8. See, e.g., Kuhar, *Addicted Brain*, 95, commenting about the impact of drug use on brain chemistry and how addictions force us to chase artificial constructs of wellness.

presence of other people, especially a greater social context, we become vulnerable to the lack of reciprocity in our valuation methodologies through not identifying pain and suffering associated with our low self-worth due to asymmetries in our emotional perceptions, expressions, and receptions. Basically, most of us formulate a sense of self-worth that we eventually fall in love with in some capacity as the pursuit and attainment of that particularized self-worth erroneously comes to represent an optimal valuation reality. The asymmetry originates and persists in this valuation strategy from the fact that we ignore whether or not that sense of self-worth can actually produce and *sustain* the emotions we believe it can. We also do not consider the broader implications of the romanticized self-worth beyond the *Self* in terms of a societal context and that context's impact on our optimal valuation reality. It sort of resembles the situations where we might have fallen in love with someone who does not love us in return, or even worse, generates a destructive emotional attachment.[9]

Hopefully, this chapter will help illuminate those areas in our self-worth valuation techniques that can benefit from the presence of an expanded perspective beyond the *Self* to help identify similar asymmetries between our romanticized optimal valuation and our real optimal valuation. As we contextualize this problem between our *personal narratives* and the *Grand Historical Narrative*, we can better integrate the reactions and comments from others who, in some ways, can better see the asymmetries in our thinking processes since they will be experiencing our implemented valuation methods as reflected in our attitudes and other interactions with them. After all, we have yet to figure out a way to look at or behind our eyes without a mirror or other third-party apparatus. So, why should we close our eyes and optimize our self-worth without similar reflective benefit from those who can reflect back at us the nuances within our optimization strategies.

Most importantly, we must craft an optimization strategy for valuing our self-worth that adequately reflects our valuation's dynamic, ever-evolving nature. To ensure we place proper emphasis on this dynamic nature, we embrace the multivariate nature of the "self" in self-worth and allow ourselves to appreciate the comings and goings involved with our societal interactions. We can be certain that should we assume that there exist any constant variables in our valuation methodologies, we

9. Adams, *Fragmented Intimacy*, 96, discussing the emotional ramifications of unreciprocated compassion.

are actually pursuing suboptimal valuation strategies. Here, the transactional paradigm between "our" *Self*, "the" *Self* and others in the pursuit of a maximized valuation strategy warrants perpetual modifications to those transactional components, as well as those components interaction within a societal context. The multifarious correlations between psychology and religions exemplifies how two distinct disciplines can be intertwined in a co-evolutionary process of exploration and realization for an individual and the societal reality in which that individual dwells.[10]

For the purpose of this chapter's objective, we consider that every variable comprising our valuation methodologies requires us to be diligent to recognize their evolutionary changes as the interplay between "our" *Self*, "the" *Self* and others change over time through various societal interaction. In this way, we can improve our ability to reckon with our doubts about how former and current efforts to increase our self-worth can create sustainable, long-term self-confidence and self-assuredness in our futures.

Despite the numerous benefits of the expanded "self" in self-worth as set forth above, some of us may have difficulty moving beyond the limits of our former and current valuation methodologies. Regardless of whatever else we learn from this chapter, we must always remember that the maximization of our self-worth requires us to adopt an optimistic approach to our creative capacities. Without acknowledging and appreciating love for our inherent creative capacities, we will have tremendous difficulty in formulating an effective self-worth optimization strategy. When we ignore our creative capacities and their significance in our overall self-worth valuation exercises, we create cognitive dissonance between "our" *Self* and "the" *Self* as we begin to offset our own valuation inadequacies from others who lack similar creative capacities. Some clinicians have examined this phenomenon within the context of sadist-masochistic behavior engagements where sadistic and masochistic tendencies pair individuals who lack creative potential and prevent the removal of psychological barriers within a socialization context.[11] Rather than utilizing love and power dynamics within a constructive context, sadomasochism reinforces the rejection of creative capacities

---

10. Havens and Bakan, *Psychology and Religion*, 123, citing R. D. Liang and his research regarding the interplay between mental illness and religion.

11. Rosenfels, *Homosexuality*, 122, discussing role of sadomasochistic tendencies in individuals lacking creative growth potential.

in recognizing any constructive potential of "the" *Self* due to "our" *Self*'s sense of low self-worth.

Avoiding a *Fifty Shades of Grey* reference, we should understand how relational power dynamics and control issues separate us from experiencing our "full" creative potential. We are all innately attuned to create. Everyday when we wake up, we create another episode within our *personal narrative*. We also create ways to interact with the *Grand Historical Narrative* through various moments throughout our day. Yet, somehow we surrender our creative capacities to numerous derivative sadomasochistic paradigms in our personal and professional realities, especially where we experience low self-worth and self-confidence in "our" *Self* and its expression by "the" *Self*. Most of us who experience distorted self-worth valuations cling to emotional situations that we erroneously believe could improve our self-worth and confidence.

These situations reflect our *aspirations* to access our creative capacities, rather than our *applications* to employ our creative capacities to constructively create real improvement to our self-worth and self-confidence. As in the case of *Fifty Shades of Grey*, we all substitute pain, power, and control to remind us about our inferior ability to experience the abundance of our own creative abilities in sustainable, emotionally nourishing situations as we struggle for the instant gratification of an artificial, perverse pleasure. Whether or not we share Christian Grey's physical proclivities, we all employ some permutation of them in our daily emotional discourse when we derive some sort of pleasure from being disenfranchised from our constructive creative abilities.

Within these notions of control and power, we can finally understand and appreciate why maximizing self-worth requires the differentiation between "our" *Self* and "the" *Self* and our creative capacities being exercised therein. First, we equate our low self-worth and self-confidence to a form of a suffering since either "our" *Self* feels disenfranchised from the positive reinforcement and nourishment from our personal and professional encounters. Our internal suffering conditions us to relate to suffering with a whole new purpose, especially as we seek ways to compensate for our feelings related to low self-worth and confidence. Second, we transmit various manifestations of the internal sufferings of "our" *Self* to our circumstances, conditions and encounters with "the" *Self* in numerous relational settings. Basically, "the" *Self* allows "our" *Self* to confirm and to manifest an emotional reality related to our internal suffering. We can all recall our a negative attitude or self-perception about ourselves infiltrated, as well as precipitated, a personal or professional confrontation that was deliberately established to confirm our lack of self-assuredness in our decision-making. These scenarios include our perceived inability to perform our work tasks satisfactorily or to satisfy our partners' relational needs. We have all been subject to these types of situations that have significantly influenced the estimation of our self-worth in a negative direction.

So, for purposes of this chapter's objective, we must recognize the interplay between the internal suffering in "our" *Self* and the expressed suffering in "the" *Self* to determine how and why we utilize that suffer in calculating our self-worth, especially with interactions beyond "the" *Self* with others. When we feel down and our self-worth trending toward zero, we misappropriate our suffering associated with those *de minimis* valuations to create a sort of artificially inflated sense of self-worth. We accomplish this task through leveraging our most potent emotional as-set—suffering. In times when we feel the lowest sense of "our" *Self* and the most ineffectual sense of "the" *Self*, we often busy ourselves with other people's problems. Whether our fellow coworkers, friends, family members or acquaintances, we find ways to distract "our" *Self* from feeling pain associated with depressed feelings of self-worth and to reorient "the" *Self* from feeling ineffectual in its interactions with others through escaping into others' sufferings. This escape comes in various forms and names, ranging from performing acts of charity, assuming unrealistic workloads, listening to others' problems, resolving others' dilemmas, or engaging in similar communal suffering endeavors. All of these activities share some common form of emotional pain and suffering that allows us to utilize the suffering of "our" *Self*, experienced by "the" *Self*, for the alleged benefit of others. Before we continue with this reasoning, please take a moment (only if some of us can currently possess the emotional fortitude) to re-visit an episode in our *personal narratives* where we were experiencing a profound emotional suffering related to an underestimated sense of self-worth and how we became entangled into someone else's suffering to avoid our own. Almost certain, we all have at least *one* (if not many) such moments throughout our *personal narratives*.

Our misappropriated creative capacity motivates us to get involved with other peoples' problems as we seek ways to express that capacity and to connect with others while suffering through our bouts of low self-worth.[12] Hence, we apply the suffering of "our" *Self* and "the" *Self* to the pursuit of an *imaginary heroism* in which we will assume the suffering of others to help us transcend our own unhappiness, to allow "our" *Self* and "the" *Self* to experience compassion for another and to inflate our sense of self-worth with an imported, artificial emotional accomplishment. In essence, if "our" *Self* cannot muster the creative capacity to save "the" *Self* from its ineffective and marginalized feelings of insignificance, we can find some value enhancement for our self-worth and self-confidence through allegedly helping others with their suffering. Obviously, the whole exercise comports with notions of a zero sum arrangement since swapping out our own suffering with a foreign suffering cannot possibly maximize any valuations, never mind our own feelings of self-worth or self-assuredness. Rather, we continue to marginalize "our" *Self* through isolating the core of our psychological perceptions to "the" *Self*'s ability to exercise its creative capacity in a diminished state without any real basis to determine how successful our involvement with others will improve our own sufferings (besides postponing our inevitable confrontation with them).

Moreover, an effective optimization approach to our self-worth requires us to know the emotional limits of "our" *Self* and the creative limits of "the" *Self*. Unfortunately, our desires to escape within other peoples' problems usually prevent us from fully knowing and appreciating those limitations as we begin to increase variables in our optimization methodologies through adding outside suffering into the overall equation. For example, our effectiveness in dealing with other peoples' problems becomes an important variable in our valuation efforts. However, being dependent on others' reactions for our sense of self-worth, we further weaken our optimization methodologies for our self-worth and self-assuredness. This problem becomes amplified where we have unrealistic expectations about someone else's gratitude for our assistance that causes us to have unfulfilled, broken expectations with additional dampening effects on our self-worth. As a result, we must try to avoid escaping into others' suffering to avoid our own suffering so as we will truly know and appreciate our self-worth and find constructive ways to express and to enhance it over the course of our *personal narratives*.

12. See, e.g., ibid., 86, discussing how our creativity drives us to bring truth and right into our relationships and societal institutions.

OPTIMIZED SELF-WORTH—A DYNAMIC SUPERLATIVE

While we have set forth some stimulating and difficult concepts throughout this chapter, we must now add some convergence to this convolution to ensure we can effectively maximize our self-worth in different circumstances throughout different moments in time throughout our *personal narratives*. We should understand that our current realities operate as the preliminary stage in the development and optimization of our self-worth. After all, our current realities teach us about aspects of "our" *Self* and "the" *Self* that describe why our self-worth requires accurate valuation and enhancement.

As we conceive of our self-worth beyond the limitations of our current realities, we begin to identify vulnerabilities in our valuation methodologies that require us to revisit and to revalue our self-worth and self-confidence with that clarity and that objective. Thereafter, we can complete the optimization process of our self-worth through integrating our self-awareness about its vulnerabilities with our understanding about its dynamic, ever-changing nature to safeguard against unnecessary depressions in its valuation. To accomplish this dynamic superlative, we will borrow a Buddhist construct known as the three mental poisons—desire, hatred, and delusion[13]—to demonstrate how best to create a self-worth optimization methodology. These three mental poisons reflect a sort of flowing stream in our emotional process that will help keep us mindful of our own ever-changing, ever-evolving emotions and their influence on our dynamic self-worth valuations. As our desires, our hatreds and our delusions change over time, we will become more attune to the factors that weigh upon, rather than elevate our sense of self-worth.

A major negative weight upon our self-worth valuation is our desire, especially desires based on the unattainable or grounded in envy. When we taint our self-worth valuation with "the" *Self* and its desire to possess unattainable fantasies or to envy others' possessions or successes, we allow an evil poison to enter "our" *Self* that pollutes all our desires and prevents us from healthy, creative pursuits.[14] Clearly, we will not continually envy someone's possession or success until we attain a suitable substitute. Rather, we will condition ourselves to accept envy as a normal component of our desires and to permit ourselves to limit our self-worth

---

13. Rinpoche, *Three Levels of Spiritual Perception*, 280.
14. See, e.g., Capps, *Jesus: A Psychological Biography*, 229.

valuations based on the fulfillment of our envious desires. Some of us may be already trapped within this vicious cycle, especially urban professionals, who base their self-worth on acquiring and maintaining the material possessions/successes of their wealthy neighbors and/or coworkers. What makes desire such a vicious poison in Buddhist tradition is its overall impairment on our thinking process since it elevates our own finitude above others and distracts us from perceiving our common plight.[15]

More importantly, desire that is motivated by envy over tangible expressions of material worth preempts superlative decision-making processes that will reveal far superior pursuits. A great example of this conundrum can be found in the Bible when King Solomon requested wisdom, "a perceptive heart," rather than wealth or other material possessions.[16] King Solomon's wisdom represented an innate expression of "our" *Self* with express benefit to "our" *Self* with tremendous implications for "the" *Self* and its interactions with others. Rather than requesting instantaneous power, privilege, and wealth that would have exposed Solomon to scrutiny and to envy of others, Solomon requested a perceptive heart to determine good and evil—far-reaching and profound beyond its *prima facie* categorizations. As a result, we can further appreciate the pitfalls associated with acting upon and fulfilling our desires when they pursue material ambitions.

Despite its ability to evolve and to grow with us throughout our *personal narratives*, our self-worth will become subject to various detrimental impairments as we seek external satisfactions to increase our self-worth valuations. Desires change over the course of lifetimes, just as King Solomon's desires changed as he desired foreign wives that caused him to worship foreign gods with dire results for himself and the Israelites. Luckily, most of us will be learning from our Buddhist brethren about the poisonous effects of desire and why we must employ other motivating factors to increase our self-worth valuations and to safeguard ourselves from destructive capriciousness.

When we consider the largest emotional factor preventing us from experiencing the maximum valuation of our self-worth, we would most likely identify that as some form of delusion—the most potent of the three

15. See, e.g., Stolorow, "Individuality in Context," 60, discussing Heidegger's theory on how finitude individualizes us and strengthens the commonality among all peoples.

16. See Twerski, *Wisdom Each Day*, 2, citing 1 Kgs 3:9 and elaborating on the personal growth implications related to King Solomon's decision.

mental poisons in Buddhism. We have all deluded ourselves in some capacity at some moment, or moments, in our *personal narratives* to accept a delusion as a reality. We may have formed an attachment with a person, a situation or a circumstance that we deluded ourselves into believing would bring us infinite joy and satisfaction. Instead, when we eventually realized the consequences of our deluded thinking processes, we probably experienced a negative impact on our self-worth valuations. We should recall those episodes from our *personal narrative* and consider that our delusions were not just a singular, isolated phenomena, but a result of disorganized decision-making processes that made us incapable to perceive reality outside our delusions. Neuroscientists have considered that the brain requires an extensive conditioning process that must be reorganized to overcome similar types of mental deterioration in mentally ill patients.[17] Hopefully, our delusions were not as clinically severe. For purposes of this chapter's objective, we are contemplating *only* those types of delusions that are not attributable to any underlying psycho-pharmacological treatable condition (which is outside the purview of our analysis).

As we generate and control these delusions, we become acquainted with our disdain for various aspects of our realities that we want to unrealistically change through the power of our mental perceptions. Within the Buddhist context, we can extract the basis for a delusion's classification as a mental poison and can benefit from that context's contribution to optimizing our self-worth valuation methodologies. For example, delusions generally allow us to interject certain aspects of the *Grand Historical Narrative* within our *personal narratives* through aiding and abetting our *modus operandi* to escape our current realities. Historically, we can appreciate that the psychotic nature of delusions did not exist until the nineteenth century, but delusions have always been consistently influenced by time and geography.[18] Hence, our delusions will correlate with our location and our particular experiences at a particular moment in time. The Buddhists would consider these factors as poison since they create additional impediments to access the higher self. For this chapter's objective, we will extrapolate such reasoning to understand how delusions impair our self-worth valuations because our delusions cause us to

17. Aleman et al., *Hallucinations*, 167, discussing the mechanics of a hallucinating brain and how neural networks became configured to accommodate those hallucinations and must be reconfigured to avoid such conditions.

18. See, e.g., Slade and Bentall, *Sensory Deception*, 79, discussing patients who suffered from delusions and hallucinations.

create a narrow, excessively circumstantial self-worth based on our residential and professional location at a particular moment in time. Clearly, any optimization strategy requires more universal scalability than those narrow constrictions.

Most importantly, self-worth cannot be valued based on an escape from our realities since that will only confound our valuation methodologies. For example, delusion will not help us reconcile the current allocation of intellectual abilities, physical possessions, psychic gifts, professional successes, or spiritual favors.[19] Because we cannot reallocate those components of our lives that trigger our delusional thinking, we cannot undertake any self-worth optimization efforts tainted by delusional thinking. This chapter's objective to attain a superlative sense of self-worth contains an element of delusion thinking regarding a realistic assessment of our ability to attain that superlative. That said, we are attempting to achieve this objective for the purposes of bettering our current and future realities, not running from them. Hence, we cannot unduly influence our valuation methodologies through delusional decision-making processes that prevent us from valuing *and grounding* our sense of self-worth in reality!

Our final Buddhist mental poison, hatred, will help ensure that we can successfully achieve this chapter's objective since love, not hatred, will help all of us to create and to attain an optimal valuation for our self-worth. Optimality requires us to achieve the highest *Self* and to experience the divine through positive emotional experiences. Hatred, like the other two mental poisons, separate us from the divine as our emotions become trapped within our realities and anchor us to places of embitterment and disappointment. Most scholars and clergy, as well as lay folk, would concur that the inner life of God is love.[20] When we allow hatred to pervade our emotional landscape, we begin a downward descent away from God into the mundane, base nature of creation. The result is really catastrophic in the sense that we relinquish the full potential of our creative capacities to change, to empower or to improve our current realities.

As we review our *personal narratives* for episodes that demonstrate our creative capacities to improve our circumstances and conditions

19. See, e.g., Kakar, *Mad and Divine*, 135, discussing Freud's *Future of Illusion* and his appraisal of Marxism in light of religion's potency to help humanity reconcile their "current lot" against disparities in wealth and power.

20. See, e.g., Drobin, "Spirituality, the New Opiate," 238, noting how God as love is a universal theme in all religions or spiritual oriented practices.

from their predecessors, we should notice a clear pattern. Usually, positive movements between different moments in our *personal narratives* require positive attitudes and emotions. Have we ever improved anything with our madness or rage? Did we ever create anything lasting and beneficial with our hatred? Could we consider hate and disdain principal motivators within the development of our *personal narratives*? Most of us would concur that the best moments in our *personal narratives* are the opportunities, relationships, and circumstances that we created with love! Hence, it is imperative that we pursue an optimal sense of self-worth from a place of love and avoid all three mental poisons, especially hatred, in maximizing our self-worth valuations and their consequential benefits for our overall well-being.

So, before we leave this chapter this time, we must be mindful about the presence of three Buddhist mental poisons (desire, delusion and hatred) in our decision-making processes. Whenever we doubt or question why we are not increasing our self-worth, we must think about how these mental poisons are keeping us from our creative capacities to create relationships, circumstances, and conditions to experience the fullness and abundance of all of God's creation and to reflect that abundance in our own self-worth!

We are all strongly encouraged to read ahead through reading back so that we all can discover how best to access this abundance of the divine and dispel these mental poisons from our mind.

PART 3

Our Inner Messiah as Quintessential Divine Character

8

Defining Our Inner Messiah

THIS CHAPTER WILL HELP us to understand this book's title through defining and identifying our *Divine Character*—the *Inner Messiah*. So we have read and read and read, thought and thought and thought, reflected about and reflected on, all that filled the pages of this book till this point. Yet, the fundamental purpose of this literary exercise for author and reader may seem more evasive than when we started our undertaking. Do you feel your attitude about your life, especially your personal and professional relationships, has become empowered or improved in any way? Hopefully, some of us can provide an affirmative answer to that question, though many of us probably have opposite feelings about the efficacy of this writing creating a positive attitudinal shift, even in its slightest manifestation. This self-deprecatory tone does not undermine any endorsement for the quality of scholarship or the purity of intention of the arguments and insights presented throughout the book. Rather, we are all called to remind ourselves that true, effective transformation in any aspect of our lives requires nothing short of miraculous intervention of divine proportion.

After all, we have dedicated our time and effort to review this book in our quest to empower and to improve some aspect of our life, if not our perspective and attitude for our entire life. Our motivation to undertake this quest may have been related to a personal or professional disappointment that induced profound feelings of despair within our psyches. While it may be possible that our lives are quintessentially perfect by all conventional standards, it is far more probable our lives lack something (or someone) that prevents us from appreciating and living the abundance of perfection *accessible* within all creation. More poignantly, we have all acquired this book and studied it meticulously for some kernel of transformative knowledge to overcome something we identify as less than optimal in our ordinary reality. Well, the time has arrived in our literary, self-help journey to evoke some magical thinking in our language and perspective to grasp our untapped potential and to transform our lives into an optimal existence.

The term *messiah* will be our linguistic gateway to explore why our daily routines require some salvation from the various permutations of despair that plague us and prevent us from interacting with the fullness of the Divine presence in ourselves and all creation. Unlike other terms associated with self-awareness and self-help, *messiah* allows us to empower our *personal narratives* with an extraordinary dimension of importance that elevates our own mundane despair to the realms of the *Grand Historical Narrative* and beyond. Within the context of messianic movements throughout history, especially those of Jewish origin, e.g., Jesus Christ et al., the Hebrew term *messiah* (מָשִׁיחַ) encompasses the convergence of three anointed biblical figures and their narratives—the king, the prophet and the priest.[1] This convergence fulfills many functions within our *personal narrative* and its relationship to the *Grand Historical Narrative*, especially the interaction and tension between the mundane and the miraculous. We constantly search for new ways to describe our suffering, whether manifested as a profound sense of grief, an intense longing for an unfulfilled desire, or an incessant physical and/or emotional pain without any relief.

Whatever the cause or effect of our suffering, our need to describe it and to escape it warrants the creation of a special descriptive language that assembles thoughts, desires, hopes, dreams, and mysteries into a convergent panacea that heals mind, body, spirit, and soul in all dimensions, both seen and unseen. For example, one of the few times our literary expressions converge between our *personal narrative* and the *Grand Historical Narrative* deals with our reaction to extreme suffering that compels us to reach to the heavenly realms to acquire the adjective, *evil*, whose "true" meaning is as elusive as the cause for its existence, literary or otherwise. In looking at some of the Jewish history that has shaped

---

1. See, e.g., Lenowitz, *Jewish Messiahs*, 13.

the theological implications for Jewish messianic thought, especially the destruction of the Second Temple, the massacre after the Bar Kochba revolt, and the subsequent expulsion from the Jewish homeland,[2] we can appreciate the Jewish people's need to embrace and to empower a linguistic term *messiah* (מָשִׁיחַ). The term *messiah* (מָשִׁיחַ) demonstrates compassion from the heavenly realms and concentrates hope on a tangible, miraculous persona that can pioneer new and "other ways" to deal with our personal misfortune and our collective suffering.[3] We can also ascribe this term *messiah* (מָשִׁיחַ) with a correlative functional purpose in our individual and collective quest for empowerment and improvement.

To help us achieve our empowerment and improvement objectives, we must individualize this term *messiah* (מָשִׁיחַ) with respect to our individual suffering contained within our *personal narrative*, as well as our individual reaction to our collective suffering within the *Grand Historical Narrative*. In analyzing our reaction within these contexts, we will appreciate how best to expand our strength against and to reinforce our hope to overcome such suffering from individual and societal perspectives.

To properly frame our analysis, we must embrace some new thinking about common narrative behaviors, such as convergence and divergence, and their application in understanding messianic thought. In particular, we must appreciate how such behaviors have the ability to craft a personalized redemptive character, known as our *Inner Messiah*. To demonstrate this phenomenon, we first must agree that any convergence methodology associated with the messianic ideal must originate from a common source that can unite our *personal narratives* with the *Grand Historical Narrative*.

Second, we must further agree that narrative divergence takes place when we look outside the common source to empower certain elements of our *personal narrative* with unfounded and irrational extraordinary significance in relation to our ill-conceived desires to integrate more illustrious and inspiring elements contained within the *Grand Historical Narrative*. In keeping with our messianic theme and its historical multicultural and multi-spiritual relevance, we will agree to agree (at least for the purpose of this chapter) to put aside our religious differences and our spiritual convictions contained within our personal religious traditions and their scared textual foundations. Though we will heavily draw upon

2. See, generally, Jagersma, *History of Israel*.
3. See, e.g., Bloom, *Jewish Mysticism and Magic*, 159.

Jewish and Jewish-Christian thought to illustrate the concept and its potential benefits, our *Inner Messiah* can originate in many sacred textual traditions, including but not limited to, Buddhism, Hinduism, Islamic, and various other spiritual and mystical traditions. Regardless of our sacred textual preferences and their impact on our religious beliefs, customs, and practices, we shall refer to these texts as the common source text for our analysis, e.g., the Tanakh and/or Bible. We shall classify this common source as our coherent narrative construct, known as the *Sacred Textual Narrative.*

So, before our eyes roll up to the heavens with a disbelieving stare, let us try to approach the construction of our *Sacred Textual Narrative* to define our *Inner Messiah* within an authentic self-empowering and self-improving literary context. As a threshold concern, we should be mindful about the impact our *Sacred Textual Narrative* on the *Grand Historical Narrative* despite our own efforts to expunge scriptural influences from our *personal narratives* that may not resonate with our own conception of the Divine. That said, we must concede the term *messiah* and its promise to save us from our enemies through superhuman deeds and other extraordinary modes of deliverance[4] are uniquely embedded within our *Sacred Textual Narrative.* Any notion about encountering the transformative power of the messianic idea, especially encountering our *Inner Messiah*, must utilize scriptural concepts from our *Sacred Textual Narrative* to determine where and how our decision-making processes either converge or diverge with the messianic mandate and its relationship to the Divine in our *personal narrative.*

We can also consider the messianic construct as a creative empowerment exercise to bring about a "visionary leader" to heal our weaknesses and sufferings and to bring about an extraordinary reality in which we can *all* experience a connection with the Divine through an intermediate messianic figure.[5] Some scholars have opined that this messianic figure, who operates to gather up all souls and "particles of creation" back to God's exclusive jurisdiction, requires an individualized form of redemption that relates the superhuman messianic figure to our individual efforts to converge with the Divine and diverge with the mundane.[6] As a

4. Mathews, "Permanent Message of the Messianism," 270.

5. See, e.g., Elior, *Jewish*, 7.

6. See, e.g., Idel, "The Tsadik and His Soul's Sparks," 196, noting that "true" messianism may require a more individualized form of redemption that requires the individual to play a major role within the messianic enterprise.

result, the application of messianic repentance requires us to embrace our human nature, to confront our demonic and other psychic enemies and to encounter our *Inner Messiah* in a sort of cosmological convergence for our own empowerment and improvement.[7] It also requires the gathering of our lost ideas, dreams, and hopes, just like the twelve tribes in the Jewish messianic tradition,[8] to converge our past sense of completeness with our present sense of incompleteness. The encounter with our *Inner Messiah* further will help us grasp a descriptive language of hope from the heavenly realms set forth in our *Sacred Textual Narrative* that will help us to create a beneficial literary convergence between our *personal narrative* and the *Grand Historical Narrative*. That convergence will help us create a future containing a superlative expression of the *Self* and an extraordinary reality with *direct* access to the Divine.

A messianic theological framework provides an important operational methodology to help approach our self-analysis with a similar effectiveness of counseling, especially our efforts to appreciate the mysteries of our unconscious that can be analyzed outside traditional clinical settings.[9] Some times, our desires and goals for our self-improvement and self-empowerment may extend beyond the boundaries of meaningful clinical dialogues as we may *actually* benefit from understanding those desires and goals from a "supernatural perceptive."[10] Thus, our pursuit to encounter our inner messiah can represent a constructive spiritual pursuit to help us access a loving and supportive notion of the Divine, as well as offer us additional emotional confidence, to overcome obstacles from preventing us from manifesting our superlative existence.[11]

As demonstrated by the New Age spiritual marketplace,[12] the social and cultural interest in the miraculous or the Divine outside con-

---

7. See, e.g., ibid., 213.

8. See, e.g., Jackson-McCabe, "Messiah Jesus," 719, 724.

9. See, e.g., Jackson, "Pastoral Counselor," 255, noting how Freud's unpacking of the mysteries of the unconscious should not be left to the psychiatrists alone as theology in a pastoral counseling strategy can allow greater integration of theological insights.

10. See, e.g., Romme and Escher, *Accepting Voices*, 214, discussing how certain problems might be perceived of originating within a supernatural context and require modification to traditional clinical modalities.

11. See, e.g., Drobin, "Spirituality, the New Opiate," 236.

12. Some current market valuations identify the New Age / Self-Improvement market as high $11 billion. See, e.g., Marketdata Enterprises, Inc., http://www.marketdataenterprises.com/studies.

ventional organized religious institutions, rituals, and customs further confirm our need for an experiential spirituality that makes us feel good, avoids restrictive encumbrances, and imbues us with special powers/ insights.[13] Our *Inner Messiah*, by its definition and application to our *personal narrative*, will help us avoid futile commercialized spirituality and its self-serving ideologies. For example, our *Inner Messiah* can provide psychological benefits through spiritual insights and religious awakenings to help transform our outlooks, especially the weaker components of our *personal narrative*, away from the ordinary into the extraordinary.[14]

Our revised relationship with the *Grand Historical Narrative* through a new interpretation/appreciation of our *Sacred Textual Narrative* will greatly alter our creative capacities as they begin to recognize and to integrate creation motifs from our *Sacred Textual Narrative*. In other words, whatever we identify as the "beginning" of *all* creation, whether Divine Act, scientific phenomenon, or otherwise, will assume extraordinary influence in the rethinking and redeveloping our *personal narrative*. Even if our personal spiritual and religious belief systems reject the factual basis of the creation story in sacred texts, like Genesis, we will extract basic, common themes from our own *Sacred Textual Narrative* to access the presence of the Divine (or whatever mysterious, cosmological noun resonates with our *personal narrative*) to define our *Inner Messiah* through the convergence of our perspective about the principle elements of creation within our *Sacred Textual Narrative* and its representation within the *Grand Historical Narrative*.

CONVERGING PERSONAL NARRATIVE WITH SACRED TEXTUAL NARRATIVE VIA CREATION ELEMENTS

The origin of our *Sacred Textual Narrative* provides a powerful image for us seeking an encounter with our *Inner Messiah* to transform our lives from their mundane and suffering incarnations into an entirely new creation with new promise, hope and unbound possibility. Let us turn to the creation story portrayed in Genesis to appreciate this characterization

13. See, e.g., Drobin, "Spirituality, the New Opiate," 230.

14. See, e.g., Jeserich, "Can Sense of Coherence Be Modified," 3, enumerating the religious and health nexus in interdisciplinary research regarding the impact of religiosity and spirituality on mental health.

and center our analysis on the biblical foundation of our messianic character. If the breath of God, the *ruach*, created dust from chaos and transformed that dust into life,[15] that breath, whether in the *Sacred Textual Narrative* or its description of *creation*, is still present within all *creation* for us to encounter. In this vein, the promise of our *Inner Messiah*, like the prophesied biblical character, will help provide us with a deeper, more profound understanding of God's life-giving spirit and its ability to liberate us from the mundane, ordinary encumbrances within our daily routine that prevent us from accessing the Divine's animating force present in all creation.[16]

To help us relate to this esotericism, let us begin to notice our breath while we are reading these words and try to decipher how much of that breath represents our mere need for oxygen or our spiritual quest to reconnect with the breath of God. Hence, we will examine the creation story set forth in Genesis as a preliminary exercise to learn how to converge our breath with the breath of God that animates all life to its highest creative purpose in our quest to define our *Inner Messiah* and its transformative power within our *personal narrative* at the time of our own creation.

Genesis and Its Biblical Description of Creation as Common Creative Source of Our Sacred Textual Narrative in the Quest to Define Our Inner Messiah

Considering the characters present in the creation narrative at Genesis 1:1–3, God, Time and the "Narrative Voice," we can fashion our own *personal narrative* around similar characters as we prepare ourselves to undertake this quest to define our *Inner Messiah*. For example, we all have something within our lives that we can classify as God, whether it's a biblical notion of God, its our personal preference for something worldly as our God, i.e., money, fame, celebrity or success, or its some otherworldly form of the Divine. Whatever our personal preference, we can understand how that particularized, personal form of God has factored into our current existence, especially our current location and the state of affairs at this particular moment.

15. See, e.g., Novello, "Created Reality," 61.

16. See, e.g., ibid., 63.

To provide a deeper dimension to this notion of God, take a deeper and longer breath than we usually do as we read through these sentences and think about how that personalized God animates our current existence—eating, sleeping, working, playing, crying, or whatever other activities comprise our daily reality.

Next, we must consider this moment from *within* the moment and from *outside* the moment, i.e., time! Are we all commencing our *personal narratives* at t_0 to describe the events in our lives? Or are commencing them from a particular moment in time, t_x, where our age and our life experience are going to represent a significant factor in our creative enterprise and our ability to define our *Inner Messiah*? Most likely, we are undertaking this creative enterprise with some measurement of time as a co-creative force in the process, just as time itself represented an enigmatic character in the beginning of our *Sacred Textual Narrative*. Whatever we conclude, we can analyze our *personal narrative* to determine how we conceptualize time and utilize it within the evolution of our *personal narrative* and its definition within our *Inner Messiah*. In this regard, we can determine how much pressure we feel in accomplishing our self-awareness to empower and to improve our attitudes within a realistic timeframe. We can also appreciate the power of patience to liberate us from perceivable constrictions of time that our *Sacred Textual Narrative* alludes to as self-created, self-limited demarcations in this overall creative enterprise. Rather, the origin of creation encourages us to embrace time as an ally in our creative ventures and consider time's more constructive applications in achieving our highest purposes, such as contributing to our *Sacred Textual Narrative* through our own *personal narrative*.

Most importantly, the "Narrative Voice" provides the most empowering vehicle throughout the *Grand Historical Narrative* through which God spoke all creation into being. We must always remember the power of this "Narrative Voice" in formulating our own intentions and goals within our *personal narratives* since the power of the narrative voice to speak intention into creation will inspire us to narrate appropriately. Thus, the convergence of the narrative voice present within our *personal narrative* with the "Narrative Voice" in the Biblical creation story will empower our creative intentions with a similar effectiveness, at least some semblance of that effectiveness in the pursuit of encountering our inner messiah.

Historical precedence offers a potent example of narrative convergence and its evolutionary consequences as we consider the Genesis creation narrative as an exemplary convergence of our *Sacred Textual Narrative* with the *Grand Historical Narrative*. This convergence and its accepted narrative about creation can be considered the longest surviving, continually recognizable creation story—its endurance over the centuries alone warrants appropriate deference to the power of its narrative. As our own conundrum with time to identify the initial moment of focusing our creative efforts to empower and to improve our lives beyond the ordinary, the actual date of Genesis, like the beginning of eternity itself, warrants much conjecture since no definitive answer can be secured. Time's role in the creation narrative presents numerous ambiguities and creates an interesting subtext to the historicity of the *Sacred Textual Narrative*. First, the actual length of time between evening and morning is not clarified in Genesis. Second, the actual length of time from day 1 through day 7 cannot be ascertained from the text. Third, some early Church fathers, such as Clement of Alexandria and Origen, advocated an "instantaneous" creation scenario in which God created everything simultaneously.[17]

Most importantly, St. Augustine believed beyond a doubt that the world was made "with time" because the world could not have existed from eternity since he expounded that time had a defined beginning.[18] These ambiguities create a tension within our *Sacred Textual Narrative* that transforms time into a principle character with which God appears to co-create. Time might also operate as an allegory for other creation traditions or pagan gods that battle with God to affirm God's supremacy within this particularized and Genesis-packaged *Sacred Textual Narrative*.

Most scholars concur that Genesis was written for the Israelites around 1400 BCE as they were wondering in the wilderness en route to reclaim their promised land.[19] Some scholars have opined that the *Sacred Textual Narrative* foundation of Genesis represents a convergence of various pagan creation narratives. For example, we can revisit the story of a fourth-century BCE priest of Bel in Babylon, Berossus, who wrote a similar creation story on tablets entitled, "The Heaven and the Earth," also known as "Babylonica."[20] Berossus also wrote about the Babylonian legend, Oannes, a version of Ea, the Mesopotamian, who "for six days in-

---

17. Mackey, "First Book of Moses," 5.
18. Ibid, 6, citing St. Augustine's *City of God*, book XI.
19. Waltke, "Literary Genre of Genesis," 2.
20. Mackey, "Six Days of Genesis 1 Explained," 1–2.

structed Alorus," the first man who reigned on earth.[21] That story contains a similar phrase with parallel narrative tempo from Genesis—Berossus wrote that: "When the sun went down he [Oannes] withdrew till the next morning."[22] Ancient Egyptian creation stories also contain two of the three creation devices employed by God in Genesis—divine word (Gen 1:3–2:3) and fashioning form (Gen 2:4–25).[23] Unlike the Egyptians who personified the elements of nature, the Israelites portrayed God with complete dominion over nature that obeyed God's commands. Furthermore, the Egyptian creator-god, Atum-Re, created himself out of the pre-existent water, rather than God being eternally existent throughout time.[24]

Some of us might be curious as to why we are revisiting these historical creation accounts outside the parameters of our *Sacred Textual Narrative*. Well, simply put, we are looking for various narrative tensions outside our *Sacred Textual Narrative* in other traditions and how the *Grand Historical Narrative* may or may not have utilized these tensions. Regardless of the variations between our *Sacred Textual Narrative* and the *Grand Historical Narrative*, history provides us with important lessons about the power of narrative convergence to help us to create our own effective narratives to understand how to manifest our intentions and ambitions throughout time and within all creation. In particular, we are encouraged to embrace the elements of the creation story within our *Sacred Textual Narrative* to remind us about the awesome, infinite power of the Divine some of which we can access through our eventual encounter within our *Inner Messiah*. Starting with the initial Hebrew word of Genesis, *bereishit*, בְּרֵאשִׁית, God assumes control and dominance over all creation. Translating בְּרֵאשִׁית [25] as "Within the beginning," the main characters God and Time appear to coexist simultaneously within creation's beginning and the interaction between them propel the entire narrative.

This opening word, בְּרֵאשִׁית, also reflects a superlative state of being that our search for our *Inner Messiah* attempts to attain for our own *personal narrative*. This term also ensures convergence with other

21. Ibid., at 3.

22. Ibid., at 3.

23. Shetter, "Genesis 1–2," 6.

24. Ibid., 6–7.

25. The "within" translation comports with the initial בְּ referring to the limits enclosing a space. Brown et al., *Brown-Driver-Briggs Gesenius Hebrew and English Lexicon* [BDB], 881. Here, Time is the limitation enclosing both the beginning of the creation story and the emergence of the main characters, God and Narrative Voice.

superlative expressions throughout our *Sacred Textual Narrative* and their convergence with our *personal narrative* to remind us about God's ability to create this superlative state of existence. Biblically speaking, for example, Jacob used this term in Genesis 49:3 to describe his relationship with his firstborn, Rueben as "the beginning of [Jacob's] strength." Also, in Exodus 34:26, God commands the Israelites to bring only "the very first" of the first fruit of the soil as sacrifices in God's house. This command about the "first fruits" is also reiterated throughout the Torah in Leviticus 23:10, Numbers 18:12 and Deuteronomy 18:4. Wisdom narratives, such as Proverbs 3:9, summarize this notion best: "Honor the Lord with your substance and with the first fruits of all your produce." As a result, God's creation *itself* can be construed as God's greatest gift from which all existence originates. Perhaps, we will experience a similar wonderment within the initial moments of the identification with our *Inner Messiah*.

Regardless of the timing of our encounter with our *Inner Messiah*, whether our first time, last time or any time in between, we have great latitude to revisit that timing within our *personal narrative* to reflect its impact on our creative capacity as set forth in the creation component of our *Sacred Textual Narrative*. For example, God, appears to allow Time to participate in creation without any celestial time measuring mechanisms until the Fourth Day. Without such celestial time markers, previous references to "evening" and "morning" throughout the Genesis creation Narrative (Gen 1:5, 8, 13) did not have actual, tangible meaning in either the *Sacred Textual Narrative* or its parallel application to the *Grand Historical Narrative*. Until the creation of an actual measurement device to demarcate day and night (Gen 1:16), Time only existed "within the beginning" and subsequent references to "morning" and "evening" were meaningless outside God's divine order (Gen 1:5, 8, 13). While this fact may seem a distant esoteric literary enigma, it provides us with great hope about the Divine's ability to manipulate Time within the overall creative scheme.

That said, we should be mindful about the possibility to access similar time-altering properties within our *personal narrative* through the phrase "in the beginning" as an essential component of the creation story from our *Sacred Textual Narrative*. We possess the power, as God so powerfully and eloquently demonstrated, to reset our time measuring mechanisms to converge our *personal narrative* and the *Grand Historical Narrative* with the "beginning" of our empowerment and improvement endeavors. Even more importantly, this resetting capability within our narrative structures should help us to avoid unnecessary time pressures and anxieties about attaining our empowered and improved *Self*, as well as the optimal timing to define and to encounter our *Inner Messiah* and to experience the benefits associated with that encounter.

The foregoing should encourage us to think about how we will coexist with God, Time and our *Self* at the completion of our creative undertakings; at the conclusion of our efforts to empower and to improve our ordinary existence. As we ponder some historical ambiguities within our analysis and spiritual obfuscations regarding the accounts of creation, we should try to identify individuals within our *personal narrative* that demonstrate the benefits of convergence and the detriments of divergence with the *Sacred Textual Narrative*. For example, we should all know at least one friend or professional acquaintance that has been seeking to create some romantic fulfillment and to settle down with a life partner. That person's hunt can persist for an extended period of time and result in all types of consequences associated with an unfulfilled romantic desire or a frustrated procreative mandate. We can also appreciate how such circumstances create heightened anxieties and contribute to the suspension of rational decision-making in favor of outlandish mating solutions that borderline on half-baked messianic fantasies.

Our friends in metropolitan areas, in particular, reach a certain age and determine that their single status is a result of a disastrous dating record that requires an immediate and miraculous remedy. How many people do we know who look to the Internet as their ultimate destination for love, whether for a nighttime or a lifetime? How many stories do we hear about our successful friends paying outrageous sums of money to professional matchmakers who are retained to vet out potential dates and to procure a suitable mate? Have we ever balked at the details of our friends' efforts to find love? Whatever their stories, these friends truly confirm how divergence from a *Sacred Textual Narrative* moves us away from defining and encountering our *Inner Messiah* as they search for external remedies for their romantic ills that preempt accessing the full power of their creative capacity inspired by beneficial narrative convergence.

CASE STUDIES IN MISAPPLIED MESSIANIC IDEALS AND THEIR IMPACT ON NARRATIVE DIVERGENCE

Metropolitan areas present extraordinary challenges in convergence upon any common source, never mind the *Sacred Textual Narrative*, since the pace of life constantly reinforces our need to control our life and to maintain whatever illusory quality of life we have embraced. New York City residents, like other urban dwellers, have intense personal and professional pressures as the pursuit of the superlative is defined outside the *Self* within the exclusive domain of the City's most celebrated, successful wealthy denizens. The main consequence from such externalized social incubators to define and to maintain success is the disenfranchisement of the *Self* and its reliance on its *Inner Messiah*. Unlike other non-urban demographics, New Yorkers do not look inward to resolve any cognitive dissonance between their dreams and hopes and their attainment in their realities. We have two case studies that demonstrate how some New Yorkers forfeit any possibility to encounter their *Inner Messiah* for the sake of "purchasing" a messianic solution to their personal and professional problems.

Case Study—Metropolitan Messianic Mating Hunts

Some of us may know that single people over the age of 40 who live in New York City approach the mating hunt game as a true blood sport as their ability to commandeer younger competition and fluid sexualities require extraordinary skill and determination. Dating websites offer a modicum of hope for meeting eligible mates for potential love connections that extend beyond a single night. Lo and behold, numerous commercial solutions have emerged to help people find their appropriate mate, such as celebrity matchmakers who charge exuberant sums of money to introduce wealthy men to eager women looking for eligible bachelors that remain hidden from their sphere of possibilities. In some cases, these matchmakers are decades younger than their clients and, despite the age disparity and relevant life experiences, these mate-seeking clients ignore all rational concerns to pursue their hope for finding the perfect mate. While some people may find their true happiness through such commercialized acquisitions of love and life partners, both women and men have relinquished their own creative capacity to generate love and to find an appropriate mate through embracing these dating strategies. Clearly, these strategies are void of any convergence with the *Sacred Textual Narrative*, especially the wonderment and divine purpose to settle down for procreative purposes. Most importantly, they confirm the need to encounter our *Inner Messiah* to overcome our fears and anxieties about those aspects of our personal life that require some miraculous intervention, rather than to seek external solutions that do not ultimately converge with our *Sacred Textual Narrative* and the extraordinary benefits associated with that convergence.

Case Study—Institutional Messianic Metaphors and Their Power to Deceive

Beyond New York City, we can all relate to some story about the pursuit of institutional affiliation that some of us believe will transform our lives and will provide infinite opportunities for future success. This institutional pursuit generally ranges from academic institutions, especially secondary schools, undergraduate and graduate colleges and other academic research programs, to corporations; corporate organizations, such as Fortune 500 companies and leading Wall Street banks; to elite social institutions, like private social clubs, country clubs and professional societies; and even extending to religious and cultural institutions, such as historically significant places of worship, illustrious performance arts centers and other magnets for social, political and cultural change.

No doubt, certain institutional affiliations could transform our lives through permitting us to access important people, ideas, and societal movements. Before we become distracted by the lure of potential success and opportunity, we must analyze those institutional pursuits as an expression of our vanity to seek an opportunity, no matter how illusory, to converge our *personal narrative* with the *Grand Historical Narrative*.

While we can think about the successful, celebrated people we know who graduated from ivy leagues, work at Goldman Sachs-type companies, sit on various prestigious Boards, and assume leadership positions in religious organizations, we should exercise care to think about the deceptive element associated with the pursuits of this institutional affiliation. In particular, we examine those successful institutional affiliations from an emotional distance that reflects not only our detachment from the institution, but our personal feelings of longing associated with that detachment. But, we substitute the success of the celebrated people who have attained institutional affiliation as an emotional benchmark for their actual personal and professional satisfaction. Despite the obvious benefits associated with certain institutional affiliations, even if its as mundane as access to Super Bowl tickets, wealth generation, or celebrity award galas, we cannot assume institutional affiliation alone (or even as a major influence) will operate as a determinative factor in creating an extraordinary life.

Simply put, if every person or individual associated with a particular institution achieved our perceived notions of success, then we would know *every* person affiliated with a particular institution throughout its *entire* institutional history. That argument may seem oversimplified in its articulation, but its ramifications are clear. Seeking a particular institutional affiliation to align our future personal and professional opportunities with some alleged exclusive gateway to success, our desires have deceived us to some institutional realities that produce less success and generate more stress. Professional careers, for example, may trap us working for particular abusive bosses or oppressive corporate cultures as we justify the present discontent with the future, yet uncertain, career possibilities from our personal and professional sacrifices. In this process, we choose to focus our attention on the success stories of previous workers who have attained alleged career satisfaction as we purge the stories of our unsuccessful predecessors from our professional purview. Even more disturbing, we even blindly discount the institutional interest in promulgating the promotion of successful predecessors to current discontent workers as a mode of exploitation and manipulation.

Regardless of the overall value of the institutional affiliation, we must keep the pursuit and attainment of our affiliation in proper perspective to safeguard our dreams, hopes and goals from unnecessary external impairments. Without maintaining a proper perspective between our *Self* and our institutional affiliations, we can destroy any beneficial effects derived from participating with a prestigious institution. More importantly, we will enter into a vicious cycle that compels us to seek solutions and outlets to achieve our personal and professional dreams outside of the *Self* over which we can exercise limited control. Furthermore, we will move further away from the possibility of encountering our *Inner Messiah* and the benefits and opportunities we can derive from that encounter as we seek convergence with our *personal narrative* and the *Grand Historical*

Narrative based on non-common, temporal sources that negated any successful convergence, especially with the common biblical source.

THE POWER OF EFFECTIVE NARRATIVE CONVERGENCES WITH THE SACRED TEXTUAL NARRATIVE AND ITS TRANSFORMATIVE ABILITY

As mentioned in our discussion above, when we consider encountering our *Inner Messiah*, we are referring to a well-developed messianic notion developed within the Jewish tradition and set forth in the Tanakh / Old Testament. The historicity of that fact, that is, Jewish spiritual and mystical thought, cannot be underestimated in our analysis, as well as the origin and its subsequent evolution in psychoanalytical research and treatment. Most researchers concur that Jewish history and culture play a significant role in Freud's analytical thought.[26] For example, some scholars, like David Bakan, opine that Freud identified with Joseph from Genesis as an interpreter of dreams and as a warrior figure to proclaim the future messiah.[27] Even significant messianic figures in Jewish history after Jesus Christ, such as Sabbatai Zvi, represent psychoanalytical prototypes about social and emotional functions within messianic thought, notably the role of social, cultural, and emotional depravity and its influence on the instigation of extraordinary, mystical solutions for such depravity.[28]

Other potential Jewish messianic claimants, like Abraham ben Samuel Abulafia, operate within a messianic paradigm, according to Freud, through a method of free association.[29] This Freudian notion of free association demonstrates its power to unleash the soul from the ordinary and mundane and helps us to appreciate of the role of mundane anchors to prevent an inquiring soul from being overwhelmed by the "divine stream" outside our ordinary existence.[30]

Freud utilized these messianic principles of free association within his psychoanalytical treatment to understand how the mind makes, acts upon and reacts to "jumping and skipping" between thoughts and other

26. See, e.g., Bakan, *Sigmund Freud*, 11.

27. Ibid., 173.

28. Ibid, xii.

29. Ibid., 75.

30. Ibid., 75.

ideas, especially when subject to a deep meditative state.[31] More significantly, Freud's psychoanalytical perspective regarding his logic associated with accessing the unconscious appears to parallel certain aspects of Jewish mystical thought about discovering God's secret names to access the heavenly realms.[32] Freud appears to have converged that *Sacred Textual Narrative* with his contributions to the *Grand Historical Narrative* through revisiting and rearranging the relationship between God and its creation, like the doctor-patient relationship.[33] Just like rearranging the letters of God's divine name to discover hidden names, Freud rearranged the elements and boundaries of conscious and subconscious to access hidden places with extraordinary functions beyond common reason and rationale.[34] The relevance of this phenomenon to define our *Inner Messiah* will be discussed below as we revisit the magical properties of Ancient Jewish mysticism on our imaginations.

Furthermore, Carl Jung exercised similar reliance on Jewish scripture and spiritual thought, including his seminal work *Answer to Job*, which some scholars believe represent a turning point in psychoanalytical thought.[35] In particular, Jung's attempt to reconcile religion and science through psychology was a direct result of his identification of scientific and religious enterprises as self-definitional activities. These self-definitional activities appear to contain emotions and impulses that function within major portions of manifest reality and reach out toward portions of an unmanifested reality.[36] According to Jungian thought, the active imagination and our dialogue with its images to define our emotions and impulses with transformative meaning that produce a self-reflective, conscious response can best resolve any tensions between narrative divergences associated with those emotions and impulses.[37] To demonstrate, the convergence present within Freudian and Jungian thought upon a *Sacred Textual Narrative*, especially based on Jewish scripture and spiritual thought, further confirms the psychotherapeutic effects and benefits associated with narrative convergence, especially for the express purpose

31. Ibid., 76.
32. See ibid.
33. See ibid.
34. See, e.g., ibid.
35. See, e.g., Spiegelman, *Judaism and Jungian Psychology*, 71.
36. See, e.g., Bakan, *Duality of Human Existence*, 5.
37. See, e.g., Huskinson, *Dreaming the Myth Onwards*, 110.

to define and to encounter our *Inner Messiah* and its ability to facilitate our *personal narrative* with the *Grand Historical Narrative* through our *Sacred Textual Narrative* (*hereafter,* "Complete Narrative Convergence").

An important realization of this Complete Narrative Convergence is that imagination can have actual, tangible beneficial consequences for our lives, including a reasonable, rational basis to correlate our spiritual beliefs emanating from our *Sacred Text Narrative* with various challenges throughout our lifetime.[38] Generally speaking, we *all* have experienced some spiritual crisis, whether instigated by personal loss, professional disappointment, or spiritual angst itself, that has required us to access the deepest recesses of our imagination. The application of imagination to access the Divine realms requires us to think about prior historical events that empower and improve individuals enduring extreme suffering and seeking innovative ways to overcome that suffering in *both* a personal capacity, i.e., *personal narrative*, and a societal context, i.e., *Grand Historical Narrative*. We will try to relate this phenomenon to a tangible historical event that has produced a radical new language and perspective on our relationship with the Divine, as well as how our individual and societal exercise of imagination can extract transformative power from that new language and perspective. Suffice it to say, we must identify an historical occurrence that demonstrates how the convergence between *Sacred Textual Narrative* and our *personal narrative* can help us define and imbue the definition of our *Inner Messiah* with empowerment and improvement properties to help us overcome our personal and collective sufferings, disappointments and other psychic ailments.

INNER MESSIAH DEFINED AS COMPLETE AND SUPERLATIVE EXPRESSION OF INNER SELF

Before we commence this section, we must check up on our breath and see how we are still breathing. What do we feel within our breath, if anything? Or, do we just breath as an automatic action to sustain life? Have any of the words or points raised throughout this book had any impact on your breathing pattern? Hopefully, we are breathing easier about how we contemplate the challenges and disappointments throughout our *personal narrative*. The time has come in our literary journey together to extract some tangible benefits for our own journeys toward empowering

38. See, e.g., Bakan et al., *Maimonides' Cure of Souls*, 262.

and improving our attitudes. As we breath through, in, above, below, with, and within the words positioned on the remaining pages, we should really try to compel our breath to seek the remnants of the breath of the Divine as preserved within our *Sacred Textual Narrative*. For if we can nourish our inner *Self* with these remnants of Divine breath, God's *ruach*, we might be able to derive a sort of Divine strength to facilitate our efforts to define an effective, transformative *Inner Messiah*. Let us think back to opening scenes of creation in Genesis and recall how the Divine breathed his spirit of life into dust to create life.[39] No matter our faith tradition or spiritual distance from this creation account, we should understand the generic elements of its narrative. The interaction between the Divine and its creation points to a specific action—*the creation of life.*

More specifically, that interaction reminds us about the creation of *our* own life. A discursive about the philosophical and biological notions about the *creation of life* in a universal context can easily distract us, but *the creation of our life* greatly narrows the focus to a singular act in time and its *direct* consequences upon *our lifetime*. Hence, this reasoning provides the impetus to ponder our inner *Self* and how our *Inner Messiah* gives expression to that *Self* and its sense of wholeness and extraordinariness.

The *Inner Self* represents an important component of our ability to interact with externalized influences, including our externalized notions of the Divine and its miraculous, mysterious powers. Some spirituality studies have found a robust correlation between strong spirituality and connectedness to the inner *Self*.[40] Many potential factors weigh upon the degree and strength of this correlation, such as deriving comfort from our own presence *and* experiencing an inner calmness.[41] To achieve this connection with our inner *Self*, we must ensure what we relate to as our inner *Self* without *any* dependence on external factors or influence—our own completeness with the singularity of our *Self* within that particular moment.

In this regard, we can define our *Inner Self* as a tangible expression of our spirit, soul, essence or other appropriately, descriptive word that transcends our ordinary realities and permits us to touch another realm of possibility void of any limitations, whether physical constraints, or emotional obstacles. We have connected with the internal essence

39. Gen 2:7.

40. See, e.g., Raftopoulos and Bates, "It's That Knowing That You Are Not Alone," 159–60.

41. Ibid.

instilled within our being that *directly* connects us with the *Grand Historical Narrative*, via the our *Sacred Textual Narrative*, that ensures us that God, Creator, Divine, or other self-aggrandizing cosmic force name has created us at the "true" beginning.

We must reorient our conception of time beyond the conventional restrictions of linear time contained within our *personal narratives* as we realize that essence that comprises the *Inner Self* was present before the commencement of our *personal narrative* and relates back to the beginning of the *Grand Historical Narrative*—the aspect of our *Self* that witnessed all creation unfold. Hence, our breath—each ounce of air we ingest—helps connect us with the remnants of God's *ruach* (breath) that resides in all creation and, in turn, allows us to experience that commencement event so eloquently set forth in the creation account embodied by our *Sacred Textual Narrative*.[42] Yet, as we breathe breath after breath over these words, are we able to find any of this *ruach*? Is there any remnant of God's creative action from our *Sacred Textual Narrative* that can be found any where within our sight or sense? Reflect upon this notion deeply and sincerely, close the eyes and put the book down, look to the heavens and gaze to the floors. What is the simple lesson from this exercise?

As we refocus our attention onto this paragraph and the remainder of the book, let us take the experience we all just had in our unique way and manner, dependent on our geographic location, faith journey, personal and professional struggles, and other unique circumstances. Despite the multitude of variations between all of us, we can probably identify *at least* one central common theme from this exercise—*feeling*. When we attempted to find God's breath in creation, in our very decision to undertake this spiritual hunt, we all *felt* something—even if our feelings are wildly divergent. Whatever emotions we felt, whether fear, awe, wonderment, or joy, all feelings were generated from the same place—the *Inner Self*. Although we cannot adequately describe the actual emotive cause behind that feeling or even its operational purpose for our spiritual quest, we can, at least, all identify a common source—the *Inner Self*.

Our spirituality, that sense of interconnectedness with the Divine, may have its origins within our personal devotions and public ritual practices that we have internalized over the course of our lifetime in overcoming intrapersonal obstacles in formulating a spiritual belief system

---

42. Novello, "Created Reality," 61.

contained within our *personal narrative*.[43] For example, some of us may have crafted our belief system to contain a notion of God as *strictly* omnipotent and omniscient to help us encounter our life's more challenging moments with less anxiety, fear, and angst because God, as functioning within such belief systems, has already plotted out our destiny and no human action, effort, or industry can alter the content and outcome contained within our *personal narrative*.[44]

Even in those of us who do not endorse a pronounced existence of God or particular religious affiliation, we *all* most likely shared a common emotive experience, an "internal emotional rumbling," whether as ardent people of faith or staunch believers in agnosticism, as we hunted for that *ruach* remnant. Researchers call this phenomenon a "stereotyping process," that is, our exposure to the stereotypes of various social groups can impact our behavior in similar ways, even though some of us do neither endorse nor embrace any validity associated with that stereotype.[45] Hence, any exposure to religion and spirituality, and their representations throughout secular culture, will generate the commonality within and between our emotional reactions regardless of the degree of our personal belief.[46] That said, we are all familiar with the creation story in *Genesis*, even if only through our staunch opposition to creationism and its contemporary political implications. No doubt, our familiarity with Genesis influences the development and application of the shared, common elements within our *Sacred Textual Narrative* that contributed to our common emotional reactions generated by our hunting exercise. Hopefully, our *Inner Self* alone generated that emotional reaction without any external influences.

For the purposes of this chapter, we must translate that emotional reaction, feeling or sense into the cornerstone of the definition of our *Inner Messiah*. After all, our *Inner Self* represents the aspect of the *Self* whose origins are most far removed from the exigencies of our ordinary, daily routines, and are closest to God, our Divine Creator. We can access the power of creation, i.e., the *ruach remnants*, through appreciating

---

43. See, e.g., Luquis et al., "Religiosity, Spirituality, Sexual Attitudes," 602, describing factors that affect religiosity and their impact on intrapersonal faith encounters.

44. See, e.g., Laurin et al., "Divergent Effects," 6, noting how themes of omnipotence and omniscience in conceptions of God factor into behavior patterns, such as inner peace and calm, as well as submission to failure.

45. Ibid., 18.

46. Ibid.

their proximity to the Divine and extracting from our *Inner Self* what we will need to identify and define as our *Inner Messiah*. The *Inner Messiah* will enable us to utilize God's gifts present within us, i.e., the *Inner Self*, through animating an aspect of our nature that we have surrendered to various types of spiritual auditors, cartographers, historians, scribes and other fiduciaries of our souls, whether presented within the panoply of religious options, dogmas, interpretations, institutions, or other man-made, manufactured salvations. In adhering to the messianic traditions within our *Sacred Textual Narratives*, we must always remember that a messiah will lead people in singular purpose for a singular end—attainment of the full purpose and abundance of creation.[47]

More importantly, most scholarly opinion and prophetic consensus distill from our *Sacred Textual Narrative* that any prophesied messiah will elevate all of God's creation to a higher level,[48] i.e., complete knowledge of God,[49] establishment of a profound, everlasting peace,[50] and emanation of a universal purity/relationship with the "Divine Oneness."[51] This notion of "Divine Oneness" contained within our *Sacred Textual Narrative* will become the principle attribute of the definition for our *Inner Messiah*. We will define *Inner Messiah* as the complete unification of *Self* and *Inner Self* that facilitates a direct, experiential mode of communication with the God, our Divine Creator, from our *Sacred Textual Narrative*. Furthermore, our *Inner Messiah* will enable us to achieve this unification through revealing to us what we cannot discern within the narrative relationship between our *personal narrative*, the *Grand Historical Narrative* and their interconnectedness via our *Sacred Textual Narrative*. In particular, we must visit two key components of the creation account from Genesis that we have deliberately reordered for our discussion purposes set forth below.

Adam, the First Sin and Its Consequences. We have some preconceived images associated with the events surrounding the fall of humanity in that proverbial garden of creation. Countless artists, poets, scholars

---

47. See, e.g., Novello, "Created Reality," 63.

48. Ibid.

49. See, e.g., Isa 11:9, noting "...for the earth will be filled with knowledge of the Lord."

50. See, e.g., Isa 55:12–13, noting "...go out in joy, and be led back in peace" and how all nature will shout with joy."

51. See, e.g., Zeph 3:9–13, describing the purification of all speech so that *all* may call upon the name of the Divine Creator, God, in one accord.

and ingénues have imagined and reimagined this event as the dreaded snake tempting Eve to eat of the forbidden fruit tree and gain perception to be "like God."[52] Let us not confound our inspired predecessors with yet another tiresome account of our "fruit eating, wisdom seeking" progeny. Rather, let us concentrate on the immediate consequences of their actions to help shed some additional light on why their actions contribute to our detachment from our *Inner Messiah*.

First, Adam and Eve realized that they were naked,[53] they were frightened by the sound of God approaching them,[54] the man blamed the woman for his disobedience,[55] the woman blamed the serpent for being tricked into eating the forbidden fruit,[56] and God got pissed![57] God's anger was so extensive that God cursed the snake among all the creatures,[58] God put enmity between the man and the woman and their offspring,[59] God increased the pain associated with the woman's birthing process,[60] God condemned the man to hard labor to produce his livelihood from the land,[61] and God cast them out of the garden.[62] Despite the magnitude of God's fury from Adam and Eve's disobedience, this *Sacred Textual Narrative* contains critical details about how to define our *Inner Messiah*. For example, their disobedience did not prevent them from hearing God calling to them, as well as directly communicating with them—"But the Lord God called to the man, and said to him, 'Where are you?'"[63] The fact that Adam could still hear God calling his "name" and was able to respond demonstrates that *God did not remove Adam's knowledge of his Divine Name, that is, the sacred name by which God and God alone called unto him.* Furthermore, we can derive a better understanding about the power of this name and how this name helped Adam not only hear God's call, but ensured that this name would generate peace and harmony with

52. Gen 3:5.
53. Gen 3:7.
54. Gen 3:9–10.
55. Gen 3:12.
56. Gen 3:13.
57. Gen 3:14–24.
58. Gen 3:14.
59. Gen 3:15.
60. Gen 3:16.
61. Gen 3:17–18.
62. Gen 3:23–24.
63. Gen 3:9.

the land and all creation. Examining the situation from God's perspective, we can conjecture that Adam and Eve's disobedience subjected all of creation, not only themselves, to God's wrath and anger as God placed *enmity* between the various components of creation, especially man and woman and their offspring.

As we settle into this notion about God's perspective looking onto God's creation, especially the disobedience of its two principal characters, we should appreciate the practical consequences of God's action to remedy this schism within the Divine Oneness present in all creation. Rather than obliterate and eradicate all traces of their presence from the *Sacred Textual Narrative* preserved by Genesis, God made "garments of skins for the man and for his wife, and clothed them" before expelling them from the garden of Eden.[64] These "garments" and their spiritual properties have inspired the imaginations of mystical scholars since the inception of this *Sacred Textual Narrative*. For our purposes, we shall regard God's garments as the "imperative narrative membrane," the "INM," that separates the *Grand Historical Narrative* of creation from our *personal narrative* and its disobedient disposition originating with the two principal characters and their offspring from our *Sacred Textual Narrative*. The INM also operates as a vessel or husk (*kelipot*), as described in Jewish Mystical tradition, and contains the disobedient essences/souls of these principal characters.

Another practical consequence of our INM is its impact on the evolution and development of our *personal narrative*. For example, the INM operates to filter our *personal narrative*'s interaction with the *Grand Historical Narrative*, as well as the *Sacred Textual Narrative* contained within our INM and moving outside our INM. In order words, we are always functioning under some recognition, conscious or unconscious, about our separateness from the Divine Oneness that, in some ways, splinters our own *personal narrative*. Rather than fully integrating our interest and curiosity about God, Divine Creator, our *personal narrative* accepts a multitude of our divine revelations through our *Sacred Textual Narrative* and God's *ruach* moving through that narrative on both sides of our INM.

Besides severing their Divine Oneness from all creation, i.e., the complete narrative convergence, the INM concealed the sacred names of Adam and Eve and prevented them, as well as all their progeny, from

---

64. Gen 3:21–24.

hearing God's *direct* call unto them. In turn, the INM fractured the Divine Oneness in creation through detangling the Divine Oneness of all creation's shared, singular narrative and creating a boundary between the bound disobedient essence/soul (sinful) and the unbound obedient essence/soul (repentance).

The twentieth-century kabbalist attributed with many miracles, Rabbi Yehuda Fetaya, developed a profound *Sacred Textual Narrative* about our INM that he referred to as a husk.[65] He taught that our own personal sins and pursuit of worldly pleasures not only wraps us tighter within our INM, but they add additional thickness to our INM and additionally encumber our narrative divergence with all creation.[66] Without repentance, we have no chance to break free from under the narrative dissonance under our INM to reclaim our hidden sacred name to resume direct communications with God. Rabbi Fetaya taught every one of us has two names—one name comes from the side of "holiness" within the husk, i.e., behind the membrane, and the second name gets affixed to the outside of the husk, i.e., outside the membrane.[67]

Through discovering the hidden name from the side of "holiness," we will have the opportunity to know the origins of our concealed essence/soul within our INM and, extrapolating from Rabbi Fetaya's teachings, we will acquire the power to remedy our disobedience and to repair our direct communication with God.[68] It would appear that Rabbi Fetaya's teachings can help us to develop an effective strategy to reclaim our hidden, sacred name to resume direct communication with God, the Divine Creator, through our own *Sacred Textual Narrative* and its power to converge our complete *personal narrative* with the *Grand Historical Narrative* in reestablishing that Divine Oneness.

God's Breath Moving among the Nothingness. Ironically, if any of us felt that foregoing argument was vacuous, we can rest assuredly that we have found some of the remnants of God's *ruach* within that sentiment. Jokes aside, as we retreat behind our INM in our hunt to discover the remnants of the *ruach*, we must recall the power and vastness of shear

---

65. See, e.g., Fetaya, *Minhat Yehuda*, 279, noting that the garment covers the soul as a direct result of Adam's sin in the garden.

66. Ibid., 279–80.

67. Ibid., 282.

68. Ibid.

nothingness from which God made and called forth all creation—*form-less void and covered in darkness*.[69]

Moving above and over all that nothingness, the *Sacred Textual Narrative* tells us that *only* God's *ruach* was present among all that shear nothingness.[70] Hence, our task to complete our hunt successfully is to recapture that similar essence of "nothingness" within our creation as tightly wrapped within the trappings of our INM. Meaning, we must completely detach all our notions about the creation of our *Self* and its expression via our *personal narrative* from any external influences and forces. Our bounded *Inner Self*, our holiness contained within our INM, allows for that complete "nothingness" as we retreat inward with this singular attention to recapture the remnants of God's *ruach* that have been left untouched by the burdens and ambitions that dwell outside our INM. Just as God as cut us out our *personal narrative* from creation with our INM, we must appreciate our own efforts to preserve our *Self* on the outer side of our INM as our *personal narrative* interacts with the *Grand Historical Narrative* and our *Sacred Textual Narrative* within this exter-nalized context. In other words, we must pinpoint some of nothingness that moves between and exists within INM to strategize how most effec-tively to overcome any impediments caused by our INM to our narrative convergence efforts.

Ironically, this theme of "nothingness" to understand and to define the Divine even extends beyond our *Sacred Textual Narrative* to other eastern philosophical traditions, such as numerous lineages within Ti-betan Buddhism.[71] Further studies, whether academically or spiritually motivated, could help us appreciate the universal message and hope con-tained within appreciating the lessons of empowerment and improve-ment present within the "nothingness" of our daily existence. But, due to the constraints of this chapter's message and our own narrative choices, we will consider the lack of further studies as an example of nothingness that can help us learn something about nothingness and its impact on our *personal narrative* moving between, outside and inside of our INM. De-spite our potential findings associated with these studies, or lack thereof, we must always recall that any external source materials, including this

69. Gen 1:2.

70. Ibid., describing how "a wind from God swept over the face of the waters."

71. See, generally, Gyaltsen, *Parting from the Four Attachments*, emphasizing the illusion of the material world and the liberating power of embracing the "nothingness" within reality as contained within *Sakya* teachings.

book, will be an inferior encounter with the scope and vastness of the nothingness contained within our *Inner Self* wrapped within the INM. To that end, we must encounter the power of "nothingness" within the *Inner Self* and extract from it the remnants of God's *ruach* to assemble and to create a definition of our *Inner Messiah* that transforms that "nothingness" into our *Inner Messiah.*

Remember, we must all keep breathing because our encounter with any form of "nothingness" is anything but "nothing." So, let us approach the finality of our hunt for the remnant of God's *ruach* with all the emotional capacities that will empower and improve our definitional objective and enable us to concretize our individual power to experience the Divine Oneness present in all creation and to reclaim the divine character of our *personal narrative* through our *Inner Messiah.*

OUR INNER MESSIAH—THE DEFINITIONAL CONCEPT AND ITS FUNCTIONAL CONSEQUENCES

As we previously discussed a few paragraphs back, we must conceptualize the messianic message as the embodiment of an important transformative figure to empower and to improve our lives. Among the many messianic compasses contained within our *Sacred Textual Narrative,* scholarly research, and religious doctrine, we will follow an *unorthodox direction* to achieve an *orthodox destination.* Looking behind our INM and inward to our *Inner Self,* we will find and experience the fullness of nothingness present at the commencement of the creation account in Genesis for our *Sacred Textual Narrative* and, from that "nothingness," we will fully understand the transformative power of the messianic claims to empower and to improve our lives. The four most relevant messianic attributes are discussed above, but we can spend time with various other sacred texts, including those in other traditions, that may help us accelerate our hunt for the remnants of God's *ruach.* Hopefully, we will all experience the disintegration of boundaries and decisive spiritual constructs that separate us from the Divine Oneness as we turn inward on our journey together and embrace the possibilities of the infinite contained within our inner, untainted holiness and its direct proximity to the Divine.

Revisiting Messianic Attributes

The messiah will have a "complete knowledge"[72] about God according to the messianic message within our *Sacred Textual Narrative*. Such completeness will be unique not only to the sheer quantity of information about God, but the messiah's ability to transmit that knowledge to all of God's creation—sort of an *erudite ruach* that moves through all creation with the expressed purpose to educate creation about its Creator—the reunification of creation with its Divine Oneness. This "erudite ruach," unlike the remnants of God's *ruach* for which we are searching, moves *through* all creation *from* all creation, not nothingness. As history taught us, our individual beliefs in messianic claimants (including our attachments to salvific persons, objects, and messages) does not *completely* converge our *personal narrative* with our *Sacred Textual Narrative* or the *Grand Historical Narrative*. Rather, our sense of completeness might parallel our current sense of "Divine Oneness" as our INM dilutes the development of any universal, fulfilling messianic message. Our INM creates tensions between our curiosity about the Divine through our ego *and* fuels our decisiveness to claim exclusive ownership over our *Sacred Textual Narrative* through our religious beliefs and doctrines moving between the INM and contributing to the current Divine Character within our *personal narrative*.

Regardless of some of the beliefs contained within our *personal narratives*, we should appreciate the boundaries/limitations of those beliefs when we encounter disagreement and/or opposition to our conceptualized presence of the current Divine Character within our *personal narrative*. The presence of any boundary and/or limitation within our knowledge about the Divine should tell us something about how, why and for what purpose we have decided to adopt that conception of the Divine within our *personal narrative*, as well as demonstrate the filtering functions of our INM and its impact on our *personal narrative*. At least, we should wonder about the nature of some of our teachings and beliefs if they are suppose to envelope a "complete knowledge" of God within this "erudite ruach" that only breaths knowledge to some of us, *not all creation*. Or, does our INM consume God's *ruach* to preserve our *Inner Self* to protect our sacred holiness from reconnecting with the Divine Oneness, especially since not all humanity within creation can access their inner holiness? Can this truly

72. See, e.g., Isa 11:9, noting "...for the earth will be filled with knowledge of the Lord."

be "complete knowledge," especially if it requires *all* of us to acquire more knowledge to understand its completeness? Keep breathing and let us appreciate the involuntary nature of that breathe—something inherently complete *of* itself, *in* itself and *through* itself, that cannot be taught only acquired for the purpose of sustaining life.

Rather, this particular messianic attribute, "complete knowledge," confirms our need to be steadfast in our search for the remnants of God's *ruach* from our initial creation—the point of nothingness that cannot be tainted by the subsequent evolution of creation as portrayed within the *Grand Historical Narrative* and separated by the Divine Oneness through our INM. Our *Inner Self* contains such "nothingness." To understand this phenomenon, we must recall how we portray both our spirituality and religious beliefs (or lack thereof) within our *personal narrative*. The moment we include those two components of the *Self* on our *personal narrative*, not only to we immediately compare them in relation to the kaleidoscope of spiritual and religious possibilities within our culture, especially their relative congruity within the *Grand Historical Narrative*. We also expose our personal spiritual and religious beliefs to the scrutiny of others and their judgments will have consequences, even benign consequences, such as the acquisition of additional information about our personal beliefs.

Generally speaking, our INM allows us to shelter our knowledge about God and the Divine from external influences and forces that would disrupt our inner, untainted holiness and its complete knowledge of the Divine. In other words, we have the capacity to access a "nothingness" within us that closely parallels the "nothingness" from which God created creation set forth in our *Sacred Textual Narrative*. So, our hunt for the remnants of God's original *ruach* at creation should take us to this place of "nothingness" within us and, from such nothingness, we can begin to reconnect with our pure inner holiness and to build a "complete knowledge" about the Divine, i.e., God, as imparted within our own individual creation. After all, our INM and its covering of our inner holiness will obliterate any destructive influences from external sources as we begin to breath in accord with those original *ruach* remnants to create a definition of our *Inner Messiah* that will elevate us to empower and to improve all aspects of our existence.

Before we clearly define the term *Inner Messiah*, we should briefly revisit the power of "nothingness" to help us extract the power of the messianic message contained within our *Sacred Textual Narrative*. In particular, let us revisit the message's emphasis on peace.[73] The *Inner Self* contained behind our INM provides an excellent place for the existence of this type of "messianic peace" because, as we encounter the "nothingness" with the remnants of God's *ruach*, we become far removed from any external influence to disturb or to upset any feelings of peace. Most profound, our inner holiness wrapped within our INM, provides us with direct access to Divine Oneness we experienced before Adam and Eve's expulsion from the garden of Eden. The access to the Divine Oneness will enable us to manifest a relationship with Divine and all creation that eradicates all decisiveness and separateness. "Nothingness," with regard to creating a definition for our *Inner Messiah*, contains so much experiential benefit for understanding the Divine's presence within our *personal narrative* as the remnants of God's *ruach* can be released and reunified from both sides of our INM.

INNER MESSIAH: A DEFINITION

Well, hopefully, we are still breathing with an empowered and improved sense of wonderment about our status in the Divine's overall creative scheme. More importantly, we have successfully hunted and captured some of the remnants of God's *ruach* as we retreated behind our INM to appreciate our innate holiness and its proximity to the Divine. With those remnants, we will participate in an aspect of creation as set forth in the *Sacred Textual Narrative*, namely, we will create a definition of our *Inner Messiah* that will allow us to participate more fully in the original Divine Oneness present within God's overall creative scheme.

The creation of this definition requires us to recognize the fundamental components of our own creative capacities. Specifically, we must produce a definition that is *both* an original and unexpected application of the *Sacred Textual Narrative and* an appropriate and useful construct to empower and improve our lives.[74] Prima facie, this Herculean linguistic exercise sounds more daunting than searching for the remnants of God's *ruach*. That said, we should remember that a linguistic definition of *Inner Messiah* generally inspired our collective participation on this page in the

---

73. See, e.g., Isa 55:12–13, noting "...go out in joy, and be led back in peace," and how all nature will shout with joy.

74. See, e.g., Gino and Ariely, "Dark Side of Creativity," 445, describing creativity as an exercise in novel and useful innovation.

first place. With this in our minds, we shall approach this definitional construct in reverence and humility.

Drum rolls and fanfares aside, our *Inner Messiah* is our internal spiritual force that removes the INM and allows us to reconnect with the original Divine Oneness. The formulaic representation of this phenomenon is set forth below for our contemplation.

		Ability to Perceive Our Internal Holiness		Ability to Reunite That Holiness with the Original Divine Oneness
Inner Messiah	=	Perceive Our	+	That Holiness with the

Through perceiving our inner holiness and commencing the process of reunifying that holiness with the Divine Oneness through our narrative convergence, we will expand our creative capacity as we access the power to create our individual messianic era within our *personal narrative*. The solution to our *Inner Messiah* equates with a simple, yet profound, identification of our sacred hidden name that dwells within us behind our INM—the name which God and God alone knows and by which God calls us. Once we have discovered that solution—the alignment of divine and temporal convergence of our narrative identity, we can fully understand and identify *all* aspects of the *Self* and its expressions within our *personal narrative* as a fulfillment of our mandate to participate in the Divine Oneness at the beginning of creation as our Creator calls out to us, individually and uniquely by our newly perceivable inner holiness, our sacred name, to accept the Divine's invitation to participate in *all* creation.

Even more simply put, our *Inner Messiah* is just our sacred, hidden name and the powers contained within that name to clearly and obediently hear our Creator calling us. In this regard, we can recapture the pure essence of original creation at the very beginning and combine creation's creative efforts with its Creator's creative munificence to transform the entirety of our daily existence and our *personal narrative* into an original act of creation without any prior disappointments, sufferings, or prejudices that prevent us from accessing our *Inner Messiah* and the original Divine Oneness. With regard to the Genesis account, our complete narrative convergence, that is, our *personal narrative's* convergence with the *Grand Historical Narrative* through our *Sacred Textual Narrative*, will dispel the cherubim guard and the fiery ever-turning sword from their guard posts and will allow our complete return to the garden of Eden.[75]

Let us keep breathing as each breath allows us to spark the creativity contained within the remnants of God's *ruach*, as we further develop this concept of our *Inner Messiah* and understand its impact on the Divine Character in our *personal narratives*.

---

75. See Gen 3:24, noting that God stationed the "cherubim and the fiery ever-turning sword" to guard the path to the tree of life.

9

Encountering Our Inner Messiah

THIS CHAPTER'S OBJECTIVE IS meant to help us discover our sacred, hidden name that will operate as a catalyst to unify our narratives and to encounter our *Inner Messiah*. Our name, last, first, middle and everything in between and beyond, provides us with the most powerful tool to break through the separateness created by the our *Imperative Narrative Membrane* (INM) and to encounter our *Inner Messiah*. Whatever we call ourselves and whatever others call us, that calling is embodied in a singular expression of language. That powerful word, our name, allows us to know when someone or something wants our attention as we hear a simple utterance. Our emotions and feelings may churn in all directions when we hear our name mentioned in a particular way or by a particular person. Albeit, we all have a singular, universal reaction to the mention of our name, that is, we focus our attention on the source of its mention.

No matter what we are doing, where we might be or whom is with us, the moment we decide to respond to someone calling our name, we disengage ourselves from all endeavors of that moment in time and engage with its caller. Similarly, most of us spend the majority of our lifetimes empowering and improving our names, whether with professional successes and accomplishments, personal achievements, or acquisition of wealth and/or celebrity. A subtle motivation in the elevation of our name within particular personal and professional groups may be our desire for "recognized visibility." "Recognized visibility" is the empowerment of our name to the point that when we contact anyone we want *directly,* the person we are calling already knows who we are before our initial contact. For example, a hallmark of a powerful name in the entertainment/media business is the ability to call any agent, producer, director, studio, or other bigwig and bypass their assistant to get that person on the phone or to call you back. To industry outsiders, such phone politics may seem superfluous and vain. Yet, if you received a call from your favorite celebrity or historical figure at dinnertime, would you treat that call in the same manner as the annoying, anonymous telemarketer? The "recognized visibility" of our name operates as a sort of universal mode of communication that allows us to utter our name and to anticipate a particular result. As we increase the "recognized visibility" associated with our name, we adjust our expectations upon its utterance. So whether or not our name will enable us to have a choice table at a famous restaurant, courtside seats to our favorite basketball teams, or access to world class doctors and healthcare, the instantaneous response upon just hearing our name will demonstrate how much and what type of an investment we have made into its "recognized visibility."

Somewhere among all our strategizing efforts to maximize the "recognized visibility" associated with our name, there exists another aspect of our name that operates according to different functions and purposes, our *Inner Messiah*. Before we explore the power associated with that aspect of our name, we must address some of the less fortunate situations some of us may be facing within (or have faced throughout) our *personal narrative*. Namely, some of us may have felt total disenfranchisement from our name due to family dysfunction, abuse, molestation, addiction, or other soul-crushing phenomena, any of which totally preempted our efforts to empower or to improve our name. Rather than worrying about "recognized visibility," some of us may have desperately sort to avoid any mention of our name to avoid confronting and/or dealing with our despair as we surrendered any hope to empower and to improve our name. In this scenario, some of us may have been inspired to read this book by our desire to disappear, that is, we may desire our name to be eradicated completely from any mention, e.g., the complete deletion of our *personal narrative* from the *Grand Historical Narrative*. We must all remember that such dire circumstances are avoidable if we can discover our sacred name to encounter our *Inner Messiah* hidden behind our *INM*.

The diverse feelings associated with succeeding or failing at maximizing the "recognized visibility" associated with our name will facilitate the encounter with our *Inner Messiah*. For the purposes of facilitating this

encounter, we will rely heavily on the mystical musings of two major figures in psychology, Carl Jung and Sigmund Freud. As we read over their
names, we should reflect upon the feelings and thoughts they conjure
within our mind. Both names have the power to conjure intense visceral
reactions associated each name's "recognized visibility." More importantly, the mention of their names alone prepares us to anticipate the imminent themes emerging from this chapter. Whether or not any of us attain
the same "recognized visibility" as either Jung or Freud, we will always
have our *Inner Messiah*, to optimize our "recognized visibility" within the
universal, metaphysical convergence of our *personal narrative* with the
Grand Historical Narrative through our *Sacred Textual Narrative*.

To encounter our *Inner Messiah*, we will need to exploit the energies
from two opposite perceptions of our name—maximized and minimized
"recognized visibility." These opposite perceptions will help us appreciate
the "phenomenon of energy" contained within our name.[1] According to
Jung, this energy phenomenon requires a tension of opposites because
everything exists with its opposite and the greater the tensions between
those opposites, the greater the energies we can extract from them.[2] From
his observation, Jung helps us to play with the inherent power of our
name and instructs us to conceive of our name's power in two, diametrical opposed scenarios. First, maximized "recognized visibility" will most
likely generate positive feelings of accomplishments associated with our
name as we revel in being as lauded as some of the greatest historical
figures, like Carl Jung himself. Second, minimized "recognized visibility"
will most likely generate negative feelings of despair and anxiety as we
associate our name with complete failure, like being buried in a pauper's
unmarked grave. Whether history embraces our existence or completely
eradicates it, our name and the feelings it conjures within our *Self* and
within others represents the *only* constant in both scenarios. Therefore,
we must think about where does the power of our name originate and
can we encounter our *Inner Messiah* at the source of its power?

---

1. See, e.g., Huskinson, *Dreaming the Myth Onwards*, 26, noting that Jung believed
everything is a phenomenon of energy in 1917.

2. Ibid.

REVISITING ANCIENT MAGIC IN WORDS

The power of our name and encountering that power via our *Inner Messiah* can be considered an exercise in active imagination, a Jungian construct, which permits us to confront hidden emotions and images and to collaborate with God, the Divine Creator, in the development of our *personal narrative*.[3] The formless image of our *Inner Messiah* will empower and improve the creation of our *personal narrative* as we converge various forms of consciousness present within the *Self* with our subconscious desire to understand the inner instability of the Creator within all *creation*.[4]

The *INM* also preserves our inner holiness from any impure influences caused by any instability and any tensions regarding narrative divergence. Our name stabilizes us with regard to such Divine instability because our name places us within particular *loci* of all creation and allows us to move about that space with an identifiable *Self*, especially between our successes and failures, our hopes and fears and all other energy-generating opposites. For example, famous fraudsters, like Bernie Madoff, had a name that facilitated easy access to money within well-defined, wealthy, and influential circles until their names became infamously associated with thieving and fraud. Just as in the case with our name in overall creation, the reputational shift associated with such fraudsters' names, both allowing and barring access to particular sects of society and culture, demonstrates the limitations about "recognized visibility" based on a particular success or failure in any mundane undertaking. As with Madoff, his name alone retains its power to connote either his success or his failure and the access inherent within those two diametrically, opposite reputations, i.e., he literally "made-off" with others' money. This example teaches us that we must be always mindful of the inherent power of our name, even above and beyond its ability to communicate our successes and failures, as we seek to encounter our *Inner Messiah*.

We need to encounter the hidden power of our name that derives its power directly from its Creator.[5] This power can be classified as a sublime certainty about all aspects of our *Self*, extending from the depths of our soul all the way to creation's outer boundaries. We can utter this aspect of

3. See, e.g., Schlamm, "Active Imagination," 109–11.

4. See, e.g., ibid., 116, quoting from Jung's *Answer to Job* that creation's interaction with its Creator changes the Creator.

5. See, e.g., Rosenfels, *Homosexuality*, 10, discussing the improvement of *Self* hinges on the capacity for inner growth and development beyond human success or failure.

our name and know we own that identifying word and that identifying word owns us without any uncertainty. Such complete liberation from uncertainty enables us to encounter our *Inner Messiah* as we recognize what we need to effectuate that encounter and to extract the benefits from complete emancipation from all uncertainties.[6] So, as we uncover that hidden aspect of our name, we will come to understand its ability to emancipate us from uncertainty through its direct reconnection to the Divine Oneness at the beginning of our *Sacred Textual Narrative* before becoming bound within the *INM*. Remember, that hidden aspect of our name reveals to us the name the Divine calls to us no matter what we do to modify our "recognized visibility." Most spiritual scholars concur that our spiritual pursuits require an inner confidence in God's love and power over us to ensure we personally receive his care and concern.[7] Hence, we can think about our hidden name, i.e., *Inner Messiah*, being a trigger for accessing that inner confidence since God, our Creator, alone calls us by that name.

Sigmund Freud eloquently reminds us about the power of words, such as names, and how some scholarly investigations into the ancient world deals with the nexus between linguistic powers and magical customs.[8] For example, Freud classifies the Ancient Egyptian language as a unique relic that contains numerous words with two opposite meanings[9] and with two reversible pronunciations.[10] These opposite tensions, as suggested by Jung, imbued the Ancient Egyptian language with powerful magical properties that were revered throughout the ancient world. Ancient Egyptian theology/mythology illustrates the power of words and names. Ancient Egyptians believed Isis, the goddess, tricked Ra, the supreme god, to tell her his "hidden" name through inflicting a painful snakebite and only relieving him from the pain after he disclosed his "hidden" name.[11] Once Isis obtained Ra's "hidden" name, she become the most powerful magician in all history, including the power to resurrect her deceased husband, Osiris.[12] Within Ancient Egyptian theological

6. Romme and Escher, *Accepting Voices*, 56, defining personal growth has a process of emancipation from uncertainty.

7. See, e.g., Drobin, "Spirituality, the New Opiate," 236.

8. See, generally, Freud and Strachey, *Introductory Lectures on Psychoanalysis*, 20.

9. See, e.g., Freud, "Antithetical Meaning of Primal Words," 45.

10. Ibid., 49.

11. See, e.g., Assmann, "Magic and Theology in Ancient Egypt," 5–7.

12. Ibid.

practices and beliefs, such holy names were needed to add potency and efficacy to spells and their magical properties.[13] Both the hidden name and its correct pronunciation were critical to unleash the full power of Ancient Egyptian magic.[14]

Magic, expressed in words and names, explained how the Ancient Egyptian gods exercised their power within that *Sacred Textual Narrative*. That said, magical power throughout the ancient world appears to have operated as an important narrative construct that allowed its users to access their full capabilities, whether real or imaginary.[15] For the purposes of this chapter, we must think about how the identification of the hidden aspect of our name can operate as a sort of magical construct within our own *personal narrative*. When we stumble upon the hidden aspect of our name, we will have complete access to all our capabilities to achieve the fullness of our potential due to its connectedness with the power of the original Divine Oneness.

The inherent power of words becomes even more amplified when the word assumes an identifying function for our *Self* and mobilizes all aspects of the *Self* in response to its utterance. Words, according to Freud, have retained much of their magical power since words have retained their ability to empower their speaker with various dominions over their listeners/recipients.[16] Among the magical properties of words, Freud enumerates the following properties:

> By *words*, one person can make another blissfully happy or drive that same person to total despair, by *words* teachers convey their knowledge to their pupils, by *words* the orator carries his audience with him and determines their judgments and decisions. *Words* provoke effects and provide a means of mutual influence among humanity.[17]

Freud's eloquent enumeration should help us appreciate the "magical power" of words to shift our emotions, as well as our perceptions of reality, between polarized extremes. Basically, words retain their property

13. See, e.g., Budge, *Egyptian Magic*, 57.

14. Ibid., 128, describing the myth of Thoth, scribe of the gods, who made Osiris king of the underworld through teaching Osiris words and pronunciations to unleash magic's power.

15. See, e.g., Schafer, "Magic and Religion in Ancient Judaism," 21.

16. Freud and Strachey, *Introductory Lectures on Psychoanalysis*, 20.

17. Ibid., emphasis added.

to induce a metaphysical mood swing that could position our feelings downward to the depths of despair and/or elevate them upward to the heights of ecstasy. Our name, like any word, helps us to convey information about our *Self*, especially the anticipated reaction to our name being spoken and heard.[18] For example, when we hear and/or read about a celebrity's name or an important historical figure, we generally have some preconceived notions about that name. These notions could be based on a plethora of factors, such as tabloid exploits, former media projects, political affiliations, culture contributions or personal prejudices.

Whatever the source for the casual link between a name (celebrity or otherwise) and our perception of the name, we will most likely always taint new facts and circumstances we learn about that name with our own preconditioned perceptions.[19] So, as we think about the names that dominate our popular culture, like Kardashian, Madonna, Clooney, Obama et al., we must reflect upon the images they invoke and how our current name evokes similar/dissimilar images in others and ourselves.

Before we continue with our esoteric discourse about the magical power within our hidden name, we should pause and check in with our breath. Are we still breathing and thinking about the remnants of God's *ruach* within all creation? Do we still remember the importance of narrative convergence, especially between our *personal narrative* and the *Sacred Textual Narrative*, to access the full power of creation? Well, now might be a good time in our literary journey together to recall both notions before we delve into another mystical exercise to encounter our *Inner Messiah*. Breathing aside, we should converge our thoughts on the *Sacred Textual Narrative* regarding the diametric opposites present within the messianic message, such as the imagery of valleys being lifted up, mountains being made low and uneven ground made even.[20] This imagery provides an important hallmark for our encounter with our *Inner Messiah* as we think about what name may be hidden within our name

18. Ibid, 19, noting Freud's observations about how medical training conditions a doctor's expectations between an applied stimulus and its induced reaction and language within a clinical environment may not always comport with conventional medical training.

19. See, e.g., ibid., discussing Freud's analogy about how people feel convinced of new facts based on their own perceptions as museum visitors discern new facts from exhibited objects based on their preconditioned perceptions.

20. Isa. 40:4.

that can help us to adopt a similar type of topsy-turvy spiritual perspective for our ordinary reality.

As we approach this conundrum, we must remember that any messianic figure identified (foretold or fulfilled or whatever) within our *Sacred Textual Narrative* will embody a "newness" that all humanity has never before witnessed. If we visualize the encounter between the Divine, God, and the Israelites in Deuteronomy,[21] we can appreciate Moses' description about God's particular interaction with humanity at that time. Beyond its explicit "newness," Moses reminds us about the sheer awesomeness and danger of this interaction, i.e., "no people have ever heard the voice of God speaking from fire and lived."[22] Whatever the novelty of this encounter, we should truly avoid the interjection of our prejudices and expectations from influencing our encounter with our *Inner Messiah* and its potential consequences.

Freud himself utilizes the *Sacred Textual Narrative* to interpret certain aspects of the messianic message, especially how to interpret its antithetical descriptions in light of the vast power contained within the messianic promise. For example, Freud identified with Joseph from Genesis as an interpreter of dreams and also has a warrior figure to proclaim the messiah.[23] Recalling how Joseph interpreted Pharaoh's dream and acquired a powerful position in Egypt,[24] we can appreciate why Freud would utilize this *Sacred Textual Narrative* to emphasize aspects of the messianic message with regard to Ancient Egypt and its magical customs. Like Freud identified regarding the antithetical meanings and pronunciations of Ancient Egyptian words, he stressed how dream interpreters of antiquity, like Joseph, made extensive use of the supposition that anything in a dream may mean its opposition.[25] Most importantly, Freud informs us that dreams, regardless of their interpretation, have a "special tendency" to reduce two opposite elements to a single unity and to represent two opposite elements as the same element.[26] Freud's proposition regarding both dreams and their abilities to converge two opposite

---

21. Deut 4:33–34.
22. Deut 4:33.
23. Bakan, *Sigmund Freud*, 173.
24. See, generally, Gen 41.
25. Bakan, *Sigmund Freud*, 44.
26. Ibid.

meanings is crucial to discover the hidden aspect of our name and its impact on our encounter with our *Inner Messiah*.

Let us commence another exercise with our "literate" imaginations as we seek an encounter with our *Inner Messiah*. The "literate" adjective describes our imaginations since we have *just* learned about the magical power of words and the interpretation of dreams, their ancient origins, their relevance in Freudian and Jungian analysis and their assigned function to uncover our hidden name. Moreover, our hidden name, or some other unrevealed aspect of our name, is the name by which God, our Divine Creator, calls us. Some of us may recall moments when we were sitting in silence, watching a football game or walking down the street when we heard someone shout out a name. Since we did not identify the name as something someone would call us, we ignored it and kept going about our business. Perhaps, God, our Divine Creator, has been calling to us throughout our lifetime but we have never heard the call because we did not recognize the name by which God has been calling to us. Regardless of how outrageous and imaginative this scenario may sound to some of us, we can all appreciate its most simple thought—the absence of evidence is not the evidence of absence! If any of us question the presence of God, the Divine Creator, in our lives, we must ensure that we have absolutely ruled out all possible sources of an encounter, especially our own misidentification of the *Self* and the name attached thereto.

Taking inventory of the components and tools we have at our disposable, we may accept, even only grudgingly, that we have our name and God has a name for us, even if those two names are completely opposite and share no coincidental meaning. The power of our name, like any word, requires us to articulate our name and to appreciate our name's meaning, to us and to others. Let us speak our name aloud at this point. Say it over and over and over again like a mantra until we understand what feelings it stirs, what images it creates and what mysteries it contains. Repeat this exercise how often as needed to glean as much information about our name as possible. Do not worry about abandoning this book for a while until we have gathered up all the necessary information to maximize the benefits from the final part of our literary journey together. Once we feel that our name has spoken all its secrets to us and we have a modified sense of *Self* as we hear our name, *only then* let us continue with this chapter.

Now, with this expanded meaning of our name, we must continue our exercise to empower our name with the capacity to encounter our

Inner Messiah and to deal with the ramifications of that encounter. While most of us still retain our same pre- and post-exercise name, we now have begun to understand how that name identifies us within our daily realities and, for some of us, within all creation.

To ensure we grasp the magnitude of this discovery, we will utilize Freud's observation about dreams having the capacity to unify two opposites. In that vein, let us allow ourselves to dream about our names possessing two very extreme, opposite hidden meanings. The first meaning should correlate with any mention of our name being associated with complete failure and feelings associated with being considered "less than nothing." The second meaning should correlate with the complete opposite of the first so that when we speak or hear our name, we associate it with the highest success and feelings associated with being considered even "more powerful than God." As we imagine and embrace both extremes, we can thank Freud for encouraging us to dream about both impossibilities to settle upon a suitable possibility!

Whatever meanings we have attached to our name in both scenarios, we should appreciate their impact and contribution to acquaint ourselves with the potential of our name outside its usual boundaries. Did some of us learn something about our name that we never knew as we enhanced its meaning? Do we appreciate the inherent power within our name from helping us avoid a "less than nothing" existence? Have any of us discovered that hidden name within our name that brings us closer to God or our Divine Creator? What did feeling more powerful than God actually feel like outside our dreams? Were there any striking similarities between the two extreme conceptions of our name that made us question the boundaries of the extremes? Regardless of the overall outcome, we hopefully will understand something new about our name that will help us encounter our *Inner Messiah*.

Our previous discussion about our name, hidden name, its uncovered meaning and its magical power will help create a mystical dimension to our *personal narrative* and, in turn, empower and improve our attitude and perception about our past, current, and future placement within the *Grand Historical Narrative*. An encounter with our *Inner Messiah* will utilize this mystical dimension, distilled through the *Sacred Textual Narrative*, to transform how we process, utilize, exploit and even recognize the "recognized visibility" of our own name. Without finding the name by which God, Divine Creator, calls us, we will have never mastered our full capabilities to appreciate how our name *alone* connects us with something much bigger than just ourselves.

Let us think about what has kept us form accessing the power within our hidden name and how we can utilize a mystical dimension in our *personal narrative* to access the power before the encounter with our *Inner Messiah* and its transformative consequences.

JEWISH MYSTICAL LITERATURE: CHICKEN SOUP FOR THE IMAGINATION

As we prepare for that transformative encounter with our *Inner Messiah*, we must think about our perspectival assumptions regarding our messianic expectations. In particular, we should evaluate what aspects of those expectations converge with our *Sacred Textual Narrative*, how those expectations inspire our imaginations to overcome adversity, and why those expectations enable us to encounter the Divine. While many of us have some exposure to Jewish messianic thought as presented in the Judeo-Christian context, we may find messianism a messy intellectual pursuit due to the term's loaded history, especially Jewish historical tragedies. That said, we will look to a piece of early Jewish mystical literature, composed sometime between 200 CE and 600 CE (i.e., the "Talmudic Period"),[27] known as the *Hekhalot Zutarti*. This mystical story nurtures our imagination with four gifted rabbis and esteemed Torah scholars who entered a mysterious garden, the *Pardes*, and attempted to ascend and to descend successfully to Heaven to behold God sitting on his throne.[28] Although four rabbis entered the *Pardes*, only one, Rabbi Akiva, was able to ascend and to descend successfully and tell us of his experience about accessing the direct presence of God at his holy throne in heaven. The *Hekhalot Zutarti* contains this heavenly ascent account along with Rabbi Akiva's detailed instructions about the entire process. Contemporary clinical scholars have opined that *Hekhalot literature* portrays the enemy of humanity's attempt to access the Divine as "perplexity" that creates destructive symptomatic tendencies, as with the three unsuccessful rabbis, that preempt our divine encounter.[29]

27. See, e.g., Boustan, *From Martyr to Mystic*, 4, noting Gershom Scholem's dating of this literature in the Talmudic period between 200 CE and 600 CE.

28. Ibid., 95.

29. See, e.g., Bakan et al., *Maimonides' Cure of Souls*, 95.

Furthermore, some of us avoid dealing with resolving such perplexity with our defeatist tendencies to destroy not only our access to the Divine, but the Divine within us through allowing such needless perplexities to develop, to embrace, and to reify our imaginations.[30] Eventually, our *INM* becomes so thickened with this perplexity that some of us may become permanently isolated from the possibility of breaking through our *INM* and reconnecting with the Divine Oneness. For example, we exploit the more comforting nature of this perplexity as we can imagine our unfulfilled intentions as *directly* resulting from this perplexity. Rather, we may want to consider identifying less perplex causes associated with our inabilities, sufferings, and disappointments as some of us justify them with the *Grand Historical Narrative* and/or the *Sacred Textual Narrative*.[31] Stories from the *Sacred Textual Narrative*, for example, provide an outlet for our feelings and emotions to channel pain and suffering into a timeless heroic figure that we believe can feel our pain and relate to the entirety of our human condition, along with our needs and desires about escaping from *all* our temporal discomforts.

On the other hand, the *Sacred Textual Narrative* empowers our ability to describe our feelings and emotions, even if we have to do strenuous work to align our *personal narratives* with the *Sacred Textual Narrative*. This alignment should help us to understand how God may be working through our pain and suffering to not only empower and improve our lives through the disappointments in our *personal narrative*, but empower and improve all humanity through exploring ways to bring complete narrative convergence between our *personal narrative* and the *Grand Historical Narrative* through the *Sacred Textual Narrative*. The commonality of feelings associated with pain, destruction, suffering, disappointment, and all forms of temporal injustice demonstrates the possibility and importance of narrative convergence to return to our common origin—Divine Oneness. So, regardless of the intellectual density of the foregoing, we can understand the importance of avoiding theological prejudices in conceptualizing our relationship with God, Divine Creator, especially where biblical stories imprint our imaginations with particular mental images or sentient expectations about that relationship.

Let us imagine our name superimposed above, below, within, and through the name we call the Divine and the Divine presence in our

---

30. Ibid., noting errors in reifying imagination as aberrant sexuality.

31. Ibid., 160.

life. Does this superimposition create any tangible changes with our name? Or, does this superimposition modify our name's meaning or significance within our *personal narrative*? Whatever we determine, we can understand that the importance of our imagination in this exercise. After all, the connection between our imagination and our *personal narrative* is our hidden name and the power we imagine associated with that name. Through our imagination, our hidden name imbues our *personal narrative* with a dynamic flexibility that permits greater interaction with the *Grand Historical Narrative*. We can embrace this name with its own magical properties to mutually convey information between both narratives and the *Sacred Textual Narrative* to help us encounter our *Inner Messiah*, i.e., the transformative power of our hidden name, within our imaginations.

Applying these messianic themes, we will turn to Jewish mystical literature to inspire our imagination about the Divine and to demonstrate that our survival, as both an individual and as within a collective culture, depends on our ability to encounter our *Inner Messiah*, to speak its name aloud, and to hear and respond to its mention. Even in our most despair-filled moments, such as our perceived inability to uncover our hidden name and to encounter our *Inner Mesisah*, Jewish mysticism will foster our imagination to dream new ways to interact with and to encounter the Divine through the power of the "name" (*shem* [שֵׁם]).

The *Hekhalot Zutarti* ("Hz") will provide the blueprint for our imagination to dream about the power of our hidden name and its relationship to the Divine.[32] More specifically, we will dream up the fundamental elements of our hidden name, reinforce them with our imagination, and test them against our everyday realities. This process will enable us to discover more Jungian synchronicities between our dreams and our realities.[33] In exploring our imagination in this way, we will eventually reveal many aspects of our hidden name, our *Inner Messiah*, that generate a profound, immutable sense of peace and completeness. With this in mind, let us create a *pardes* (a metaphoric garden of Eden) in our imagination that we will *figuratively* enter in peace and leave in peace with the wisdom from encountering our *Inner Messiah*.

32. See Rowland and Morray-Jones, *Mystery of God.*

33. See, e.g., Begg, *Synchronicity*, 77, noting how our dream mind has access to a higher and different order of intelligence to identify synchronicities between dream and reality.

Building upon the words within our *personal narrative* and their witness to our dreams, hopes, frustrations, weaknesses, and strengths in our current ordinary reality to date, the Hz encourages us to create a "visionary reality" in which we will experience an immediate, almost instantaneous connection with the Divine presence.[34] We will focus on the practical objectives of the Hz as a mystical writing that was used to help the Jewish people to remain connected with the Divine presence in light of the Second Temple's destruction, its impact on destroying sacred ritual, and its displacement of all centralized, religious authority.[35] In particular, we will consider the success of one of the four rabbis to ascend to and to descend from God's Holy Throne, the Divine presence, as nourishment for our imagination to empower and to improve the elements of our *personal narrative*. Basically, Rabbi Akiva, the only successful rabbi, will demonstrate the importance of converging our *personal narrative* with the *Sacred Textual Narrative* to uncover our hidden name and understand its miraculous (and magical) power.

Regardless of the variation in our ultimate destinations, we *all* have undertaken this literary journey together for the common objective to change our ordinary reality for the better. The success or failure of this journey will depend on *not only* what we learned from reading through these pages, *but* how the words on these pages inspired our imaginations

---

34. See, e.g., Kraemer, "Mishnah," 299–300, arguing that the Jewish rabbinic texts, such as the Mishnah, constitute a vision of an ideal world—a messianic world, in which both the Temple and Jewish polity coexist in accordance with *common Biblical source*. See also Harris, "Midrash Halachah," 364–65, discussing the importance of creativity in rabbinic enterprise of studying the *common Biblical source*.

35. The Hz builds upon rabbinic literary techniques to unify Jews and to form a common community through addressing three major voids created by the Temple's destruction: (i) the holiness of Jerusalem temple; (ii) the legitimacy of its priesthood; and (iii) the proprietary of its rituals (the "Major Voids"). See Cohen, *Significance of Yavneh*, 45. These Major Voids warranted an effective response to resolve the "incompleteness of God" as the Jewish faith, people, and state suffered immeasurably after the Second Temple's destruction. Ibid. These Major Voids warranted an effective response to resolve the "incompleteness of God" as the Jewish faith, people, and state suffered immeasurably after the Second Temple's destruction. See, e.g., ibid, 27–28. For example, chief among effects about the destruction of the Second Temple in 70 CE were: the cessation of the sacrificial cult, the loss of the sacred center of the cosmos, the destruction of the physical symbols of God's protective presence, the public display of the power of Rome and her gods and of the impotence of Israel and her God, and the failure of apocalyptic dreams and prophecies, the economic difficulties caused by the massacre or enslavement of enormous numbers of people and the loss of the central institutions of the state. Ibid.

to perceive beyond the limitations and boundaries of our ordinary existence. Because the Hz represents the ultimate arrangement of words and the power they contain, especially "names," the Hz will help us illustrate how we can encounter our *Inner Messiah* through our name.

Sounding like the beginning of a bad joke, the Hz describes how four rabbis enter a garden, the *pardes*, and only one goes in and out in peace, while the others go in and come out in pieces! The four rabbis are Akiva, Ben Zoma, Ben Azzai and Aher, all of whom undertook a perilous journey to the heavenly realms to behold God and God's glory. Akiva's success and the others' failure turn on their knowledge of the *Sacred Textual Narrative* and God's hidden names to gain access to God's presence. Certainly, these elements can excite our imaginations to conceive various scenarios within our *personal narratives* about how the proper names attached to our goals and ambitions can facilitate their achievement. Yet, before we indulge our creative capacity with such musings, we should consider what the Hz could help us understand about the name associated with the source of our goals and ambitions, that is, our name as it exists at the formulation of goals and as it exists at the achievement of them. Unlike the other three rabbis, Akiva had attained the ultimate "recognized visibility" of his name through converging his *personal narrative* with the *Sacred Textual Narrative* to the point that God, Divine Creator, called Akiva directly into his holy presence.[36] Would we know if God, the Divine Creator, called us into this presence? Especially, what name God would use to call us? Perchance, Akiva's ability to maintain his peace upon entering and departing God's presence demonstrates something unique not only to Akvia's mastery of God's hidden names, but to Akiva's knowledge of his hidden name and its connection to God's hidden names. The fate of the other three unsuccessful rabbis will confirm our proposition as we revisit the Hz as an extended mystical portion of our *Sacred Textual Narrative*.

---

36. The Hz references the *common Biblical source* at Song of Songs 1:4 to describe how God called forth to Akiva and brought Akiva into his chambers, i.e., the heavenly halls of his dwelling place. See Hz, §345e. God's explicit invitation—"The holy one, blessed be he, said to the [Angels of Destruction who dwell at the heavenly height], 'Leave this elder [Akiva] alone, for he is worth to behold my glory.'" Ibid., §346b.

Lack of Physical Stamina (Ben Azzai)

Ben Azzai did not have the physical capacity to avoid the fatal distractions of the heavenly halls in his quest to behold God and God's glory. Unlike Akiva who kept his focus on God's presence through concentrating on God's name, Ben Azzai was seduced by the "brilliance of the air of the marble stones" within the heavenly halls to ask about their brilliance.[37] His inquiry precipitated his death because, as he gazed upon the stones, Ben Azzai's *body could not bear* their brilliance.[38] Ben Azzai's mystical demise teaches us that we can become distracted beyond our physical capabilities as we seek God and God's presence. For our purposes, Ben Azzai appears to have sought knowledge about the brilliance of the stones, rather than to have discovered his own hidden name (i.e., the name God called him).

In his attempt to acquire this knowledge, Ben Azzai further teaches us that when we seek an answer from God about God's mysterious ways, we, like Ben Azzai, may receive an answer with unexpected consequences. As a result, we may want to ask God more relevant questions about God's mysterious ways that have a direct impact on us, such as what is God's unique name for us by which God alone calls us, i.e., our hidden name. More importantly, our quest to encounter the Divine or any aspect of the Divine, especially our *Inner Messiah*, requires us to apply our physical strength to discover the Divine's mystery working with us, sort of making us as brilliant as the stones in God's heavenly halls, which can be *better* understood through our hidden name.

Imaginative Interpretation. Can magical stones that contain mysteries about the Divine actually strain our physical body to the point of death as we attempt to uncover our hidden name and its meaning for our life? Actually, yes! Let us apply this mystical lesson to a modern day scenario in our search to uncover our hidden name through searching for its meaning within the distractions of physical appearances, especially our own appearance, with dire consequences.

The author of *The First Wives*, Olivia Goldsmith, had much success with her book and its movie adaption. Despite the "recognized visibility" associated with her name, Olivia still sort her hidden name through her physical appearance. In other words, the pursuit of her physical appearance distracted her from uncovering her hidden name and its power to

37. Ibid., §345b.
38. Ibid.

attain a sense of completeness beyond the "recognized visibility" associated with her literary achievement contained within the *Grand Historical Narrative*. Tragically, Olivia died from complications during plastic surgery—the removal of loose skin from under her chin.[39]

Ben Azzai's story, while more magical and mystical, shares a similar fate with the peril of the pursuit of the aesthetic at the detriment of encountering the Divine. Basically, Olivia teaches us that had she encountered her hidden name, she might have been focused on the Divine and had a sense of completeness that transcended her physical appearance and other temporal considerations foisted upon humanity by the *Grand Historical Narrative*. Many of us have become distracted throughout our life as we search for the real, uncovered meaning behind our name, just like Olivia. Instead of losing our life, we might have lost something just as precious—the sense to live out the full meaning of our name in our personal and professional existences. Hopefully, this chapter will help us encounter our hidden name and its ability to help us to redirect our attention beyond the *Sacred Textual Narrative* that will help us to discover our hidden name, its connection to the Divine and its potential contributions to our life.

Lack of Mental Stamina (Ben Zoma)

Similarly, Ben Zoma did not have the mental capacity to avoid the fatal distractions of the heavenly halls in his quest to behold God and God's glory. Like Ben Azzai, Ben Zoma had a similar reaction to the brilliance of the stones in God's sixth palace—Ben Zoma's body *could bear it, but his mind could not*, and he was "smitten."[40] Ben Zoma's demise warns us that we can become distracted beyond our mental capabilities, despite our physical strength, as we seek God and God's presence. For our purposes, Ben Zoma appears to have overloaded his intellectual capacity with extraneous knowledge about the brilliance of the stones, rather than any knowledge about his hidden name (i.e., the name God called him).

In his attempt to acquire this knowledge, Ben Zoma teaches us that when we believe our ego and intellect can engage God in a meaningful

39. See, e.g., Kornblum, "There's a Risk to the Beauty of Surgery."

40. Ibid., §345c. In this case, Ben Zoma goes crazy in beholding the brilliance of the stones of God's sixth palace. Scripture refers to Ben Zoma through Prov 26:16 as "Have you found honey? Eat what is enough for you..." Ibid.

exchange of knowledge about God's mysterious ways, we, like Ben Zoma, may become victims of our own overestimated sense of *Self*, especially our physical prowess. Hence, we may want to think about our intellectual limitations before we formulate any questions about God and God's mysterious workings that do not have a direct impact on us. Once again, Ben Zoma could be used to teach us about the importance of knowing our hidden name as a precursor before we encounter the Divine or any aspect of the Divine, especially our *Inner Messiah*.

Imaginative Interpretation. Can any of us retain and process information about the secrets of creation without suffering a similar fate as Ben Zoma? Doubtful, especially when we think about how difficult it is for us to retain knowledge contained within our *personal narrative* and to apply that knowledge to create our own lives. Let us think about an overachieving college graduate named Joshua, a great Hebrew name with messianic meaning—savior. Joshua knew or had to reason to know about the Hebrew meaning of his name since he studied at Hebrew school, but even with knowledge about his name's Hebrew meaning, he could not save himself with knowledge of that meaning alone. Rather than look for his hidden name for his *personal narrative*, Joshua surrendered his fate and allowed his family to distract him from that quest. He submitted to his parents desire and pursued a legal career, even though Joshua became addicted to Adderall in law school. He functioned as a top student feigning his ADHD for prescription after prescription. Eventually, his achievement in legal scholarship could not offset the wear-and-tear upon his mind and Johsua fell into a deep depression. Additional psychopharmacological medications were needed to treat his condition.

Today, Joshua is a successful attorney based on his legal practice and his family approval. Yet, Joshua replaced the search for his hidden name with the fulfillment of his family's ambition and his professional achievement. While his name may conclude with an "Esq.," his name's conclusion does not compensate for his lack of knowledge about his hidden, real name that could have helped him avoid mental distress, along with the pain and suffering associated with his legal career. Though he honored his parents through submitting to their career wishes for him, Joshua's legal knowledge to create a professional career did not leave sufficient space within his mental capacity to seek ways to uncover his hidden name through the *Sacred Textual Narrative* since his alleged ADHD confined him to the success standards promulgated by the *Grand Historical Narrative* with neither interest nor mental capacity to seek the Divine, his hidden name and their relationship to his personal and professional life.

Lack of Correct Perception (Aher)

Unlike the previous two rabbis, Aher beheld a false image due to his great rush to see God and God's glory through "cutting the shoots"[41] and, in turn, became an arch-heretic.[42] Most scholars would interpret "cutting the shoots" in light of other Jewish mystical literary traditions as Aher's impatience to behold God that caused him to incorrectly identify an angel as God and to suffer the consequences of that error—Aher's exclusion from the world to come, i.e., eternal damnation or some variation thereof.[43] His failure to extract knowledge about either God's hidden name or his own name from his *Sacred Textual Narrative* made him very disruptive whenever he visited places of worship or Biblical study houses to ensure no others would obtain the knowledge that he could not possess.[44] For our purposes, Aher appears to have gazed upon something that made him believe it was God, the Divine presence, and his acceptance of that presence without properly questioning its Divine authenticity caused him to forfeit his access to the world to come, i.e., his salvation. That forfeiture can be used to confirm his lack of ability and/or interest in "earnestly" seeking the Divine presence since he attempted to take a shortcut to see God and to elevate what he beheld to God's status. More interestingly, once Aher knew that he was denied access to the "world to come," he decided to extract all the potential pleasure from the *Grand Historical Narrative* without regard to its moral consequence (due to his lack of morality and anticipated eternal damnation).

With his inability to correctly discern God, the Divine presence, Aher teaches us that when we search for a shortcut to our intended goal, we will lack the preparation to achieve our goal and to avoid being deceived by our desire. In addition, our deception will have far-reaching consequences as we attempt to spread the results of our deception to

---

41. Ibid., §345d, referring to Aher as Elisha b. Avuya.

42. Schäfer, *Origins of Jewish Mysticism*, 189.

43. Ibid., discussing Aher in the context of other Talmudic and mystical literary sources.

44. See ibid., at §345d, describing how Aher would speak over children succeeding at Torah study and creating disruptions in synagogues.

prevent others from extracting any important lessons from the *Sacred Textual Narrative* and to impede in their search for their own hidden name. Like with the two previous rabbis, Aher further confirms that we must spend the time and effort to discover our hidden name, as well as God's secret name, to ensure we can avoid deception in our desires and their fulfillment. Had Aher knew his hidden name and God's secret name, he could have heard God calling to him, as well as Aher being able to call to God to avoid his banishment from salvation through his *personal narrative's* complete convergence with the *Grand Historical Narrative* through complete and correct knowledge from this *Sacred Textual Narrative*.

Imaginative Interpretation. Have any of us ever attempted to find and to exploit a shortcut to attain our personal and professional ambitions? Did those ambitions represent a convergence with any aspect of the *Sacred Textual Narrative* or the *Grand Historical Narrative*? Can we appreciate the consequences of not discovering our hidden name, just a deceived, false representation of our hidden name and its relationship to God's secret name (or our concept of God's hidden name)? A contemporary story about that pitfalls of deception associated with our desires and willingness to take shortcuts is Marc Dreier, another lawyer, who graduated Harvard Law School, built a successful legal career and law firm, Dreier, LLP, and enjoyed life's finest pleasures and professional accolades.[45] Despite all the affirmation of his success, Dreier's success and his desire for more success deceived him into taking a shortcut with far-reaching consequences for his professional status, his freedom, and his family. He undertook a four-year Ponzi scheme and stole approximately $380 million from thirteen hedge funds through drafting false financial instruments on a former client's stationary and impersonating various investment officers to hedge fund managers.[46] The outrageousness of his behavior can be best understood through watching the documentary movie, *Unraveled*, in which Dreier brazenly stares into the camera and recites over-and-over again, "Don't judge me, you don't know what you would do if you had a chance to cross that line."

Like Aher, Dreier took a shortcut that had dire consequences for the people whom he encountered. First, his law firm that employed 270 lawyers and provided livelihood for their families (as well as support staff)

---

45. See, e.g., Burrough, "Marc Dreier's Crime of Destiny."
46. Ibid.

instantly disintegrated, erased their sense of professional pride associated with their careers, never mind undoing any significance associated with their personal and familial sacrifices in excoriating long days and weekends to produce their legal work product. Second, Dreier has left his New York City high life behind as he is currently serving a twenty-year prison term for his crimes. Third, and most importantly, his son, Spencer, had to bear the burden of his father's behavior that disrupted his education to the point that he sued his college roommates for defamation and assault.[47] Clearly, Dreier, like Aher, employed his own deception at seeing his "false God," his professional success, to enjoy this world's pleasure to excess without regard to the consequences on himself and others, especially Dreier's abandonment of any efforts to discover his hidden name and its relationship to God. Regardless of the bizarre circumstances of Dreier's crimes, we should all learn that the convergence of our *personal narrative* with the *Grand Historical Narrative* without any elements of the *Sacred Textual Narrative* (or other sacred text) represents a perilous shortcut. Whether grounded in mysticism or reality, such shortcuts appear to unleash a vicious deception in our individual and collective efforts to discover our hidden name and its relationship to the Divine presence.

Complete Convergence with the Sacred Textual Narrative (Rabbi Akiva)

Unlike the three previous rabbis, Rabbi Akiva successfully completed his ascent and descent to heaven and beheld God's Divine presence in peace.[48] His success could be attributed to his many deeds,[49] his knowledge of sacred scripture,[50] and his ability to apply them to find a path to God, the Divine presence.[51] As portrayed within the Hz, Akiva's success can be attributed to his "completeness" that we can conceptualize as the complete merger of Akiva's *personal narrative* with the *Sacred Textual Narrative* to

47. See Grannis, "Marc Dreier's Son."

48. See Hz, §345e, stating that Rabbi Akiva went "in (up) in peace and came out (down) in peace."

49. Ibid., §344d.

50. See, e.g., ibid., §336e, stressing the importance of the heart retaining all its heard and learnt from "scripture, mishna, talmud, halakhot, and aggadot."

51. See, e.g., ibid., §346b, noting how Rabbi Akiva made more signs on the entrances of the *rakia*, i.e., entrances to God's heavenly halls, than his own house to mark his path to God's presence.

provide him with "divine revelations" to transcend the *Grand Historical Narrative* to gain direct access to God and the Divine presence.[52] The intricacies[53] and perils[54] of this process aside, Rabbi Akiva instructs us that the hidden names of God should be invoked "in awe, in fear, in purity, in holiness, and in humility"[55] so as to receive benefits from their proper invocation, such as increased posterity and prosperity.[56] Clearly, Rabbi Akiva's miraculous journey to God's presence and its inspirational legacy for future generations confirm Akiva's heroic status as his *personal narrative* merged with the *Grand Historical narrative* through their convergence with the *Sacred Textual Narrative*. More importantly, this sense of completeness allowed Akiva to uncover not only God's secret names, but to discover his own hidden name and its relationship to the Divine as evidenced by God calling Akiva into the Divine presence.[57] With this knowledge, Rabbi Akiva had attained and maintained his "peace" regardless of where he traveled, the perils he faced, and all the trials and tribulations through his *personal narrative*.[58]

Imaginative Lessons. Have any of us received a miracle or experienced some act of "Divine Intervention"? Do some of us know people who attribute their fate to God's intervention in their lives? Or, do we just treat such occurrences as Jungian synchronicities that we can affect, directly or indirectly, through our own mental and physical efforts? Our own personal religious and spiritual beliefs will greatly influence that answer. If we google the word *miracle*, we will see over thirty-eight million references with some amazing stories of survival against the odds. Those thirty-eight million references represent a plethora of faith traditions and religious customs that have embraced the term *miracle* to describe an event as an act of "Divine Intervention." Perhaps, some of us even might qualify reading to this point in the book as a miracle since so many things

---

52. See, e.g., ibid., §335a.

53. See, e.g., ibid., §424b, enumerating the requisite purification rituals through fasting, prostrating and speaking instructions.

54. See, e.g., ibid., §424d, noting that the holy names should only be uttered during the day lest one may "make a mistake and destroy the holy one, blessed be he."

55. See, ibid., §373c.

56. Ibid.

57. See ibid., §346b.

58. Finkelstein, *Akiba: Scholar, Saint and Martyr*, 5, commenting about the evidence of Akiva's death as a martyr and his suffering through that process, including his recitation of the *Shema* at his death.

from our personal and professional lives demand our attention and distract us from our allocated leisurely pursuits, like our reading time.

Whatever we feel and however we categorize that circumstance, we may be reluctant to acknowledge some form of "divine intervention" in the outcome. For example, the simple fact that we are holding this particular book and reading this particular page at this moment in time is nothing short of miraculous. Yet, we all never agree on a singular, unified term to describe the phenomenon about why we are reading this book at this time. Even more ironic, we are reading a book about encountering our *Inner Messiah* outside of traditional sacred texts, like the Bible, that contain much more spiritual guidance on messiahs and their potential appearance within our lifetime. We read on, though, rather than pausing our literary journey here to fetch some *Sacred Textual Narrative* materials to expand our knowledge about God's mysteries in less secularized writings. Common sense and rationality, some times, have no place within our *personal narratives* when we are pursuing something that has already been attained, but yet remains invisible to us for any number of reasons, such as our hidden name and the power it contains.

Rabbi Akiva's story in the *pardes* and his encounter with the Divine presence contain many lessons that can help us uncover our hidden name. First, Akiva utilized his knowledge about his hidden name and God's secret names to avoid all distractions, unlike the other three rabbis. This means, we might want to think about events, endeavors, people and circumstances that trigger our situational ADHD and cause us to lose focus and to seek out unproductive (or even destructive) distractions. For example, we may have tremendous pressure at work and become subject to extreme anxiety. Rather than search for our hidden name to determine if we have chosen the right job, we find other distractions to dispel our efforts from finding our hidden name and a job/profession that would facilitate its discovery. So, like Ben Zoma, we may be searching for our hidden name and its connection with the Divine in a professional, or some other similarly situated activity, that strains the mind beyond its mental capacity. Here, Rabbi Akiva teaches us that if we engage in any activity that does not bring us peace, we will never succeed to discover our hidden name, never mind all the mysteries associated with it. As a result, we should carefully monitor our actions and efforts to determine their impact on our peace.

Second, Akiva maintained his physical stamina through merging his *personal narrative* with the *Sacred Textual Narrative* to ensure he possessed the requisite strength to behold God and the Divine presence. Through gaining knowledge of his hidden name and God's secret names, we can assume that Akiva avoided activities that would have diminished his physical strength to behold God and the Divine presence, unlike Ben Azzai. Akiva's physical strength to accomplish this task suggests that when we search for our hidden name to understand its relationship to the Divine, we must preserve our physical strength to avoid fatal distractions. For example, some of us may have given up all hope to ever find happiness and/or contentment in our personal and professional lives. To deal with such disappointment, we may turn to drugs, alcohol, or even high-risk sexual behaviors. While we may not instantly see how those activities deteriorate our strength, we can appreciate their potential damage to the clarity we need to uncover our hidden name and to contemplate its Divine significance.

Third, Akiva possessed a completeness of peace that must have originated from his peace with, about, and in God from the convergence of his *personal narrative* with the *Grand Historical Narrative* through the *Sacred Textual Narrative*. This peace permitted Akiva to exercise extreme control over the use of his hidden name, especially where that name was used interchangeably with the Divine presence. For example, Akiva's successful ascent to heaven could be categorized as Akiva being perceived as belonging to and being apart of God since Akiva passed safely by the heavenly angelic guardians that did not allow the others similar access. Akiva's safe passage should inspire us to share a similar love for both the Divine and the *Sacred Textual Narrative* so that we can employ our hidden name to transform ourselves into some aspect of the Divine. If our hidden name allows us to assume attributes of the Divine presence with the capability to access the heavenly realms, could you imagine what those attributes could achieve for us in overcoming our struggles to stay focused on uncovering it and learning about our original Divine Oneness?

Whether or not we will have the ability and perseverance, like Rabbi Akiva, to merge our *personal narrative* with the *Sacred Textual Narrative*, we should appreciate how our efforts to uncover our hidden name could transform our lives and make the impossible possible in ordinary and extraordinary reality.

OUR SELF AND OUR INNER MESSIAH—THE POTENTIAL ACTUAL ENCOUNTER

Somewhere between our imagination and our faith, we can find the ultimate good that God, the Divine Creator, can offer to his creation—an opportunity to *perceive* God.[59] The notion of *perception* in this context is intentionally ambiguous due to God's vastness and presence throughout all creation. We are participants in that creation and share with God some creative capacities that allow us to shape and to form our realities around our preferences and other circumstances. The development of our *Self* and the "recognized visibility" attached to the *Self* via our name confirm our autonomy in our creative endeavors, including our choice whether or not we accept God, Divine Creator, as part of this process. That said, should we decide to marginalize God and the Divine presence in our existence, then we can safely say that we will not encounter our *Inner Messiah* because our external *Self* has eclipsed any need for that encounter. Instead of our creative endeavors helping us draw close to God, we choose activities that distract us and cause us to satisfy our temporal needs without regard to our spiritual health and welfare.

Our *Inner Messiah* will help us to carve a place in our reality that will help bring us close to God and the Divine presence. In drawing close to God, we will have a profound sense of completeness that will reveal our hidden name and ensure our proximity to God as we experience the Divine Oneness in creation. As our current life affirms, none of us are really using our hidden name if we think about how we feel when certain people call our names. Most likely, our visceral reactions will vary widely based on the person calling our name and the emotions we attached to that speaker. The *Inner Messiah*, our hidden name, saves us from these emotional variations as we exercise ownership in a unified fashion that no longer will vary by circumstances, locations, and situations. In this way, our *Inner Messiah* will help us achieve the ultimate goal of creation since our hidden names will allow us to draw close to God and encounter that Divine Oneness from our very beginning.[60] After all, our hidden name reflects an aspect of God's secret names within our own name so that we too might share in the Divine's power to craft a superlative life without any external distractions to jeopardize our role in creation. Hence, our encounter with our *Inner Messiah* will not only provide us with peace,

59. See, e.g., Kaplan, *Sefer Yetzirah (the Book of Creation)*, 247.
60. Ibid.

but an extraordinary completeness, to stand in any world or dimension, including the heavenly halls, without fear of being distant from God.

The acquisition of our hidden name, sort of like a change in faith or religious custom, requires us to change and to grow in new ways as we search for deeper meaning and purpose for our lives. If we remained with the same birth name throughout our lifetime, then we most likely never grew beyond the limitations of that name. On the other hand, our hidden name does not have any limitations and encourages us to grow closer to God, or the Divine presence, as we overcome the barrier of our *INM* and revisit the relationship between the *personal narrative* and the *Grand Historical Narrative* via an empowered and improved *Sacred Textual Narrative*.

Through the foregoing and our encounter with our *Inner Messiah*, we will appreciate God's promises and their fulfillment with our *Inner Messiah* to remind us what a state of perpetual mindfulness can help us achieve.

FINAL THOUGHTS ABOUT OUR INNER MESSIAH

Whatever we call ourselves or allow others to call to us, we just undertook an extraordinary, imaginative exercise to help us to step outside the ordinary nature of our names and to seek something extraordinary within them. From this journey, we can hopefully recognize the importance to reevaluate the most basic aspect of our *Self*, our name, and how our name connects us to both our *personal narrative* and the *Grand Historical Narrative* through the *Sacred Textual Narrative* (or other sacred text). Once we have uncovered our hidden name within our ordinary name (which could even be our birth name), we will have encountered our *Inner Messiah* to help us overcome our feelings of incompleteness and dissatisfaction with all aspects of our personal and professional lives. This encounter will create a profound sense of completeness within ourselves no matter who calls our name and how we use our name to attract others' attention.

Most importantly, we will have attained a proximity to God (or our conception of the Divine Creator) that will empower our own creative efforts with a new intentionality that will help us amplify the presence of God, Divine Creator, throughout all creation. In the end, we will encounter our *Inner Messiah* in, through, and with our hidden name that allows us to transform our lives, modify our perspectives and invigorate our dreams with a new, unique, and intimate relationship with the Divine as we embrace something we always possessed, but never discovered, until now.

Before reading the next chapter, we should think of the name within our name that would make us encounter our *Inner Messiah* to allow God and the Divine presence to empower and to improve every aspect of our lives as we aspire to generate and to expand the "recognized visibility" of the Divine presence, rather than just our *Self* and its expressions, within all creation.

10

Empowering and Improving Ordinary Existence with Our Inner Messiah

OUR FINAL OBJECTIVE WILL enable us to connect and to interpret our *Divine Character* to empower and improve our *personal narrative*. We have arrived at the final twilight of our literary journey together as this chapter will set forth how we can capitalize on the positive, transformative effects of recognizing our *Inner Messiah* as a reflection of the convergence between our *personal narrative*, *Grand Historical Narrative*, and *Sacred Textual Narrative*. Now, let us take a moment to recollect those moments within our *personal narrative* that we may have felt, or in some way have encountered, a Divine presence. Regardless of our religious beliefs, most of us can reasonably concur that we have had some sort of experience with God, the Creator, whether or not we actually agree on God's ultimate existence and/or its presence in various organized religions. Though, we must adopt a universal notion that can rally our attention and our hope around a unified notion about the Divine, especially our *Inner Messiah*, and its potential impact on our ordinary existence.

To achieve this end, we will sit with our thoughts and these inspirational words to transfix our memories on specific instances within our *personal narrative* that we directly attributed an occurrence, circumstance, or other phenomenon that induced positive feelings, such as when a guilty criminal gets convicted and an innocent convict goes free. We are searching those moments from our past to revisit and to

200

benchmark as representative moments for our own Divine encounters. Most importantly, we can analyze such moments to discern how the story and their emotive effects may have inspired us to change some aspect of our ordinary existence, like pursuing alternate personal or professional stratagems. For example, we all have collected a few books and authors through our educational careers that have had profound influences on our personal and/or professional outlooks. Whether Ayn Rand enthralled or disgusted us by her capitalist sensibilities, F. Scott Fitzgerald encouraged or discouraged our romantic sensibilities, or Ernest Hemmingway inspired or frightened us from our darker creative proclivities, we can all point to an individual author or other creative work with tremendous thematic influence on our own *personal narrative*. For this chapter's objective, it is that particular type of influence we are seeking to capture from our emotions that reflect some aspect of the Divine, as well as borrow some gravitas from the *Sacred Textual Narrative*.

Do we really know what the power of the Divine feels like? Or, the potential power of our *Inner Messiah*? Do we doubt its existence? Or, our ability to recognize this power within our lives? Something compels us to explore this possibility as evinced through our academic knowledge about our *Sacred Textual Narrative* and our dedication to complete this book. Despite the myriad of reasons why some of us may or may not believe in God or an organized religion, we can all appreciate our own mortality at the conclusion of our *personal narrative*.

While the *Grand Historical Narrative* might provide an interesting collection for the memory of our *personal narrative*, our personal spiritual beliefs will determine how, when, and if our *personal narrative* concludes with our physical existence. Our personal eschatological perspective can be both broaden and narrowed by our spiritual beliefs. Some of us may feel more connected to the *Grand Historical Narrative* and its ultimate destiny through our religious and spiritual beliefs, while others of us may feel more insulated from the fate of humanity and empowered through our spiritual notions of extending our lives through an indestructible soul. Wherever we might fall within this scale, we must think about how our personal thought on this particular subject, *death*, affects how we live our lives, what we chose to believe and why we adopt certain behaviors toward ourselves, our loved ones, our coworkers and all our daily encounters and experiences contained within them. In our own time, i.e., by conclusion of this chapter, we all will come to understand how the connection with our *Inner Messiah* will empower and improve our daily encounters and interactions through manifesting the Divine within the *Self* and reconnecting with the Divine Oneness in our *personal narrative* to achieve something extraordinary.

To concretize our analysis about our *Inner Messiah's* potential benefits, we will objectively examine this proposed phenomenon. We have all desired something in our lives, such as a good grade in school, a particular job, a certain love interest, a good bottle of wine, or some other perceived pleasure. We shall classify the time our desire originated as t_0 for purposes of our analysis. Over the course of our life, most of us have somehow, whether through our personal industry or good fortune, have obtained some aspect of our desires, while others of us unfortunately were not able to achieve any of our essential desires in life. We shall classify the time regarding the realization about our desires, whether attained or forfeited, as t_1 in this analysis. Assuming we have the ability to discern whether or not we have fulfilled our own desires, we should recognize the feelings associated with our desires, since the emotions at t_1 tell us whether or not we have achieved them. Yet, some element of that feeling at t_1, regarding accomplishment or disappointment, must have existed at t_0 unless how would we know how to *connect* our emotion to our desire and how to *interpret* the feelings associated with our desire's fulfilled or unfulfilled expectations.[1]

Although theoretical physics may provide some clumsy solution to a physical version of elements moving through conventional, linear time,[2] such physics cannot adequately describe our rational, plausible conclusion. Rather, this example demonstrates the bilocative nature of our emotional capacities—our desires are not only conceived at t_0, but are both conceived and realized at t_0. As a result, we can only appreciate our mental perceptions about the future when we experience them at t_1, but by that time, we have become disconnected from our emotional basis that helps us to determine whether or not our desires were achieved. In other words, our future emotions resemble *coruscating* instants of our present feelings that our mental capacity allowed us to experience prior to their actual presence in our ordinary reality. Other scholars have examined the foregoing, known in colloquial terms as the "punctiform present assumption," as indicating that any time demarcated boundaries between

---

1. See, e.g., Sassoon, *Reality Revisited*, 56, describing the notion of the "punctiform present" where some future feeling in the brain had a trace of existence in the past that defies physics but registers as a rational, plausible analysis for this phenomenon.

2. See, generally, Gott, *Time Travel in Einstein's Universe*.

past, present, and future are useless since the present is without duration, while the past is only a collection of our mental memories, and the future is only a collage of our mental expectations.[3]

Applying this assumption to our *Inner Messiah*, we now have a powerful constructive tool to empower and to improve our narrative convergence. Mainly, we are no longer confined to the conventional time pressures that create anxieties within our *personal narrative* or unrealistic expectations about our personal achievements in relation to the *Grand Historical Narrative*. Even more liberating, we can tame our frustrations about the mysteries contained within the *Sacred Textual Narratives* as we contemplate their possible revelations and lessons for our ordinary existence. As a result, we should reconfigure our patience within this more expansive notion of the present to ensure an effective convergence with these three narratives and to understand the emergence of our *Inner Messiah* from that convergence and its potential power to transform our lives.

As discussed below, our *Inner Messiah* will unleash its transformative powers to empower and to improve our lives through helping us understand the difference between our individual and collective experiences within a particular moment in time. It will also help us appreciate how we can learn from our past errors in finding deeper meaning and purpose within our ordinary existence. Moreover, our *Inner Messiah* will increase our creative capacity to describe events within our ordinary existence that will facilitate our efforts to draw closer to the source of the *Sacred Textual Narrative*. Most importantly, these factors will directly empower and improve our decision-making process beyond its current capabilities, as we perceive extraordinary opportunities within our ordinary existence.

TENSION BETWEEN INDIVIDUAL SELF AND COLLECTIVE EXPERIENCE

Without our *Inner Messiah*, the tension between our individual *Self*, as expressed through our *personal narrative*, and our collective experience, as expressed through the *Grand Historical Narrative*, will originate from their opposite placement around our INM so as to bifurcate their

---

3. Meissner, *Time, Self, and Psychoanalysis*, 41, citing Mundle and Augustine about the "punctiform present assumption" that the present is without duration and the past and future do not exist.

energetic contributions to our personal and professional development.[4] To unlock the power of the encounter with our *Inner Messiah*, we need to embrace the uniqueness and newness of our knowledge about our name and its relationship to the Divine. This power will enable us to disentangle our *personal narrative* from the *Grand Historical Narrative* and to emerge from the INM's bifurcation to reevaluate our relationship as an individual with a Divine character. That Divine character will reconnect us with the *Divine Oneness* at the beginning of creation and help us to understand our *personal narrative* in relation to the collective efforts of all humanity to acquire knowledge and to find purpose.[5] Simply put, our *Inner Messiah* will cause us to revisit our relationship between the *Self* and the social world through the origin of the *Sacred Textual Narrative*—the beginning. Even Darwin's evolutionary observations or scientific developments cannot undermine the transformative power of the narrative, experienced within our own spiritual context rather than its historical authenticity. As a result, we can revise the independent development of our *personal narrative* based on our own interpretation of the *Sacred Textual Narrative* in terms of the other scientific, spiritual, and psychological acculturated influences and expectations from the *Grand Historical Narrative* and their impact on our *personal narrative*.[6]

Two main consequences arise from this independent and interdependent characterization. First, our appreciation for our *Inner Messiah* will cause us to reconsider the impact of the *Sacred Textual Narrative* on our decision-making process regarding our intentionality to consider the plight of others in our personal choices. Rather than just satisfying our personal needs and wants, our *Inner Messiah* helps us to appreciate another dimension to how our *personal narrative* interacts with the *Sacred Textual Narrative* to demonstrate how individual actions could generate undesirable consequence for our collective social construct and its reflection within the *Grand Historical Narrative*.[7] For example,

4. See, e.g., Kaya, "Compelled to Create," 26, discussing Jungian belief in energy phenomena being generating by a tension of opposites.

5. Adams, *Fragmented Intimacy*, 131, discussing role of separation and severing preexisting relationships to overcome obstacles in severing the addict from the addiction.

6. See, e.g., Frie, "Culture and Context," 12, citing studies by Markus and Kitayama (1991) that conceptualize the relationship between the self and the social world as independent and interdependent phenomenon.

7. Ibid., citing Markus (2008) regarding the intentional and voluntary concern for others as an unnecessary and non-obligatory phenomenon in the *Self's*

we can rely on the unfortunate plentitude of church scandals plaguing religious institutions in the late twentieth and early twenty-first centuries. The staggering statistics surrounding the Roman Catholic Church sex abuse scandals are particularly distressing. Some reports indicate that there have seventeen thousand victims of sexual abuse involving approximately seven thousand priests since 1950.[8]

In addition to the Catholic Church's $2.5 billion expenditures associated with settlement and other abuse related costs, this absolute tragedy clearly demonstrates the problems associated with individual tensions between *personal narrative, Grand Historical Narrative* and *Sacred Textual Narrative.* Any priest who would contemplate any form of inappropriate touching of an innocent youth must have possessed this inclination prior to entering the priesthood and incorrectly merged this tendency within their *personal narrative* with the *Sacred Textual Narrative* as an attempt to reconcile the "*disease*" between his identity and his desire.[9] The *Sacred Textual Narrative* provided such priests with a language to ignore their innate proclivity and, unfortunately, the ability to expand the priests' INM through the collective Catholic ritual, i.e., *Grand Historical Narrative*, provided an additional muting buffer between desire and identity and their inner holiness and external perversion.[10] Hence, such abusing priests must have never encountered their *Inner Messiah* as they allowed Catholic cultural influences within the *Grand Historical Narrative* to mask their pedophilic faults and defects with a false sense of obedience and love of the Divine.[11]

Any rational, cognitive capacity to appreciate the dire consequences of the pedophilic priests' desires on their victims, never mind the Catholic institution's role in the *Grand Historical Narrative*, must have been completely absent within these priests' mental faculties. Yet, most of these priests, along with their hierarchical protectors, maintained long

---

decision-making processes.

8. See, e.g., Grossman, "Clergy Sex Abuse Settlements," citing 2012 report from US Conference of Catholic Bishops' Office of Child and Youth Protection.

9. See, e.g., Bucholtz and Hall, "Theorizing Identity," 469, noting close relationship between identity and desire.

10. See, e.g., Twerski, *Addictive Thinking*, 29, noting culture's values and their impact on individual's perception of time and *Self.*

11. See, e.g., Rosenfels, *Homosexuality*, 115, noting how men attempt to love in an independent way without sufficient submission to power and relinquishment to object of affection so as to avoid hostile feelings toward idealized romantic interests.

careers within the Catholic Church. Like the Catholic Church and its contributions to the *Grand Historical Narrative*, the longevity of these priests' careers intimate that they must have manifested some positive aspect of the *Sacred Textual Narrative*, no matter how muted or small, within their *personal narratives*. Otherwise, these priests, along with inappropriate Church policies and practices, would have been exposed years earlier. Regardless, the Catholic Church's future portrayal within the *Grand Historical Narrative*, along with its interaction with the *Sacred Textual Narrative*, will be under strict scrutiny by believing and disbelieving individuals, if not generations.

The second consequence from our independent and interdependent characterization requires us to appreciate the power of our *Inner Messiah* to isolate the *Self* from the success or failure of any human undertaking as our *Inner Messiah* energizes our personal growth and development with our unique and new appreciation for the *Sacred Textual Narrative*.[12] Revisiting some observations from the Catholic sex abuse scandal, we can discern the importance of preserving the individual relationship with the Divine to safeguard our own independent realization and convergence with the *Sacred Textual Narrative* in our spiritual belief system without unnecessary and harmful religious institutional distractions within the *Grand Historical Narrative*. That said, we must recognize our interdependent relationship with institutional religion, or even secularized notions of the spiritual and the Divine, as an important conditioning element in the interaction between our *personal narrative* and the *Grand Historical Narrative*.[13]

For most of us, we have acquired a knowledge of what is holy, what is evil, what is spiritually nourishing, who is a psychic vampire, how to find the Divine, or why we should have a spiritual experience through some form of religious conditioning, even if our only exposure to these themes can be found in pop culture and/or literary myths. In some cases, we might have crafted our own *Sacred Textual Narrative* from various sources, like the Internet and its bricolage spiritualities that incorporate themes from fiction, film, music, television and art.[14] As one scholar

12. See, e.g., ibid., 10, noting that something within the *Self* can separate itself from the success or failure of any human undertaking.

13. See, e.g., Slade and Bentall, *Sensory Deception*, 113, emphasizing the importance of classical conditioning in observing humans conforming to a response that they are expected to make.

14. See, e.g., Robertson, "Beast Within," 13.

opines, "cyber-spirituality provides for a detached expression of the [*Self*] in various spiritual modalities."[15] In such scenarios, we should recognize by now that our *Self's* detachment from spiritual modalities does not provide the same benefits of convergence with the *Sacred Textual Narrative* since detachment weakens our *Self* and its ability to maintain its own independent expression within our *personal narrative* as we interact with the *Grand Historical Narrative* and other collective cultural influences. Basically, without knowing our identity in regard to the Divine, we will never have our own sense of completeness that enables us to utilize *Sacred Textual Narrative* to empower the evolution of our *personal narrative* around our *own unique* dreams and hopes as we seek to overcome distractive and/or destructive collective behaviors and to improve our interaction, both individually and collectively, with the *Grand Historical Narrative*.

Besides these two consequences, we must not forgot about the cultural utility contained within the *Grand Historical Narrative* to help us to create meanings and to organize experiences around a collective social construct with common symbolic interpretations and understandings.[16] The tradeoff to such organizational and communicative efficiencies is the diminished capacity of our *Self* as our personal perspectives become influenced by the dominant modes of thinking, acting, dreaming, and experiencing, whether socially constructed, personally created, or biologically based.[17] Some scholars have opined that our personal sense of finitude and its impact on all our important relationships allow us to sustain a "sense of individualized selfhood" from our deeply personal traumatizing emotions associated with this realization.[18] Rather than preserving the experiential *Self* with a sense of its own mortality, our *Inner Messiah* provides an outlet for a broader perspective to recognize the relational dynamics between the *Self* and its deep relationships through an esoteric interpretation of *Sacred Textual Narrative* to help enshrine our *personal narrative* with a mysterious uniqueness that encourages us to be mindful of our individuality and its relationship to the *Grand Historical Narrative*.

Recasting this "mysterious uniqueness" within a Jungian paradigm, we can conceptualize the process of individuation as requiring us to

---

15. Ibid.

16. See, e.g., Frie, "Culture and Context," 13.

17. Ibid.

18. See, e.g., Stolorow, "Individuality in Context," 66.

immerse our ego into the unconscious until we have reached complete "nothingness," but for a moment of identity with the Divine.[19] That moment, no matter how fleeting, helps us to expand our consciousness beyond the ordinary constraints of reality and access the origins of the state of consciousness itself that created, creates, and renews all conscious life.[20]

More importantly, the interaction between the individual and the Divine helps us to encapsulate the fragmentary nature of human existence since that interaction represents two opposite states of consciousness and perception—ordinary reality and divine reality.[21] Those two legitimate opposites require us to seek resolution in a similar fashion as we resolve opposite perceptivel states in our recognition between the *Grand Historical Narrative* and its impact on our *personal narrative*. Through our *Inner Messiah*, we can accommodate this fragmentation through encountering the Divine within us through our interpretation and implementation of the *Sacred Textual Narrative* that helps us understand our sense of *Self* from a new and unique perspective. This perception allows us to see and to hear the Divine in terms of how the Divine sees and calls to us, rather than our tainted expectations about that encounter through religious institutions and experiences contained within the *Grand Historical Narrative*.

Most importantly, once we can appreciate the full impact of how the Divine sees us as its creation, rather than the creation, us, beholding its Creator, our *Inner Messiah* will remove fragmentary influences on the *Self* and help us to redefine our relationship with the *Grand Historical Narrative*, as well as the *Sacred Textual Narrative*, to optimize all expressions of the unified *Self* within our *personal narrative*. To access the fullness of this power, we will first need to analyze, to recognize and to remedy our past errors in former expressions the *Self* throughout our *personal narrative* and its relationship with the *Grand Historical Narrative* and *Sacred Textual Narrative*. In this way, we can ensure that we possess sufficient information without threatening or overburdening our conscious mental capacities with extraneous past errors and mistakes.[22]

---

19. Dourley, *Paul Tillich, Carl Jung,* 127.

20. Ibid.

21. See, e.g., ibid., 165.

22. See, e.g., ibid., 138–39, stressing how the content of the unconsciousness does not enter into the consciousness to avoid overloading it with excess information.

REVISITING PAST RATIONALES AND THINKING-PROCESSES TO REMEDY OUR PAST ERRORS

A wonderful attribute about our *Inner Messiah* is its innovative perspective on our conception of our *Self* and its relationship to the Divine. No matter what names we have been called or identities we have acquired throughout our *personal narratives*, our *Inner Messiah* provides us with an entirely new approach to our ordinary existence as it encourages us to restructure our lives around a tangible transcendental experience to overcome previous emotional, psychological and spiritual impediments.[23] Our *Inner Messiah* allows us to connect with the totality of creation as embodied through all phases of time, past, present and future, thereby providing us with a tangible transcendental experience. As one scholar so eloquently opined about Jung's observations about *apocatastasis*, i.e., restoration of the original condition through humanity's reunion with creation at its origin:

> When Jung equates the recovered memory of one's totality with apocatasis, he is stating that such wholeness is experienced as worked by the memory itself and in the here and now. Both paradise and the end of time are to be approximated and experienced in the present as moments in natural processes of maturation and individuation, for Jung, no longer distinguishable from the divinization.[24]

These observations suggest that our *Inner Messiah* operates as a powerful filter to transcend the limitations of the here and now since we can access our original relationship not with creation, but with our Creator. As a result, we will have an entirely new perspective on our relationship with the Divine through the convergence of our *personal narrative* with the *Sacred Textual Narrative* that will provide us with new knowledge to remedy our previous ignorance and our prior erroneous judgments.

For our *Inner Messiah* to truly transform our lives into an extraordinary existence, we must "peel off" our past incorrect thinking processes about our relationship with the Divine penetrate our *INM* to ensure our past errors, especially the lack of narrative convergence, can have minimal impact on our future. We need to be diligent to safeguard future

23. Romme and Escher, *Accepting Voices*, 100, citing research that demonstrates people who suffered great loss overcame suffering through restructuring their lives around a transcendental experience with a higher purpose / spiritual component.

24. Dourley, *Paul Tillich, Carl Jung*, 129.

portions of our *personal narrative* are void of these errors because such errors are ever present throughout our ordinary existence as we repeat them in the present and recommit them to similar circumstances in the future until they are completed eradicated from our psyche.[25] Our *Inner Messiah* helps to contribute to this eradication through our new relationship with and new perspective about the Divine in our *personal narrative*, but we must be mindful not to disregard and marginalize our *Inner Messiah* and its demands upon our self-awareness for the more comfortable and familiar pre-*Inner Messiah* conduct. First, we must ensure to accept our own responsibility for our past errors and not blame our ignorance as an excuse for our past behaviors that kept us from manifesting our superlative natures in our daily existence.[26] Otherwise, we will not fully utilize our intellectual and spiritual investment in this book as we rely on our *Inner Messiah* to empower and to improve our lives.

Second, we must recognize deeply personal and intimate dysfunctional aspects of our early life that have become embedded in our *personal narratives* and may require us to deal with them through our continued personal relationships with family members or our current professional relationships with unpleasant coworkers and/or other social interactions.[27] While our *Inner Messiah* will help us deal with the former dysfunction's impact on our mental outlook, our *Inner Messiah* may not provide adequate safeguards to protect us for lapsing into former, destructive coping behaviors as we directly confront the people or circumstances responsible for the dysfunction. As a result, we must exercise additional diligence in the application of our *Inner Messiah* to remove those behavior patterns from our thought processes to ensure an effective transformation in our daily lives.[28]

Most importantly, our *Inner Messiah* contains the hope that our destructive and self-limiting behaviors that we have adopted in our ignorance can be remedied through their complete avoidance.[29] We should be

25. Sassoon, *Reality Revisited*, 129.

26. Twerski, *Addictive Thinking*, 49, discussing how projection places blame on other people or circumstances for the denial of our destructive behaviors.

27. See, e.g., Kuhar, *Addicted Brain*, 119, stressing how early life events and familial dysfunctional could lead to destructive behaviors during various growth stages.

28. See, e.g., Jeserich, "Can Sense of Coherence Be Modified," 23, discussing how to measure health-promotion effectiveness from mindfulness exercises to combat degenerative effects of stressors and destructive coping behaviors.

29. See, e.g., Kuhar, *Addicted Brain*, 93, describing how an addicted brain can

grateful that our *Inner Messiah* has afforded us an opportunity to engage in forbearance from our less than optimal behavior patterns. For example, our *Inner Messiah* can inspire us to reorient our lives around our new relationship with the Divine as we begin to trust the Divine in this relationship to introduce an extraordinary dimension to our ordinary reality.[30] The convergence between the *Sacred Textual Narrative* and our *personal narrative* also will motivate us to revisit our prior self-aggrandizing inclinations in light of how our *Inner Messiah* will modify and expand the former "self" in our "self-interest" motivations and decision-making processes.[31]

After we have encountered and unleashed our *Inner Messiah*, we can appreciate its impact on our *personal narrative* and its extra dimensionality to understand the relationship between the *Self*, the Divine and all creation. Whether we perceive those dimensions as making us less significant in terms of our potential contribution to the *Grand Historical Narrative* or more significant in terms of our interpretative importance to the *Sacred Textual Narrative*, our *Inner Messiah* guarantees that the boundaries of our *personal narratives* have forever been redrawn and reimagined according to our optimal existence as envisaged from our Creator's perspective.

As with other powerful spiritual and mystical tools, the exercise of our *Inner Messiah* does require some caution to avoid misuse and unintended consequences. Around 1700, the famous Jewish mystical healer and Chassidic leader, Baal Shem Tov, used God's divine, sacred name to perform all types of healings and miracles, as well as to expound divine wisdom.[32] His mystical teachings, along with his kabalistic predecessors, strongly caution against misusing the mystical aspects of the *Sacred Textual Narrative* without proper preparation to ensure an individual maintained complete control over its passions to avoid any misuse or abuse of

---

never truly be returned to its pre-addicted state since some drug effects last forever and most effective long-term treatment is complete avoidance.

30. See, e.g., Twerski, *Addictive Thinking*, 108–9, noting how addicts must acquire a new concept of reality to overcome their addictive behavior and this new version of reality must originate from a trusting relationship.

31. Havens and Bakan, *Psychology and Religion*, 31, describing individuals as self-seeking with individual self-interested as primary motivator in decision-making processes.

32. Bakan, *Sigmund Freud*, 79.

the Divine teachings.[33] Similarly, an ancillary purpose of revisiting the past errors in our decision-making processes is the requisite preparation to handle and to manage our newfound relationship with the Divine and its transformative power within our ordinary existence. Such preparation will help us understand how our encounter with our *Inner Messiah* affected our sense of *Self* within our *personal narrative* after its convergence with the *Sacred Textual Narrative*.

The promise of our *Inner Messiah* is to exceed conventional boundaries of achievement in our self-awareness and self-development through our understanding of the Divine's *particularized* identity for us within creation—the obliteration of the *INM* and reunification with the *Divine Oneness*. The power of this knowledge will cause us to confront and to overcome long-established limitations on this topic. For example, Jung warned us that the *Self* could only be approximated, never fully realized, in the course of a lifetime.[34] Other thinkers, like Tillich, join Jung and opine that our spirituality has limited capacity to perceive reality in full resonance with the Divine while in physical reality, except for only "ephemeral instances."[35] Daunting as our task may appear, our *Inner Messiah* could help us to defeat such claims as remnants of the superfluous emotional and spiritual myopia associated with our *INM* and its ability to divide us from the *Divine Oneness*. We can safely conclude that Jung and Tillich, along with many others, believed that any identity or sense of *Self* without a complete relationship with the *Divine*, was an optimal identity or *Self* in ordinary reality, especially since any form of extraordinary and/or spiritual reality was unsustainable. Fortunately, our *Inner Messiah* helps us to realize that our current identity or *Self* is unsustainable in ordinary reality due to our mortality and the ephemeral nature of our desires and their fulfillment throughout our ordinary existence. These repetitive, self-perpetuating accoutrements of ordinary living have previously distracted us, just like the greatest minds of many generations, from rephrasing our quest for an extraordinary and/or spiritual encounter.

The merger of our *personal narrative* with the *Sacred Textual Narrative* allows our *Self* and other concepts of identity, especially its Divine Character, to be conceived and analyzed without oppressive standards imposed by the *Grand Historical Narrative*, i.e., Jung's observations about

33. Ibid.

34. Dourley, *Paul Tillich, Carl Jung*, 175.

35. Ibid.

the boundaries of self-awareness and self-development. We can utilize the perspective of our *Inner Messiah* and our *specific* identity in creation, as given to us by our Creator and confirmed through our own diligence, to integrate that Divine Character and its purpose into all aspects of our daily routines to bring about an extraordinary, spiritual reality for our *Self* that will encourage others to join us in our collective pursuit of the extraordinary.

CREATIVE INTERPRETATIONS AND THEIR UNIQUENESS TO OUR DAILY ROUTINES

Do you ever question why we look for some profound meaning from a simple occurrence? How many of us have heard a song on the radio or in a store and ascribed a special significance to the song? Did we ever find an old letter or newspaper clipping that caused us to question the synchronicity of the timing? No matter how creatively we interpret a particular event in our ordinary existence, we all share a similar purpose in the exercise of our creativity. The impetus behind this collective purpose can be considered some innate need to find something unique from a singular ordinary moment. With this uniqueness, we have an impetus to change something about our ordinary existence[36] or to legitimate something within our reality.[37]

Whatever the ultimate application of this uniqueness, we must all recognize that something within our personality drives us to differentiate our *Self* from the other with this uniqueness. Our *Inner Messiah* represents a creative and unique aspect of the *Self* that allows us to empower our *personal narrative* with anthropomorphisms from the *Sacred Textual Narrative* and their impact on differentiating our *Self* from ordinary reality portrayed within the *Grand Historical Narrative*.[38] Most importantly, our *Inner Messiah* minimizes our conflict and disdain for being considered ordinary and helps us avoid unnecessary disputes with the *Self* and others to confirm our uniqueness so as to avoid any pejorative

36. See, e.g., Adams, *Fragmented Intimacy*, 131, noting how ambivalence can become a critical impetus for change.

37. See, e.g., Twerski, *Addictive Thinking*, 15, commenting about addictive thinking process relying on irrational conclusion to legitimate an altered state of reality.

38. Bakan et al., *Maimonides' Cure of Souls*, 160, mentioning Maimonides discussion about projection as origination from biblical anthropomorphisms.

consequences on our personal and spiritual well-being, especially our relationship with the Divine.[39]

As we adopt and settled with our *Inner Messiah* and its power to create a new relationship with the Divine, we will begin to observe the former boundaries of our imaginations dissolve and expand to accommodate the modifications to our *personal narrative* with its convergence with the *Grand Historical Narrative* via the *Sacred Textual Narrative*. While the self-help/self-awareness market space is filled with books and exercises to dispel negative thinking patterns and to adopt positive attitudes,[40] such exercises may not provide adequate instructions for us to truly overcome our destructive behaviors through the *complete* restructuring of our ordinary reality.[41] To extract the therapeutic benefits from our *Inner Messiah*, we must empower our language to accurately interpret its impact on our creative capacities and their reflections of our inner turmoil and difficulty to manifest our potential and to recover completely from our past hurts and disappointments.[42] Unlike traditional self-help and therapeutic remedies with their limited ability to maintain our attention,[43] our *Inner Messiah* represents a dynamic, therapeutic extension of the *Self* that allows us to interpret our burdens and challenges, as well as to unleash our creative potential, within the context of our relationship with the Divine. Rather than just thinking of ourselves as operating within the confines of creation, our *Inner Messiah* grants us the capacity to represent an extension of the Creator operating within us, as creation through our own unique, creative capacity.

Generally speaking, when we are confronted with job frustrations or other challenges, no matter our career phase, we profess an interest in pursuing a creative career or some other creative exercise. For example,

---

39. See, e.g., Twerski, *Wisdom Each Day*, 76, discussing Midrashic wisdom about avoiding disputes through the components of the conflicts and their place within the conflict.

40. See, e.g., Romme and Escher, *Accepting Voices*, 77.

41. See, e.g., Twerski, *Addictive Thinking*, 95, commenting on how addicts structure their behavior around their belief that their addiction will add something extra to their life as reality is "never good enough."

42. Kakar, *Mad and Divine*, 115, describing the psychoanalyst's role to enable a patient to verbalize its inner emotional states and to utilize words to promote effective healing.

43. See, e.g., Havens and Bakan, *Psychology and Religion*, 31, describing the nature of self-seeking man as an experimental science that can only maintain the attention of individuals for a certain time.

some surveys report that 81 percent of Americans profess an interest in writing a book.[44] Whatever the source or impetus for our creative impulse, our *Inner Messiah* will help us improve our creative outlook through helping us understand that any creative exercise represents an opportunity for us to participate with creation. However, our relationship with the Creator through our *Inner Messiah* will help us perceive creation from the ultimate vantage point—our Creator's perspective! Conjecturing from Jung's observations about knowing God in *Answer to Job*, we can conclude that the impact of knowing God changes the parameters of our active imagination in the creation of our *personal narrative*.[45] Our *Inner Messiah* enables us to experience the numinous power and essence of the Divine through our own creative interpretation of those experiences, as first encountered within the narrative convergence and subsequently manifested and utilized in our ordinary, everyday existence.[46]

Moreover, our *Inner Messiah* allows us to empower and to improve our ordinary reality with a divine-human collaboration for our *personal narrative* and its ability to extract and to integrate the most relevant, transformative teachings from the *Sacred Textual Narrative*. We cannot overemphasize the significance of our encounter with the Divine through both our *Inner Messiah* and the convergence of our *personal narrative* and the *Sacred Textual Narrative*, as Jung has poignantly opined:

> The inner instability of Yahweh is the prime cause not only of the creation of the world but also of the pleromatic drama for which mankind serves as a tragic chorus. The encounter with the creation changes the creator.[47]

Although Jung's statement presents a theological quagmire, we can try to distill some basic elements from its linguistic density. In particular, we can appreciate Jung's interpretation of creation as our *personal narrative* representing the fulfillment of God's presence in creation, i.e., the "pleromatic drama." Also, God's encounter with creation through that narrative and, according to Jung, within our unconsciousness,[48] provides an additional dynamic element for the *Grand Historical Narrative* and the *Sacred Textual Narrative*, as well as challenges and concessions for their eventual

44. See, e.g., Epstein, "Think You Have a Book in You?"
45. Schlamm, "Active Imagination," 109.
46. Ibid.
47. Ibid., 116, citing Jung's *Answer to Job*.
48. Ibid.

convergence within our *personal narrative*. That dynamic element allows the Divine to create and to recreate within creation to ensure that we, as extensions of creation, can facilitate the integration of the Divine's ever-changing plan into our individual and collective realities.

So, we can synthesize these themes around the central notion of our *Inner Messiah* and its impact on our creative capacity to extract innovative interpretations from our ordinary existence to strengthen our relationship with the Divine. In other words, our *Inner Messiah* has become the primary spiritual activation for our memory's Divine origin and purpose within all creation to help both individual and collective consciousness to unite to these similar memories through all aspects of our creative expression.[49] Most importantly, our *Inner Messiah* will empower and improve our creative innovations with the newness of our relationship and understanding about the Divine's relationship with creation through encouraging us to discover new manifestations and representations of Divine phenomena that have never been previously discovered or contemplated. Unlike previous hallucinations within *Sacred Textual Narrative*, such as King Belshazzar seeing a hand on the wall[50] or Peter seeing of vision of food,[51] we have concretized our imaginative vision with direct mystical experience through our *Inner Messiah*. In turn, our imaginative vision can be consider an actual act of Divine creation that helps us to live more productive lives and to fulfill our mandate to share in the abundance of creation.[52]

As long as we firmly ground our imaginative exercises and creative interpretations in well-reasoned theological and spiritual constructs from the *Sacred Textual Narrative* and ensure their healthy integration within our *personal narrative*, we should be able to effectively unleash the power of our *Inner Messiah* and to diligently preserve our mental capacity against imaginational overload.[53] Furthermore, we can determine the

---

49. Dourley, *Paul Tillich, Carl Jung*, 130, discussing ritual activation and its impact on individual and collective memory to unite opposites, like individual and collective, and ensure human consciousness can obtain its full potential in the future through this convergence.

50. See Dan 5:1, 5–6.

51. See Acts 11:5–7.

52. See, e.g., Aleman et al., *Hallucinations*, 21.

53. See, e.g., Stolorow, "Individuality in Context," 59, noting that philosophical phenomenology and its impact on individualized self-hood can be explained as a rational structure of experience.

psychological and spiritual appropriateness of our creative interpretations based on their ability to bring us, both individually and collectively, closer to the universal original of the *Sacred Textual Narrative*.

INDIVIDUAL WAYS TO MEASURE OUR PROXIMITY TO THE SACRED SOURCE

As we can extrapolate from mystics and their *personal narrative* enduring within the *Grand Historical Narrative*, most extreme encounters and relationships with the Divine present a perilous spiritual path somewhere between mystical neurosis, mental psychosis, transcendental realism, or some permutation of all of them.[54] To realize the full promise of our *Inner Messiah*, we must safeguard against the mental pitfalls some of our predecessors have encountered in their spiritual journeys. Our major safeguard, besides reliance on mental health professionals when necessary, will be our ability to discern a spiritual certainty with our *Inner Messiah* that will help to replace our more restless emotions, such as pleasure and anxiety.[55] Unlike previous religious constructs, our *Inner Messiah* does not require any segmentation between the manifestation of the Divine within externalized ritual and institutional doctrine and the direct experiential presence of the Divine within our internalized thought processes and perceptions.[56] Through the removal of this demarcation, i.e., *INM*, our *Inner Messiah* allows our relationship with the Divine to become fully integrated within the *Self*[57] and to avoid external distractions, complications, and prejudices that have previously prevented us from obtaining this relationship with the Divine through our *Inner Messiah*.

An important aspect to our authentic *Inner Messiah* is how we actually own, as opposed to disown or to disavow, other spiritual constructs in living out an ordinary existence with complete awareness of our relationship with the Divine. This phenomenon most closely correlates with Heidegger's notions of authentic existence that requires us to own our impending death as both a certain and indefinite (as to its "when")

54. See, e.g., Belzen, "Spirituality, Culture, and Mental Health," 298.

55. See., e.g., Bakan, *Duality of Human Existence*, 68, citing Freud's claims that ego has dethroned the pleasure principle as certainty, rather than surface emotions like pleasure, ensure greater success and satisfaction.

56. See, e.g., Cramer, *Protecting the Self*, 71, noting segmentation between the inside (the self, the ego) and the outside (the other) and their psychological implications.

57. Ibid.

phenomenon to recognize the influence of this constant and present threat within our thinking process.[58] In terms of our everyday existence, our *Inner Messiah* serves a particular function to connect us with the Divine that we have never encountered—completeness. While our former spiritual practices and their current influences in our religious views were/are valuable experiences, they always had finite start and stop times, such as the duration of our prayers, religious studies, or clergy interactions. Whenever we engaged the Divine under those circumstances, we were always faced with the inevitable withdrawal from the Divine presence and influence from that singular encounter.

More importantly, we have engaged in external manifestations of the messianic promise within those encounters that neither have adequately fulfilled nor represented that promise. Otherwise, we will have already encountered the Divine, have attained an optimal ordinary existence, have reconnected with the *Divine Oneness*, and have no need for this book or its observations. Rather, our *Inner Messiah* helps us to steer clear of *messianic Titanics* that promise all types of spiritual transformations and leave us worse off and more confused then when started our spiritual journey. Hopefully, our time together will not leave any of us shipwrecked or waiting on the dock for the next spiritual life preserver as this literary odyssey begins to draw to its climatic conclusion. May God spare all of us from that unspeakable fate! Most importantly, may our *Inner Messiah* preserve and further develop our perpetual relationship with the Divine to preempt any icebergs from derailing our spiritual journey.

Despite that slight digression and metamorphic indulgence, we must remember that we will face many distractions in our desire to empower and to improve our attitudes and daily routines. Our *Inner Messiah* provides us with a celestial assistant that helps us facilitate the flow of Divine ideas, perceptions, goals, and theories into our physical reality.[59] To comprehend the magnitude of our *Inner Messiah's* contributions to our ordinary existence, we must recall how its introduction into our thinking process will remove an essential anxiety from our thoughts about the impossibility of the Divine presence having any active role in

---

58. See, e.g., Stolorow, "Individuality in Context," 63, reviewing possible correlations between Heidegger's authentic existence and the phenomenology of traumatized states.

59. See, e.g., Bakan et al., *Maimonides' Cure of Souls*, 74, noting how Maimonides opined about how the active intellect creates revelations within the soul through the merger of the physical and divine sciences.

our ordinary existence, as well as the Divine presence being pushed out of our consciousness to make room for more secular interests.[60] As a result, we can confirm the successful functionality of our *Inner Messiah* in our ordinary reality when we notice our decisions and perspectives reflecting this Divine presence and our desire to manifest this presence into our ordinary reality.

With regard to *how* our *Inner Messiah* enables us to experience the Divine and to confirm this experience, we can borrow the concept of anamnesis that Jung modified to describe the depth of our inward memory to recall and to recollect our original state of "oneness with the God-image."[61] The *Inner Messiah* provides us with an immediate experience of that "oneness" as we constantly recall our relationship with the Divine through our hidden name and its revelation within that relationship. The impact of our hidden name reconfigures and restructures our consciousness to participate within our ordinary reality with a mindfulness of the Divine and the Divine's perspective on its creation, i.e., the *Divine Oneness* present at the beginning.[62] Hence, when we find ourselves detached from any religious experience as a muted sense of the Divine's presence within our decision-making capacity, we have misfocused our *Inner Messiah* away from the center of our ordinary existence and have pursued less than optimal spiritual strategies to empower and to improve our ordinary existence. Unfortunately, many opportunities exist for us to pursue less optimal strategies as our pre-*Inner Messiah* state of existence can demonstrate.

Many self-help and spiritual remedies promise self-improvement through the acquisition of spiritual knowledge and magical powers.[63] The recent popularity of shape-shifting metaphor in certain Neopagan and Neoshamanic practices illustrates this phenomenon as books, like *Animal Speak* by Ted Andrews, revisit Emile Durkheim's theory of totemism and encourage individuals to discover their "animal totem" and to access

---

60. See, e.g., Stolorow, "Individuality in Context," 65, reviewing possible correlations between Heidegger's authentic existence and the phenomenology of traumatized states.

61. See, e.g., Dourley, *Paul Tillich, Carl Jung*, 129.

62. Ibid., 175, noting impact of "oneness" on consciousness transitioning into a deeper religious experience and adopting the perspective of "eternal ground of all empirical being."

63. Robertson, "Beast Within," 13.

the power within the totem.[64] Even pop culture reflects these notions as shows like *True Blood* (HBO) showcase shape-shifting characters that use their animal shape-shifting capabilities for both good and bad purposes. Whatever our initial reaction to this particular form of spirituality, we must appreciate its ability to lure and to distract inquisitive individuals from performing necessary diligence to connect with their own innate, inner holiness.

Whether pagan, Wiccan, shamanic or other new age label, these spiritual philosophies offer products that promise to allow their consumers to transcend the ordinary and to access magical realms that were traditionally reserved for our grandest fantasies and appear to be designed to exploit our curiosity about history and myth.[65] Even if some of us have referred to the teachings associated with these spiritual modalities as foundational sources for our *Sacred Textual Narratives*, our *Inner Messiah* will even supersede their spiritual fallacies to allow our imaginations alone to confirm the pure emotional satisfaction that can be derived from a vibrant relationship with the Divine.[66] Mainstream religions, just like our *personal narratives*, have been relying on our imaginations for all types of functional purposes. For example, these syncretistic spiritualities attempt to converge our *personal narrative* with a fragmented and, in most cases, an imaginatively reconstructed version of the *Sacred Textual Narrative*.[67] These attempts draw more heavily upon the *Grand Historical Narrative* since their promised spiritual benefits are more aligned to our common emotional passions within that narrative, such as our desires for drastic, unrealistic personal transformations with minimal effort based on our observations about specific historical figures and/or celebrities.

No matter our personal or collective beliefs about the spectra of religious possibilities, we must recall our ultimate goal in all these pursuits is a better understanding of the *Self*, both the physical and spiritual components of that *Self*, within our personally- and socially-constructed cosmology, as well as the Divine's created cosmology. That means, the limitations of science should not prevent us from meaningful and beneficial conjecture about the physical and spiritual placement of the *Self* within any discernible and indiscernible part of our reality. Our *Inner*

---

64. Ibid.

65. Drobin, "Spirituality, the New Opiate," 229–39.

66. See, e.g., ibid., 232, referencing Freud's description of religious psychodynamics and their impact on the syncretistic pursuits of New Age cults.

67. Ibid.

Messiah will allow us to exercise our imaginations to place ourselves, all aspects of our *Self* externally present throughout the Universe and internally present within our consciousness, to interpret how those placements shape, refine, and develop our emotions about ordinary reality and how to pursue an extraordinary existence.[68] Through the emotions attached to that experiential exercise, we will have greater control and discipline to identify our "true" passions emanating from our relationship with the Divine, i.e., the *Divine Oneness*, rather than the distractive influences from the *Grand Historical Narrative* and its limiting historical figures and celebrity characters.[69] Thus, our *Inner Messiah* will permit our ordinary existence to reflect our authentic passions and to sustain our efforts to pursue them through the strength we derive from our relationship with the Divine.

Another important hallmark regarding our proximity to the Divine is our sense of time. If our *Inner Messiah* brings us some sense of control over time such that we do not feel unnecessary time pressures and related anxious emotions, we have successfully drawn closer to the Divine. For example, some of us may ask the Divine for patience but we want and/or need that patience right now.[70] While all of us can relate to our instant gratification impulses in some form, our *Inner Messiah* should reformulate the concept of "instant" as our relationship with the Divine will help us mature our understanding of time and its superfluous functions outside our ordinary reality. After all, whether or not we received our patience at the time of our request, t_o, or at some point in the future, t_x, its impact on the Divine is the same—nothing, no change, naught!

Through our *Inner Messiah* and our relationship with the Divine, we will eventually adopt a similar appreciation of time being a self-imposed fiction to which we voluntarily submit with great peril to our physical, spiritual and emotional well-being. Unless we have personal or professional commitments that require specific time commitments, we should always be mindful about allocating our physical, emotional, and spiritual

68. See, e.g., Bakan, *Sigmund Freud*, 79, describing feelings of ecstasy originating from knowledge about the soul leaving the body and deriving therapeutic effect from that experience.

69. See ibid., noting how overcoming fears and superfluous emotions will help remove distractions from our thought process and liberate us to pursue our passions without unnecessary distractions.

70. See, e.g., Twerski, *Addictive Thinking*, 30, discussing time pollution impairing our clarity to See the consequences of our distorted perspective about time.

endeavors in accordance with an optimal scheduling strategy that reflects the Divine's perspective of unnecessary time pressures. More important-ly, we can better manage the various activities that make demands upon our time allocations as we co-create our time management with our *Inner Messiah* and its spiritual contributions to our ordinary reality.

Finally, our *Inner Messiah* will continuously provide us with oppor-tunity-after-opportunity to fulfill its redemptive function, that is, starting over/beginning anew, in helping us deal with the burdens of our daily routines. If we cannot discern this redemptive function with our *Inner Messiah*, then we know that we must question the robustness of what we identified and embraced as our hidden name and its relationship with the Divine. For example, this redemptive function enables our *Inner Messiah* to help us recast our ordinary existence and start over with a fresh per-spective about our lives and our abilities to manifest something extraor-dinary within our ordinary living circumstances.[71] This ability to reboot our lives as if our memories and perspectives have been wiped clean of all negative residues can be only experienced through our *Inner Messiah* and its unique relationship to the Divine. Even though this thought may seem an elusive conjecture in the abstract, this thought pertains to every point raised throughout this chapter and this book. Had our *personal narrative* represented an optimal expression of our *Self*, we would have neither encountered each other nor formed this intimate relationship through these pages. Simply stated, we have all arrived at this point in our personal journeys because we desire a complete overhaul of our *personal narrative*, or at least major portions of it, to reflect some resonances with the our favorite moments from the *Grand Historical Narrative*. Hope-fully, we have all understood and appreciated how convergence with the *Sacred Textual Narrative* enables us to empower and to improve ourselves beyond our ordinary constraints to rewrite our *personal narrative* and to reconsider its relationship with the *Grand Historical Narrative*.

FINAL REMARKS

The power of our *Inner Messiah* to help us achieve something extraordi-nary within our ordinary lives will be ultimately determined by our story,

71. See, e.g., Jackson, "Pastoral Counselor," 261, discussion how people who believe in God have a mandate to create a redemptive society to enable every member to start over and to cope with life's burdens without concern about the individual's and society's finitude.

that is, how well our *personal narrative* reflects the spiritual promises and possibilities contained within our selected *Sacred Textual Narrative*. Regardless of our physical and/or emotional capacities, our own creativity will always prevail as we create opportunities to engage the Divine within our imagination to unlock possibilities we previously ignored in the development of our *personal narrative*, as well as to influence our collective contributions to the *Grand Historical Narrative*.

Conclusion

THE INEVITABLE HAS ARRIVED upon us or we have arrived at it—the conclusion of our time together. Gratitude and appreciation aside, we hopefully had a transformative time together through the pages we have just completed. Regardless of whatever we take away or leave within our individual and collective experiences, we all should have some sort of epiphany about our internal creative process and its original proximity to the Divine Oneness. Specifically, as we read and contemplated the messages contained within this book, can we clearly and explicitly hear our narrator? Who read these words off these pages and mediated their meanings some where between their intellectual placement on this paper and their order within our consciousness? That narrator and its narrative voice provide an additional dimension to our field of self-awareness[1] since we have acquired an enhanced understanding of our character, its proximity to the *Divine Oneness*, and its unlimited and unbound creative capacity.

Even more empowering, some of us may have come to identify the actual placement of our narrator and the location of our narrative voice within conventional space and time constraints within our *personal narrative*. As we extract the transformative nature of this observation, we should recognize that the difference between the "here" and "there" with our dreams, ambitions, and hopes is unnecessary fiction. Through our empowered and improved narrative perception, we understand that the fiction deprives us from recognizing our narrator and its narrative

---

1. Sassoon, *Reality Revisited*, 168, stressing how all organisms are striving to transcend space, time and self.

voice—allowing us to experience all things as being within the "here" moment in our *personal narrative*.[2] This means, we have the creative capacity to empower and to improve our *personal narrative* to reflect the optimal configuration of all aspects of that narrative, as well as its relationship with the *Grand Historical Narrative* and its eventual convergence through the *Sacred Textual Narrative*.

That said, the preservation of the narrative status quo enables us to acquire and to process information at a beneficial velocity to safeguard against overloading our narrations with excess elemental components that could permanently impair our perceptive capabilities.[3] Looking within our narrative through the *Sacred Textual Narrative*, we have crafted a self-regulating narrative safeguard to limit the unnecessary expansion of externalized characters that distract us from seeking and relying on our Divine Character—our *Inner Messiah*. This character helps us to identify the main purpose of our *personal narrative*, that is, our eventual reunification with the *Divine Oneness* present at the beginning of creation. That reunification also stresses he importance of focusing on the beginning as the source of meaningful, transformative experiences. While we may have formerly considered our purpose as within the *Grand Historical Narrative* or the *Sacred Textual Narrative*, we should now understand why those purposes never provided sufficient meaning and/or satisfaction for our *personal narrative*. Our reasoning demonstrates that any definitive purpose requires complete narrative convergence. Otherwise, any purpose we identify for ourselves will only lead to the discovery of another purpose within the original purpose as we recognize and attempt to resolve the narrative dissonance through shifting purposes between narratives and their elemental components.[4]

With our narrative convergence, we will possess the power to avoid ephemeral solutions in our decision-making efforts that, with the assistance of our Divine Character, can achieve perpetual optimality. The Divine Character within our *personal narrative* also will liberate us from the constraints of ordinary reality as we modify our perspective on creation through adopting an expansive awareness that reflects our

2. Ibid.

3. Ibid., 138–39, noting that the division between consciousness and unconsciousness helps protect the centre consciousness being inundated with excess information.

4. See, e.g., ibid, 168–69, noting every purpose seems to hold inside it another purpose and arranged like layers of an onion as we continue to peel back additional layers revealing additional purposes.

new proximity to the Creator and our new appreciation for the *Divine Oneness*. Through our *Inner Messiah*, we will have empowered and improved our *personal narrative* to maximize our freedom from distractive/destructive influences and to appreciate our contentment with an unwavering, inner confidence. Describing this phenomenon as distancing our *personal narrative* away from our ego and embracing the *Divine Oneness* associated with our *Inner Messiah*, we will have entered and embodied the "sacred" from the *Sacred Textual Narrative* and, in turn, we will refocus our pursuits for more meaningful and exalted purposes untainted with counterproductive vanity or materialism emanating from the *Grand Historical Narrative*.[5] As a result, our Divine Character will imbue our ordinary existence through an optimal completeness that has not been experienced since all creation was unified within the *Divine Oneness*.

PRACTICAL IMPLICATIONS ON OUR CURRENT DECISION-MAKING

How can we experience the *Divine Oneness* right now, today, if all creation cannot be actually unified to bring about this experience? Can our Divine Character actually be classified as our *Inner Messiah* without actually encountering our Creator within creation? What can be the most valuable lesson from all this narrative-speak about transforming our life today in the "here" and "now"? Well, all these questions are valid and should be addressed as we wind down this provocative empowerment and improvement exercise. In a nutshell, the simple answer to all these questions is the power of the answer to these questions is the power of us asking these questions in the first place. Whatever impact this book may or may not have on our future perceptions, we all must never forget we have the power now at t_0 to experience an empowered and improved Divine Character in the future at t_1 through just thinking about the feelings and emotions associated with that character no matter whatever the period at t_x. Therefore, whether we are obsessing about our dreams and hopes we want to experience at t_1 or we are rethinking and revising our personal and professional objectives at t_x, we can are always experience some tangible and real aspect of our Divine Character in our emotions

5. See, e.g., ibid., 178, noting how surrender of the ego can help us access the supreme reality where we surrender our will to our Creator's will to maximize our freedom and bliss from enabling us to achieve the ideal and its corresponding action without any inner turmoil.

and perceptions at t_0, right now! The readily accessible, transformative power of our *Inner Messiah* is our recognition of this Divine Character as a catalyst to help us overcome our psychological limitations associated through a narrative dynamic that compartmentalizes our desires, drives, and dreams in accord with a specific narrations, rather than a single, unified narrative construct.[6]

Our *Inner Messiah* unleashes our imagination to resolve the tension between possible and impossible, success and failure, and other diametrical perceptions without any weaknesses or limitations on our problem solving strategies. Maximizing the potential within opposite possibilities, we can understand and appreciate how the removal of our barriers and impediments, like our *INM*, will liberate our Divine Character to reconfigure our problems and their solutions.[7] For example, instead of wondering why we cannot achieve our personal goals and professional ambitions, our Divine Character will permit us to formulate solutions first and then ask questions to arrive at those solutions. Remember, both the questions and the solutions are simultaneously present now at t_0. By waiting for sequential revelations at t_1 in the future, we are unnecessarily limiting our creative capacity to perceive all possibilities and to maximize our strategic self-awareness within the present moment. That said, the division between problem and solution, like the dissolution of other barriers discussed throughout this book, eventually will become obsolete as our Divine Character becomes more present in our daily routines as we rely on our *Inner Messiah* to become free from our current confining notions. Ironically, according to this reasoning, our current confining notions have already been resolved since they can be accurately classified as our past confining notions.

To truly experience the transformative power of our *Inner Messiah*, we must all encounter this Divine Character on our own terms and through our own narrations. After all, we are all hearing and experiencing each word on this page and its collective meaning within the overall book's content through our own personal narrator and its narrative voice. This aspect of our individuality cannot be denied and overcome without our *Inner Messiah* to help reconnect us with the *Divine Oneness* present

6. See, e.g., ibid., 137, discussing our field of self-awareness as a psychological space to allow the mind to observe the configuration of its desires and goals within a dynamic present.

7. See, e.g., ibid., 137–38, discussing how opposite emotions help reveal particular tendencies within our personality.

at the beginning of creation to help reunite our individual narrative voice with the Creator's narrative voice. Indeed, until all of us can dial up the Creator's narrative voice as our principal narrator within the original *Divine Oneness*, we must not hasten our individual efforts to optimize our personal existence and to maximize its potential to bring about all creation's reunification with that *Divine Oneness* present at the beginning of all creation.

Our *Inner Messiah* enables our narrative voice to reconnect directly with our Creator as our principal narrator since our innate, inner holiness reflects this phenomenon. Whatever we think after reading all this, we must recognize our Creator calls us to live in the full abundance of creation and to share creative responsibility to define, to understand, and to evolve from our co-creative roles in creation. The recognition of our Divine Character facilitates this co-creative partnership as our *Inner Messiah* empowers and improves our creative capacities with greater self-awareness and peripheral perception through helping us understand the perceivable and unperceivable consequences of our actions and ideals.[8] Is our *Inner Messiah* a sufficient rational explanation for understanding our need for narrative convergence to reunite with the *Divine Oneness* at the beginning of creation? Though that answer will vary between skeptic and supporter of classifying and accessing our Divine Character, the question itself will incite the same universal reaction—a need to create a response to represent our unique perspective to this interrogatory. We can identify this singularity as representative of the numerous other singularities many of us share, but may have never considered as representative of our collective commonality.

Regardless of the timing of our Divine Character's emergence,[9] we must trust that our *Inner Messiah* has always been present in our thinking process and our own narrative dissonance preempted us from accessing its full potential. We have also recognized our potential to reorganize and to optimize our creative capacity to overcome our own destructive, less than optimal behavior patterns as our Divine Character's imaginative potential alone eclipses those behaviors. The ultimate goal to reconnect

8. Begg, *Synchronicity*, 69, noting how synchronistic events remind us that another, altogether different order of reality is intelligently operating on our behalf as if we are part of an unimaginable vast world.

9. See, e.g., ibid., 3, discussing Jung's teaching about synchronistic phenomena that has no rational explanation about the optimal timing for the emergence of a person or thing.

with the creative potential available with the *Divine Oneness* at the beginning of creation further motivates our acceptance of our *Inner Messiah* as a redemptive character trait that allows to overcome our past errors and to attain the full promise of our future. Once again, as our reasoning set forth above clearly demonstrates, we have already experienced and acknowledged some aspect of the full promise of our future as we struggled with our own weaknesses and challenges in the past and present. However, through our Divine Character, we will acknowledge and accept the power of our *Inner Messiah* to create perfect unity with our creative power to transform our ordinary reality into an extraordinary existence.[10]

FINAL THOUGHT ON THE INNER MESSIAH AND OUR DAILY REALITY

Our literary destiny together has been fulfilled. We have arrived at the last paragraph in this book and now we all must determine how to write the next paragraph to narrate our own life and its role within all creation. Whatever the *Inner Messiah* was, is, or will become depends on our Divine Character and its presence in our everyday existence. Hopefully, our *Inner Messiah* will at least illuminate the critical elemental components of the *Grand Historical Narrative*, our *personal narrative*, and our *Sacred Textual Narrative* to facilitate their convergence for our reunification with the *Divine Oneness*. In the vernacular, we can say that we must think about the most effective ways to reclaim our unpolluted *Divine Character* that does not desire mundane accolades to justify our existence. Rather, our unpolluted *Divine Character* aspires to transcend all forms of fragmentation within ourselves and all creation to unify our individual and collective creative endeavors and their linkages to the Creator. In the end, whether we hear ourselves or multiple narrators narrate our own story and its creative elements, we must always make a choice who we want to hear and how much we want to know from our principal narrator. Once we make that choice, we can focus our efforts on uncovering its source and converge that discovery to help our principal narrator fully integrate the full potential of all creation.

Let us hope that our time together will enable us to converge all our narrative perspectives so that we can conclude this sentence and this

---

10. See, e.g., Dourley, *Paul Tillich, Carl Jung*, 165, noting Tillich's thinking about unity of power between human and divine can best be experienced through creativity.

book with the promise of a new beginning that only our Divine Character, our *Inner Messiah*, can provide us. After all, whatever we do after we put down this book and start conceiving our new narrative relationships, we must always remember that we *all* have the ability to reunify our complete, optimal *Self* with its divine origins and create a life that will be beyond best!

December 7, 2013

Bibliography

Adams, Peter J. *Fragmented Intimacy: Addiction in a Social World.* New York: Springer, 2008.

Aleman, André, et al. *Hallucinations: The Science of Idiosyncratic Perception.* 1st ed. Washington, DC: American Psychological Association, 2008.

Assmann, Jan. "Magic and Theology in Ancient Egypt." In *Envisioning Magic: Princeton Seminar and Symposium, Studies in the History of Religions,* edited by Peter Schäfer and Hans Kippenberg, 1–18. Leiden: Brill, 1991.

Bakan, David. *And They Took Themselves Wives: The Emergence of Patriarchy in Western Civilization.* 1st ed. New York: Harper & Row, 1979.

———. *The Duality of Human Existence: An Essay on Psychology and Religion.* Chicago: Rand McNally, 1966.

———. *Maimonides on Prophecy: A Commentary on Selected Chapters of the Guide of the Perplexed.* Northvale, NJ: Aronson, 1991.

———. *Sigmund Freud and the Jewish Mystical Tradition.* Princeton: Van Nostrand, 1958.

———. *Sigmund Freud and the Jewish Mystical Tradition.* London: Free Association, 1990.

———. *Slaughter of the Innocents.* 1st ed. Jossey-Bass Behavioral Science series. San Francisco: Jossey-Bass, 1971.

Bakan, David, et al. *Maimonides' Cure of Souls: Medieval Precursor of Psychoanalysis.* Albany: State University of New York Press, 2009.

Begg, Deike. *Synchronicity: The Promise of Coincidence.* Wilmette, IL: Chiron, 2003.

Bellah, Robert Neelly. *Religion in Human Evolution: From the Paleolithic to the Axial Age.* Cambridge: Belknap of Harvard University Press, 2011.

Belzen, Jacob A. "Spirituality, Culture, and Mental Health: Prospects and Risks for Contemporary Psychology of Religion." *Journal of Religion and Health* 43 (2004) 295–306.

Bloom, Maureen. *Jewish Mysticism and Magic: An Anthropological Perspective.* Routledge Jewish Studies series. New York: Routledge, 2007.

Boustan, Ra'anan S. *From Martyr to Mystic: Rabbinic Martyrology and the Making of Merkavah Mysticism.* Tübingen, Germany: Mohr Siebeck, 2005.

Brown, Francis, et al. *The New Brown-Driver-Briggs Gesenius Hebrew and English Lexicon*. New ed. Peabody, MA: Hendrickson, 1996.

Bucholtz, Mary, and Kira Hall. "Theorizing Identity in Language and Sexuality Research." *Language in Society* 33 (2004) 469–515.

Budge, E. A. Wallis. *Egyptian Magic*. Books on Egypt and Chaldaea 2. London: Trübner, 1899.

Burrough, Bryan. "Marc Dreier's Crime of Destiny." *Vanity Fair*, November 2009. http://www.vanityfair.com/business/features/2009/11/marc-dreier200911.

Capps, Donald. *Jesus: A Psychological Biography*. St. Louis: Chalice, 2000.

———. "John Nash, Game Theory, and the Schizophrenic Brain." *Journal of Religion and Health* 50 (2011) 145–62.

———. "John Nash: Three Phases in the Career of a Beautiful Mind." *Journal of Religion and Health* 44 (2005) 363–76.

———. "John Nash's Delusional Decade: A Case of Paranoid Schizophrenia." *Pastoral Psychology* 52 (2004) 193–218.

———. "John Nash's Postdelusional Period: A Case of Transformed Narcissim." *Pastoral Psychology* 52 (2004) 289–313.

———. "John Nash's Predulsional Phase: A Case of Acute Identity Confusion." *Pastoral Psychology* 51 (2003) 361–86.

———. *Understanding Psychosis: Issues and Challenges for Sufferers, Families, and Friends*. Lanham, MD: Rowman & Littlefield, 2010.

Center for Disease Control. "Trends in HIV-Related Risk Behaviors among High School Students (US), 1991–2011." *Morbidity and Mortality Weekly Report* 61 (2012) 971–76.

Cohen, Shaye J. D. *The Significance of Yavneh and Other Essays in Jewish Hellenism*. Texts and Studies in Ancient Judaism. Tübingen, Germany: Mohr Siebeck, 2010.

Cramer, Phebe. *Protecting the Self: Defense Mechanisms in Action*. New York: Guilford, 2006.

Critchley, Simon, and Jamieson Webster. "The Gospel according to 'Me.'" *New York Times*, June 29, 2013. http://opinionator.blogs.nytimes.com/2013/06/29/the-gospel-according-to-me/?_php=true&_type=blogs&_r=0.

Davies, W. D., and Louis Finkelstein. *The Cambridge History of Judaism*. Cambridge: Cambridge University Press, 1984.

Dittes, James E., and Donald Capps. *Re-Calling Ministry*. St. Louis: Chalice, 1999.

Dourley, John P. *Paul Tillich, Carl Jung, and the Recovery of Religion*. London: Routledge, 2008.

Drobin, Frederick A. "Spirituality, the New Opiate." *Journal of Religion and Health* 38 (1999) 229–39.

Elior, Rachel. *Jewish Mysticism: The Infinite Expression of Freedom*. Littman Library of Jewish Civilization. Oxford: Littman Library of Jewish Civilization, 2007.

Erikson, Erik H. *Childhood and Society*. 1st ed. New York: Norton, 1950.

———. *Identity, Youth, and Crisis*. 1st ed. New York: Norton, 1968.

———. *Young Man Luther: A Study in Psychoanalysis and History*. 1st ed. Austen Riggs Monograph. New York: Norton, 1958.

Epstein, Joseph. "Think You Have a Book in You? Think Again." *New York Times*, September 28, 2002. http://www.nytimes.com/2002/09/28/opinion/think-you-have-a-book-in-you-think-again.html.

Fetaya, Rabbi Yeduda. *Minhat Yehuda.* Translated by Avraham Leader. Edited by Yehuda Herskowitz. Jerusalem: Mechon Haktav, 2010.

Finkelstein, Louis. *Akiba: Scholar, Saint and Martyr.* New York: Atheneum, 1970.

Fisher, Charles, and Howard Shevrin. *Subliminal Explorations of Perception, Dreams, and Fantasies: The Pioneering Contributions of Charles Fisher, Psychological Issues.* Madison, CT: International Universities Press, 2003.

Fitzgerald, Michael. *The Genesis of Artistic Creativity: Asperger's Syndrome and the Arts.* Philadelphia: Kingsley, 2005.

Flores, Philip J. *Addiction as an Attachment Disorder.* Lanham, MD: Aronson, 2004.

Freimuth, Marilyn. *Hidden Addictions.* Lanham, MD: Aronson, 2005.

Freud, Sigmund. "The Antithetical Meaning of Primal Words (1910)." In *The Standard Edition of the Complete Psychological Works of Sigmund Freud,* edited by James Strachey, 11:153–62. New York: Norton, 1976.

Freud, Sigmund, and James Strachey. *Introductory Lectures on Psychoanalysis.* New York: Norton, 1977.

Frie, Roger, and William J. Coburn. *Persons in Context: The Challenge of Individuality in Theory and Practice.* Psychoanalytic Inquiry series. New York: Routledge, 2011.

Gino, Francesca, and Dan Ariely. "The Dark Side of Creativity: Original Thinkers Can Be More Dishonest." *Journal of Personality & Social Psychology* 102 (2012) 445–59.

Gott, J. Richard. *Time Travel in Einstein's Universe: The Physical Possibilities of Travel through Time.* Boston: Houghton Mifflin, 2001.

Grannis, Emily. "Marc Dreier's Son Says College Roommates Bet He Would Drop Out." *Bloomberg,* July 11, 2012. http://www.bloomberg.com/news/2012-07-11/marc-dreier-s-son-says-college-roommates-bet-he-would-drop-out.html.

Greene, Jack P. "Search for Identity: An Interpretation of the Meaning of Selected Patterns of Social Response in Eighteenth-Century America." *Journal of Social History* 3 (1969/70) 189–220.

Grossman, Cathy Lynn. "Clergy Sex Abuse Settlements Top $2.5 Billion Nationwide." *USA Today,* March 13, 2013. http://www.usatoday.com/story/news/nation/2013/03/13/sex-abuse-settlement-cardinal-roger-mahony/1984217.

Gyaltsen, Jetsun Drakpa. *Parting from the Four Attachments: Jetsun Drakpa Gyaltsen's Song of Experience on Mind Training and the View.* Ithaca, NY: Snow Lion, 2003.

Havens, Joseph, and David Bakan. *Psychology and Religion: A Contemporary Dialogue.* Princeton: Van Nostrand, 1968.

Hilgevoord, Jan, and Jos Uffink. "The Uncertainty Principle." In *The Stanford Encyclopedia of Philosophy,* summer 2012 ed., edited by Edward N. Zalta, no pages. http://plato.stanford.edu/archives/sum2012/entries/qt-uncertainty.

Holzner, Steven. *Quantum Physics Workbook for Dummies.* Hoboken, NJ: Wiley, 2010.

Horvath, Adam O., and Lester Luborsky. "The Role of the Therapeutic Alliance in Psychotherapy." *Journal of Consulting and Clinical Psychology* 61 (1993) 561–73.

Huskinson, Lucy. *Dreaming the Myth Onwards: New Directions in Jungian Therapy and Thought.* London: Routledge, 2008.

Idel, Moshe. *Messianic Mystics.* New Haven: Yale University Press, 1998.

———. "The Tsadik and His Soul's Sparks: From Kabbalah to Hasidism." *Jewish Quarterly Review* 103 (2013) 196–240.

Jackson, Gordon E. "The Pastoral Counselor: His Identity and Work." *Journal of Religion and Health* 3 (1964) 250–70.

Jackson-McCabe, Matt. "The Messiah Jesus in the Mythic World of James." *Journal of Biblical Literature* 122 (2003) 719–24.

Jagersma, H. *A History of Israel from Alexander the Great to Bar Kochba.* 1st Fortress ed. Philadelphia: Fortress Press, 1986.

Jeserich, Florian. "Can Sense of Coherence Be Modified by Religious/Spiritual Interventions? A Critical Appraisal of Previous Research." *Interdisciplinary Journal of Research on Religion* 9 (2013) 1–36.

Kakar, Sudhir. *The Inner World: A Psycho-Analytic Study of Childhood and Society in India.* 2nd ed. New York: Oxford University Press, 1982.

———. *Mad and Divine: Spirit and Psyche in the Modern World.* Chicago: University of Chicago Press, 2009.

Kaplan, Aryeh. *Sefer Yetzirah (the Book of Creation): In Theory and Practice.* York Beach, ME: Weiser, 1990.

Kaya, Nihan. "Compelled to Create: The Courage to Go Beyond." In *Dreaming the Myth Onwards: New Directions in Jungian Therapy and Thought,* edited by Lucy Huskinson, 21–30. London: Routledge, 2008.

Kepnes, Steven. "Buber's Ark: The Dialogic Self." In *The Endangered Self,* edited by Donald Capps and Richard K. Fenn, 101–13. Princeton: Center for Religion, Self and Society, Princeton Theological Seminary, 1992.

Kornblum, Janet. "There's a Risk to the Beauty of Surgery." *USA Today,* January 21, 2004. http://usatoday30.usatoday.com/news/health/2004-01-21-plastic-surgery-risks_x.htm.

Kuhar, Michael J. *The Addicted Brain: Why We Abuse Drugs, Alcohol, and Nicotine.* 1st ed. Upper Saddle River, NJ: FT Press, 2012.

Laurin, Kristin, et al. "Divergent Effects of Activating Thoughts of God on Self-Regulation." *Journal of Personality & Social Psychology* 102 (2012) 4–21.

Lenowitz, Harris. *The Jewish Messiahs: From the Galilee to Crown Heights.* Oxford: Oxford University Press, 1998.

Luquis, Raffy R., et al. "Religiosity, Spirituality, Sexual Attitudes and Sexual Behaviors among College Students." *Journal of Religion & Health* 51 (2012) 601–14.

Mackey, Damien. "The First Book of Moses and the 'Toledoth' of Genesis." http://www.specialtyinterests.net/Toledoth.html.

———. "The Six Days of Genesis 1 Explained." http://www.academia.edu/3690091/The_Concept_of_the_Six_Days_of_Genesis_1_as_a_Written_Account_of_Creation.

Mathews, Shailer. "The Permanent Message of the Messianism: I. The Permanent Elements in the Faith in a Messiah." *Biblical World* 49 (1917) 267–74.

McCabe, Sean Esteban, et al. "Sexual Orientation, Substance Use Behaviors and Substance Dependence in the United States." *Addiction Research Report* 104 (2009) 1333–45.

Meissner, W. W. *Time, Self, and Psychoanalysis.* Lanham, MD: Aronson, 2007.

Muir, John. *My First Summer in the Sierra.* New York: Houghton Mifflin, 1911.

Novello, Henry. "Created Reality as the Manifestation of Spirit." *Australian Catholic Record* 90 (2013) 60–70.

O'Brien, Charles P., et al. *Addictive States.* Research Publications / Association for Research in Nervous and Mental Diseases. New York: Raven, 1991.

Ogden, Sofía K., and Ashley D. Biebers. *Psychology of Denial, Psychology of Emotions, Motivations and Actions Series.* New York: Nova Science, 2010.

Raftopoulos, Mary, and Glen Bates. "'It's That Knowing That You Are Not Alone': The Role of Spirituality in Adolescent Resilience." *International Journal of Children's Spirituality* 16 (2011) 151–67.

Rinpoche, Deshung, and Kunga Tenpay Nyima. *The Three Levels of Spiritual Perception: An Oral Commentary on the Three Visions (Snang Gsum) of Ngorchen Konchog Lhundrub*. Translated by Jared Rhoton, edited by Victoria R. M. Scott. 2nd ed. Boston: Wisdom, 2003.

Robertson, Venetia Laura Delano. "The Beast Within: Anthrozoomorphic Identity and Alternative Spirituality in the Online Therianthropy Movement." *Nova Religio: The Journal of Alternative and Emergent Religions* 16 (2013) 7–30.

Romme, M. A. J., and Sandra Escher. *Accepting Voices*. London: Mind, 1993.

Rosenfels, Paul. *Homosexuality: The Psychology of the Creative Process*. New York: Ninth Street Center, 1986.

Ross, Michael W. "Typing, Doing, and Being: Sexuality and the Internet." *Journal of Sex Research* 42 (2005) 342–52.

Rowland, Christopher, and Christopher R. A. Morray-Jones. *The Mystery of God: Early Jewish Mysticism and the New Testament*. Leiden: Brill, 2009.

Salyers, Beth, and Greg Wiggan. "Hidden Curriculum in Education and the Social Psychology of Denial: Global Multicultural Education for Social Transformation." Chapter 3 in *Psychology of Denial*, edited by Sofia Ogden and Ashley D. Biebers. New York: Nova Science, 2010.

Sassoon, Solomon David. *Reality Revisited*. 2nd rev. ed. Jerusalem: Feldheim, 1991.

Schäfer, Peter. *The Origins of Jewish Mysticism*. Princeton: Princeton University Press, 2009.

Schäfer, Peter, and Hans Kippenberg. *Envisioning Magic: A Princeton Seminar and Symposium*. Leiden: Brill, 1991.

Schildkraut, Deborah J. "The More Things Change . . . American Identity and Mass and Elite Responses to 9/11." *Political Psychology* 23 (2002) 511–35.

Schlamm, Leon. "Active Imagination in *Answer to Job*." In *Dreaming the Myth Onwards: New Directions in Jungian Therapy and Thought*, edited by Lucy Huskinson, 109–21. London: Routledge, 2008.

Sharma, A. "Psychotherapy with Hindus." In *Handbook of Psychotherapy and Religious Diversity*, edited by P. Scott Richards and A. Bergin, 359–60. Washington, DC: American Psychological Association, 2000.

Sharp, Lesley A. "The Commodifications of the Body and Its Parts." *Annual Review of Anthropology* 29 (2000) 287–328

Shetter, Tony L. "Genesis 1–2 in Light of Egyptian Creation Myths." Paper presented at the second annual Student Academic Conference, Dallas Theological Seminary, April 18, 2005. https://bible.org/article/genesis-1-2-light-ancient-egyptian-creation-myths.

Sigmund, Judith A. "Spirituality and Trauma: The Role of Clergy in the Treatment of Posttraumatic Stress Disorder." *Journal of Religion and Health* 42 (2003) 221–29.

Slade, Peter D., and Richard P. Bentall. *Sensory Deception: A Scientific Analysis of Hallucination*. London: Croom Helm, 1988.

Spiegelman, J. Marvin. *Judaism and Jungian Psychology*. Lanham, MD: University Press of America, 1993.

Stevenson, Ian, and Jurgen Keil. "Children of Myanmar Who Behave like Japanese Soldiers: A Possible Third Element in Personality." *Journal of Scientific Exploration* 19 (2005) 171–83.

Stolorow, Robert D. "Individuality in Context: The Relationality of Finitude." In *Persons in Context: The Challenge of Individuality in Theory and Practice*, edited by R. Frie and W. Coburn, 59–68. New York: Routledge, 2011.

Twerski, Abraham J. *Addictive Thinking: Understanding Self-Deception*. 2nd ed. Center City, MN: Hazelden, 1997.

———. *Wisdom Each Day*. 1st ed. Artscroll series. New York: Mesorah, 2000.

Waltke, Bruce. "The Literary Genre of Genesis, Chapter One." *Crux* 27 (1991) 2–10. http://www.creationbc.org/index.php?option=com_content&view=article&id=136&Itemid=62.